HONDA
SHOP MANUAL
and
HANDBOOK

I0303566

Super Cub Model C 100

ANNOUNCEMENT

We are happy to reproduce this Shop and Service Manual covering the extremely popular Honda Super Cub Model C100.

As publishers of over 200 books on automobiles and motorcycles, we have had an ever-increasing demand for shop manuals and handbooks covering Honda models, and we are therefore most happy to be able to supply these books to our customers — who consist of dealers, individuals, booksellers newsstands, riders, enthusiasts and collectors.

These books were originally printed in Japan and translated in that country. There are some expressions that differ from our own but we have left the wording exactly as it appears in the original books.

Floyd Clymer

FLOYD CLYMER PUBLICATIONS

World's Largest Publisher of Books Relating to Automobiles, Motorcycles, Motor Racing, and Americana

222 NO. VIRGIL AVENUE AT BEVERLY BLVD., LOS ANGELES 4, CALIFORNIA

INTRODUCTION

Welcome to the world of digital publishing ~ the book you now hold in your hand, while unchanged from the original **1970** edition, was printed using the latest state of the art digital technology. The advent of print-on-demand has forever changed the publishing process, never has information been so accessible and it is our hope that this book serves your informational needs for years to come. If this is your first exposure to digital publishing, we hope that you are pleased with the results. Many more titles of interest to the classic automobile and motorcycle enthusiast, collector and restorer are available via our website at **www.VelocePress.com.** We hope that you find this title as interesting as we do.

NOTE FROM THE PUBLISHER

The information presented is true and complete to the best of our knowledge. All recommendations are made without any guarantees on the part of the author or the publisher, who also disclaim all liability incurred with the use of this information.

TRADEMARKS

We recognize that some words, model names and designations, for example, mentioned herein are the property of the trademark holder. We use them for identification purposes only. This is not an official publication.

INFORMATION ON THE USE OF THIS PUBLICATION

This manual is an invaluable resource for the classic **HONDA** enthusiast and a "must have" for owners interested in performing their own maintenance. However, in today's information age we are constantly subject to changes in common practice, new technology, availability of improved materials and increased awareness of chemical toxicity. As such, it is advised that the user consult with an experienced professional prior to undertaking any procedure described herein. While every care has been taken to ensure correctness of information, it is obviously not possible to guarantee complete freedom from errors or omissions or to accept liability arising from such errors or omissions. Therefore, any individual that uses the information contained within, or elects to perform or participate in do-it-yourself repairs or modifications acknowledges that there is a risk factor involved and that the publisher or its associates cannot be held responsible for personal injury or property damage resulting from the use of the information or the outcome of such procedures.

It is important that the reader recognizes that any instructions may refer to either the right-hand or left-hand sides of the vehicle or the components and that the directions are followed carefully. One final word of advice, this publication is intended to be used as a reference guide, and when in doubt the reader should consult with a qualified technician.

FOREWORD

This manual is designed as a "service handbook" of the 50 cc Super Cub Model C 100.

Therefore, by carefully reading this manual, the service man will be able to perform a thorough service and the salesman will be able to obtain brief mechanical knowledge by referring to this manual.

Service in this case means to reinstate the trouble arising to its proper condition by diagnosis and repair of that part and also, to perform periodic inspections and for protection administer preventive maintenance and adjustments so that the vehicle can always operate efficiently.

This manual has 4 chapters with each chapter seperated into sections and the service contents of each item is made up by the sequence of disassembling-inspection-service-assembling.

Provision is made for service memorandum at the end of each chapter and section to enter design modifications or special notes concerning that portion, and for ready reference.

An effort has been made to produce a manual avoiding fundamental principle and theory by explaining the actual mechanism and special emphasis has been placed in illustrations and pictures to make it easy for the service man to understand without reading every line.

This manual will be revised without notice.

HONDA MOTOR CO. LTD.,
SERVICE DEPARTMENT

HONDA SHOP MANUAL & HANDBOOK
Super Cub Model C 100
INDEX

Frame Serial Number

1. Engine 1
   - 1.1 Removal & Installation of Engine 2
   - 1.2 Cylinder Head and Cylinder Head Cover ... 4
   - 1.3 Cylinder Piston and Piston Rings 7
   - 1.4 L Cover & Relative Parts 11
   - 1.5 R Cover & Relative Parts 13
   - 1.6 Crankshaft & Connecting Rod 17
   - 1.7 Lubrication System 20
   - 1.8 Cam and Valve Mechanism 22
   - 1.9 Transmission and Kick Starter 24
   - 1.10 R Crankcase and L Crankcase 29
   - 1.11 Clutch 30
   - 1.12 Shift Mechanism 34
   - 1.13 Neutral Swtich 35
   - 1.14 Carburetor 36

2. Chassis 43
   - 2.1 Steering Handle and Various Wires & Cables ... 44
   - 2.2 Front Fork 46
   - 2.3 Front Suspension (Shock Absorber) 49

| ENGINE |
| CHASSIS |
| ELECTRICAL STSTEM |
| INSPECTION, MAINTENANCE & SPECIFICATION |

2. 4	Rear Fork & Rear Suspension	53
2. 5	Drive Chain System	56
2. 6	Front & Rear Wheel	59
2. 7	Brakes	65
2. 8	Fuel Tank Saddle & Luggage Carrier	68
2. 9	Air Cleaner	72
2.10	Exhaust System	74
2.11	Polyethylene (Hiezex) Made Parts	76
2.12	Step Bar, Main Stand & Brake Pedal	78
2.13	Frame	80

3. Electrical System 83

3. 1 Ignition System 83

    A. Contact Breaker 84
    B. Condenser 84
    C. Spark Plug 85
    D. Flywheel Magneto 86

3. 2 Charging System 87

    A. Charging Coil 87
    B. Selenium Rectifier 88
    C. Battery 89

3. 3 Switches 91

    A. Combination Switch 91
    B. Directional Signal Lamp Switch & Head Dimmer Switch 92
    C. Neutral Switch 93
    D. Horn Button Switch 93

3. 4 Various Electrical Loads, Harness & Speedometer 94

    A. Horn 94

  B. Directional Signal Lamp Relay 94
  C. Speedometer 95
  D. Head Lamp 96
  E. Tail Lamp & Speedometer Lamp 97
  F. Directional Signal Lamp 97
  G. Fuse 97
  H. Wire Harness 98

4. Inspection, Maintenance & Specifications 101

4.1 Preventive Maintenance 101

  A. Engine Tune-up 101
  B. Adjustment of Drive Chain 110
  C. Adjusting Brakes 110
  D. Care of Battery 111
  E. Lubrication 112
  F. Inspection for Tightening of Various Parts 114

4.2 Periodic Inspections & Maintenance 117

  A. Daily Inspection 117
  B. Periodic Inspection 117

4.3 Diagnosis of Troubles 120

4.4 Maintenance Data & Specifications 129

  A. Maintenance Data 129
  B. Specifications of Performance 129
  C. Specifications of Parts 131

FRAME SERIAL NUMBER

In preparing forms for service correspondence, claims reports, parts orders and other inquiries, the frame serial number is always required. This number is designated in series by model year or by model for the engine or frame and by using this number in all correspondences it will enable us to give the required answer back without delay and confusion.

Frame Serial Number location and designation is as pictured below.

NOTE: Up to the number C 100 E-986179 Engine Serial Numbers are effective, thereafter the engine is provided with a production number attached to certification plate.

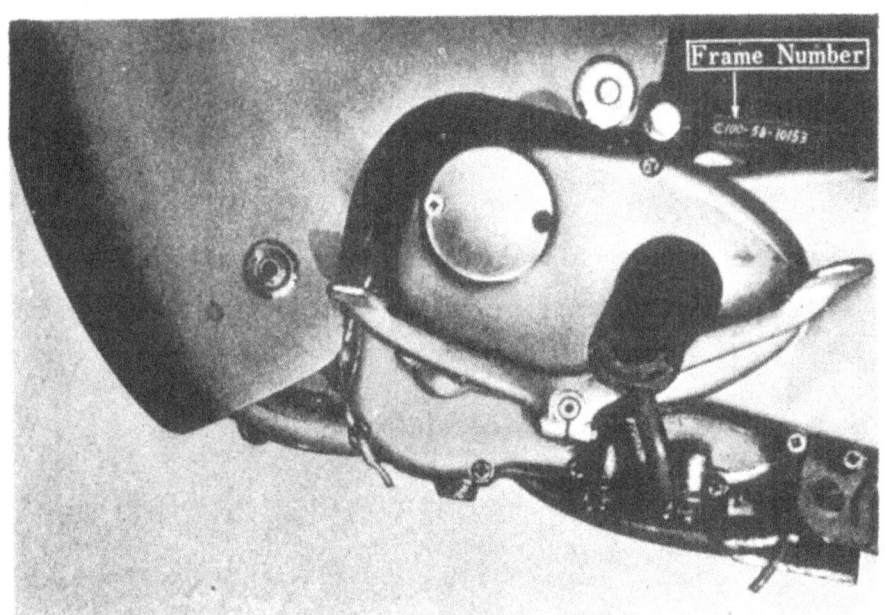

Location of Frame Serial Number

CERTIFICATION NUMBER PLATE

To certify that the vehicle is formally approved by the Ministry of Transportation the following number plate is fixed on the left hand top of the engine. This certifies that the Super Cub engine is a 50 cc displacement 'Class 1 Engine Installed Bicycle Engine'.

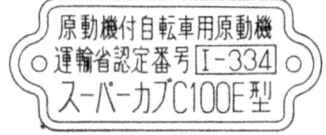

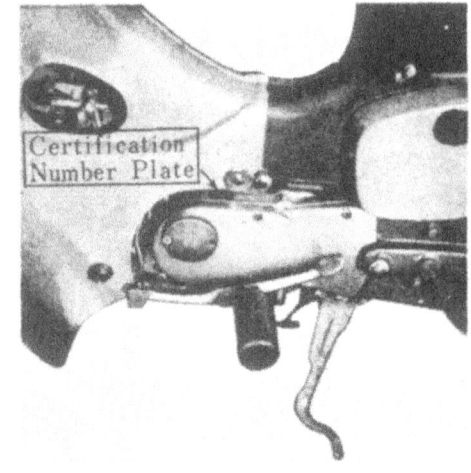

IV

1. ENGINE

The compact engine weighing 15 kg is of 50 cc displacement-4 cycle, regular over-head-valve construction.

The crankcase, united with the transmission, is made of light-alloy die cast and the compact construction enables you to inspect and service with ease.

Fig 1.1 Engine Mountings

During the process of servicing and repairs always use the tools specified (**fig. 1.3**) with care and according to the standards.

Fig. 1.2 shows the various packings used and as these are made with special care towards the material, only use genuine parts.

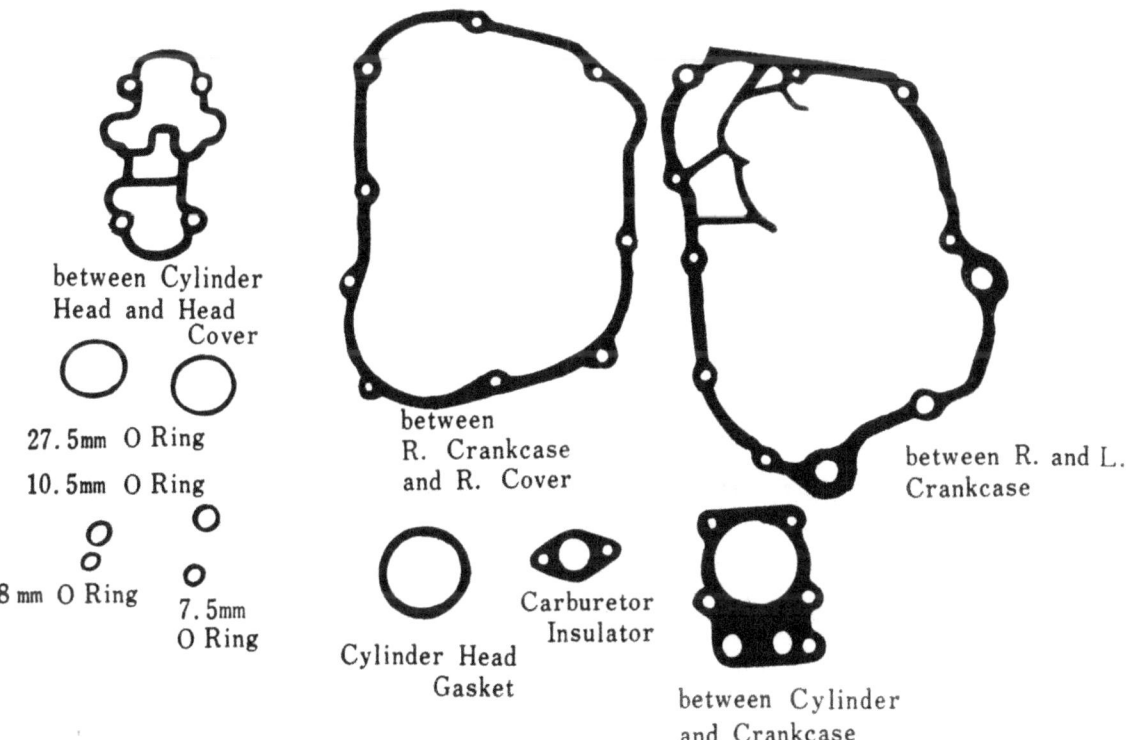

Fig 1.2 Model C 100 Engine Gaskets

1. ENGINE

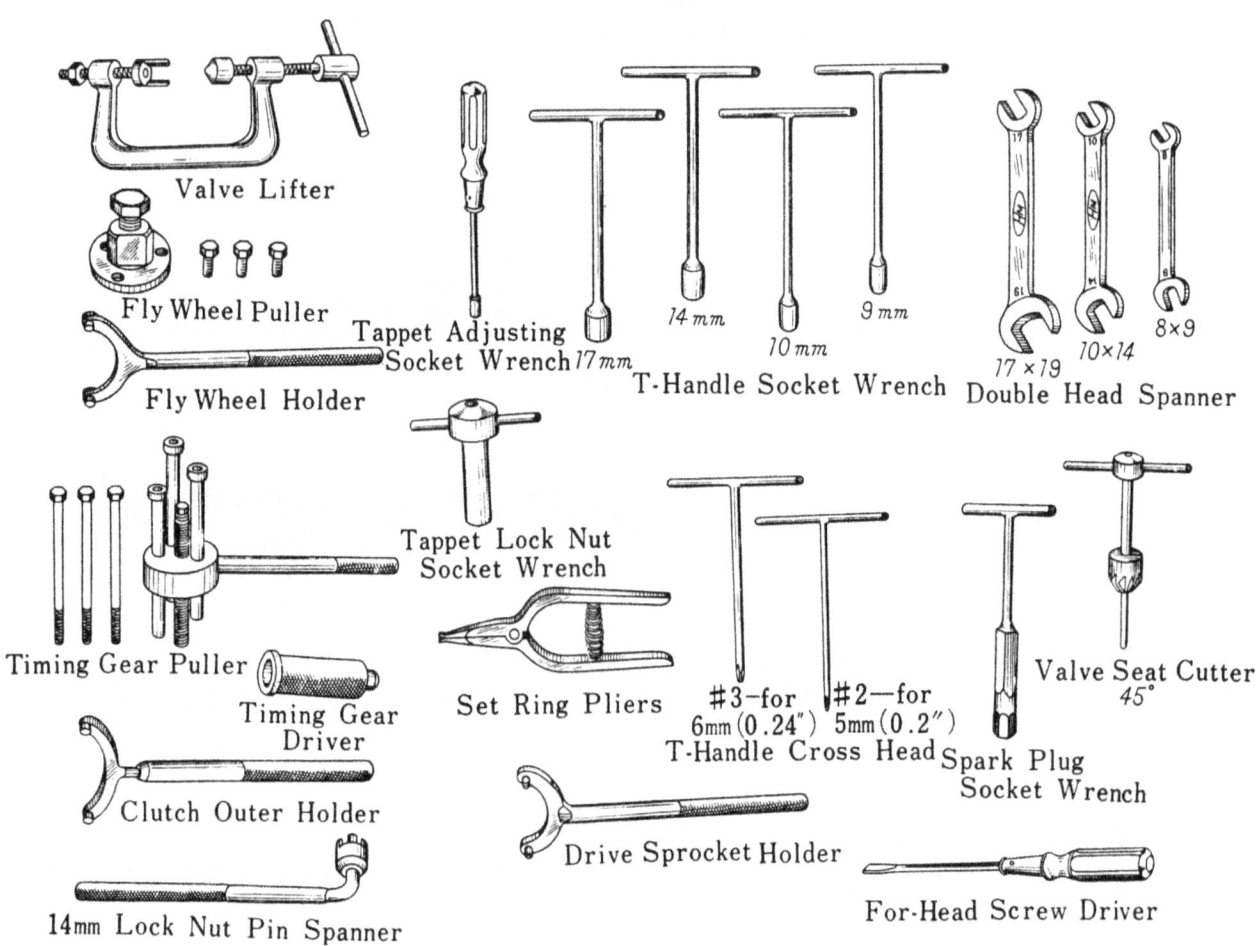

Fig. 1.3 Disassembling Tools

1.1 Removal and Installation of Engine

A. Removal of Engine

First remove the air cleaner cover (10 mm spanner), front cover (10 mm box wrench). Then follow the sequence (1), (2).... in **fig. 1.4** carefully.

> NOTE: If carburetor removal is necessary, insert clip on fuel pipe to stop fuel flow as fuel cock is attached to the carburetor.

B. Installation of Engine

Follow the numbers (12), (11)........ in **fig. 1.4** backwards. In this case special care must be given to tightening torques and the way chain joint (7) is facing.

1.1 REMOVAL AND INSTALLATION OF ENGINE

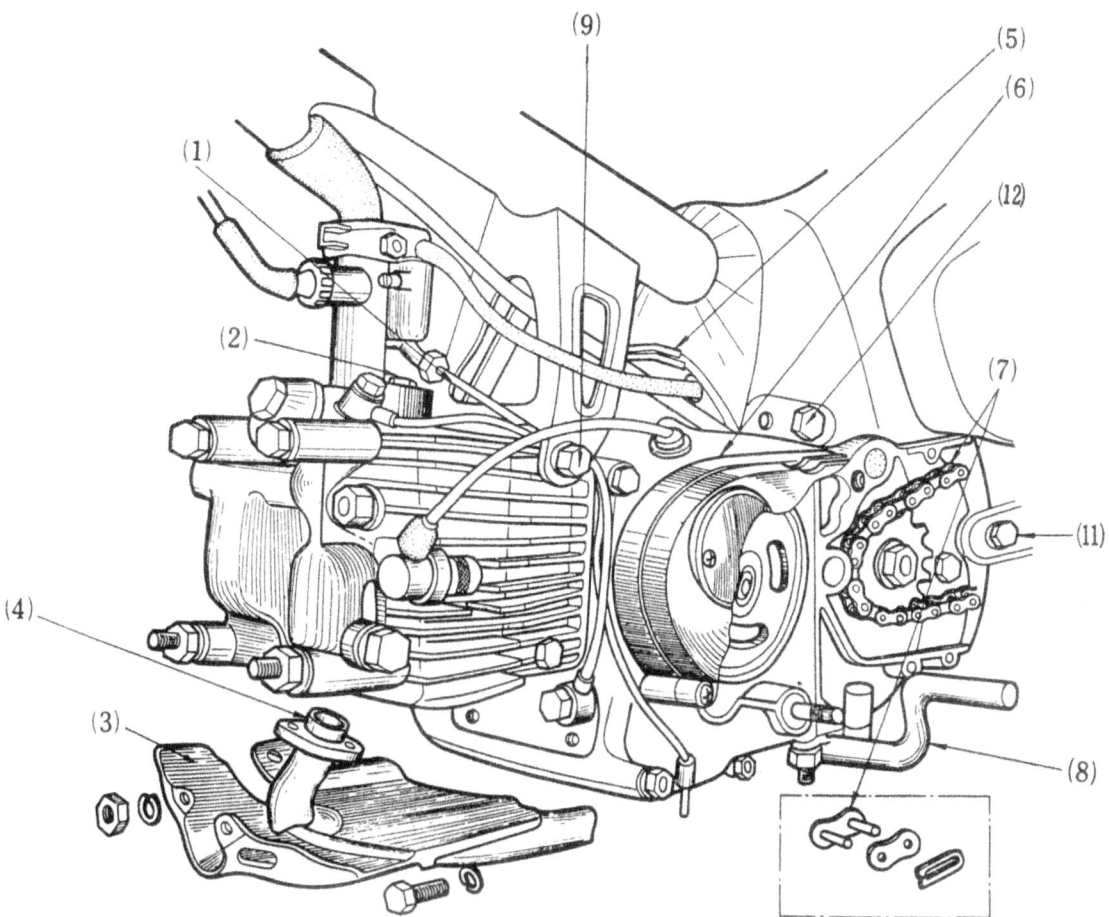

(1) Over flow pipe (with 10 mm spanner)
(2) Carburetor mounting bolts
    (with 10 mm spanner)
    Recommended tightening torque
    60 in-lb (0.65 kg-m)
(3) Dust guard (with 10 mm spanner)
(4) Exhaust pipe (with 10 mm spanner)
(5) Wiring connectors
(6) L crankcase cover screws
    (with 3 cross head screw driver)
(7) Drive chain joint clip (with pliers)
(8) Step bar (with 14 mm spanner)
(9) 8×40 mm engine hanger bolt
    (with 14 mm socket wrench)
(11) Engine support bolt
    (with 14 mm socket wrench)
    Recommended tightening torque
    10~15 ft-lb (1.5~2.0 kg-m)
(12) Engine support bolt A
    (with 14 mm socket wrench)
    Recommended tightening torque
    10~15 ft-lb (1.5~2.0 kg-m)

Fig. 1.4 Engine Removal (1)

Fig. 1.5 Engine Removal (2)

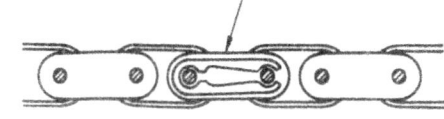

Fig. 1.6 Attaching Joint Clip on the Chain

1.2 Cylinder Head and Cylinder Head Cover

The cylinder head is made of cast iron with a compression ratio of 8.5 : 1, and has a dome shaped combustion chamber with efficient flame distribution. With a forward inclining cylinder of 10° towards horizontal top angle, this is installed to the crankcase with a 6 mm stud bolt. Valve guides and not used and the valve is directly installed to the cylinder head.

The rocker arms are assembled to the cylinder head cover, also made of cast iron and an oil pipe is firmly held in place on top by an oil bolt, for lubricating by the cam shaft journal.

A. Disassembly

Disassemble according to the steps ①, ②, ③ ...... in **fig. 1.7 & 1.8** Remove valve cotters depressing each valve with valve lifter, then disassemble valve springs, valve and valve spring seats.

Check for oil leaks, compression leaks and wear and damages while disassembling.

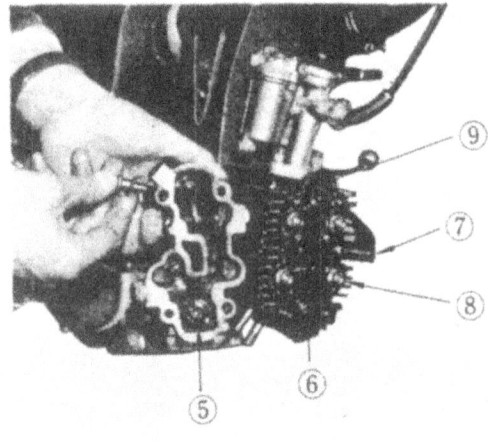

① Oil tube clamp bolt (with 10 mm socket spanner.) Rec. torque 60 in-lb
② Carburetor mounting stud nuts (2) Rec. torque 60 in-lb
③④ Cylinder head cover bolts (4) (with 10 mm socket wrench) Rec. torque 65 in-lb

Fig. 1.7 Removing Cylinder Head Cover

⑤ Cylinder head cover
⑥ Push rod
⑦ High tension wire terminal
⑧ 6 mm Cylinder stud nuts (4) (with 10mm socket wrench) Rec. torque 70 in-lb
⑨ Cylinder head

Fig. 1.8 Removing Cylinder Head

B. Inspection and Servicing

(1) Valves and valve seats

Remove valve cotter and pull out valve. Check for wear on facing, blowby and carbon accumulation. If the valve facing is not worn or pitted excessively, reface the valves with valve refacer to an angle of 45 degrees (in. and ex.).

1.2 CYLINDER HEAD & CYLINDER HEAD COVER

Replace the valve if they are warped, burned, pitted or exceed the specification (**fig 1.9**).

Replace the head if the valve guides and valve seats are not serviceable. As valve guides are not fitted but compacted of cylinder head, be careful not to mar or damage inside face of guide.

After reseating worn valve seat with a valve seat cutter and refacing the valves, lap the seat and valve together with a fine lapping compound with a light tapping motion.

Standard specifications are shown in **fig. 1.10**, but if this operation is mishandled the cylinder head must be replaced so special care must be given.

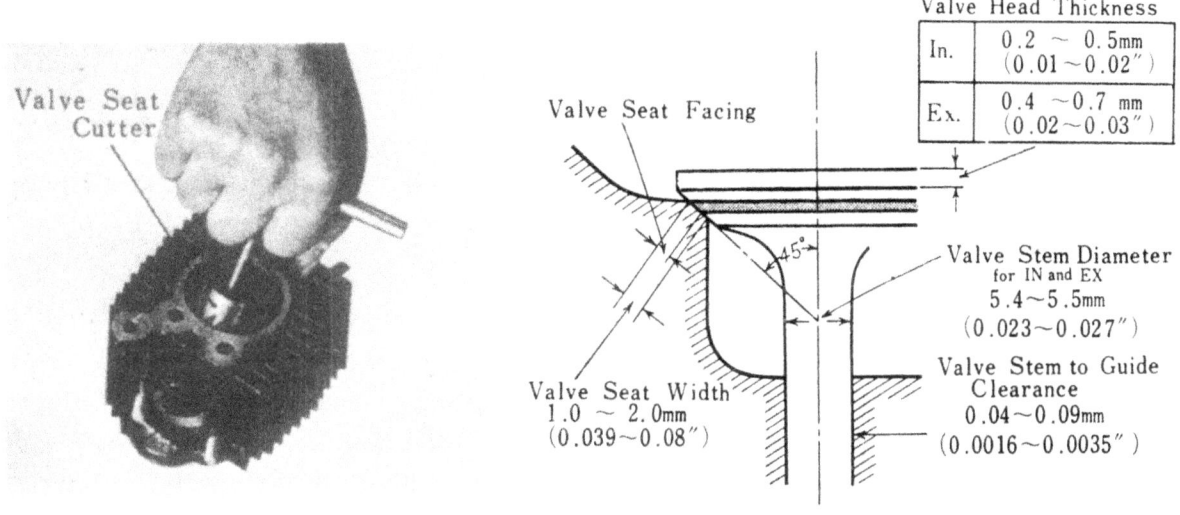

Fig. 1.9 Refacing Valve Seat   Fig. 1.10 Valve Specification

(2) Valve springs

Valve springs play an important part in keeping the valve operation mechanism, which open and close at high speed, in perfect condition. When disassembled always check to see if they are within the standard measurements.

Measurements are taken by the spring tester shown in **fig. 1.12**. The standard service tolerance is shown below and the springs out of the tolerance should be replaced.

	Test Length	Compression
Outer Spring	27.0~25.0 (1.06~0.9″)	0 kg (free length)
	23.5 (0.925″)	6.4~4.4kg (14.0~9.7 lbs)
Inner Spring	27.8~26.0 (1.09~1.2″)	0 kg (free length)
	22.5 (0.885″)	2.6~2.0 kg (5.1~4.4 lbs)

1. ENGINE

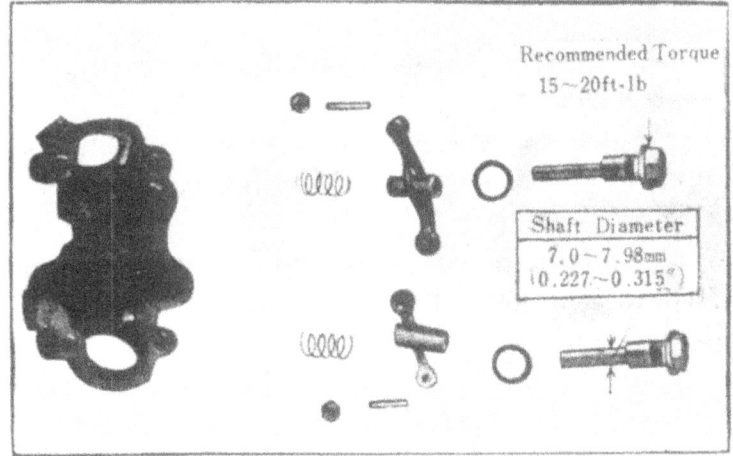

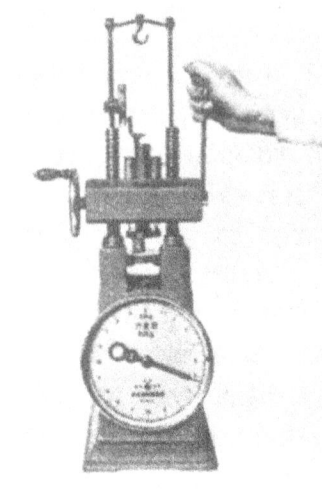

Fig. 1.11 Disassembled View of Cylinder Head Cover

Fig. 1.12 Checking Spring Tension with Spring Tester

(3) **Rocker arm**

Check the fit of the rocker arm on the rocker arm shaft.
Side play of rocker arm in correctly installed position is 0.06–0.10 mm. (refer to **fig 1.8**)

C. Reassembly

For reassembling follow the steps for disassembling backwards.
Be careful to check the 7.5 mm rubber packing, the 10.5 mm "O" ring 2 pcs. and head gasket between the cylinder and head. Especially with the 10.5 mm "O" ring, check to see "O" ring is in good condition before installing. (**fig 1.13-b**)
On installing the cylinder head, tighten the four (4) 10 mm nuts in sequence 1-2-3-4 shown in **fig. 1.13**, using a torque wrench making sure there are no compression leaks.

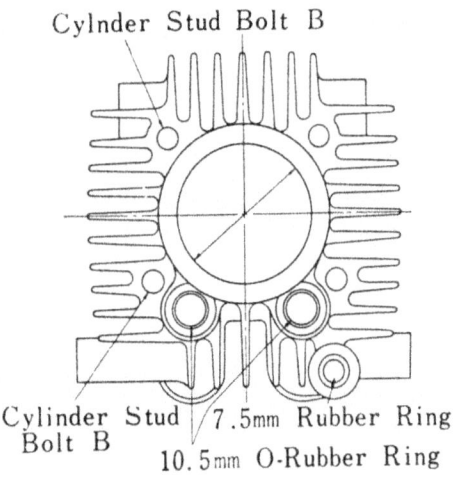

Fig. 1.13-a Location of Rubber Rings

Fig. 1.13-b Tightening of Cylinder Head

1.3 Cylinder, Piston and Piston Rings

Special attention must be given to the material and precision of piston parts, which move at maximum speeds upwards of 10 m per second. Model C 100 has aluminum-alloy piston and grey cast iron cylinder. Piston rings consist of 2 compression rings and 1 oil ring. The top ring is chrome plated, the second ring is tapered and the oil ring is grooved-tapered. Be careful of which way the piston is facing, top and bottom of rings and the angle when installing.

A. Disassembly

After removing cylinder head, the cylinder can be pulled out from the crankcase. Then remove the piston pin end clip with thin nose pliers and draw out the pin.

B. Inspection and Reassembly

(1) **Cylinder**

Check the inside diameter of the cylinder as shown in **fig. 1.14 & 1.15**. Allowable dimensions are shown in **fig. 1.16** and whenever the dimensions do not meet the allowance, boring or honing is required. Accomplished size of boring must not exceed the specific tolerance, in out of round and taper of inner face.

Available oversize is each 0.25~0.26 mm (0.00985~0.0102″) added dimensions of 3 steps. For these oversized cylinder piston and rings are prepared as supply parts.

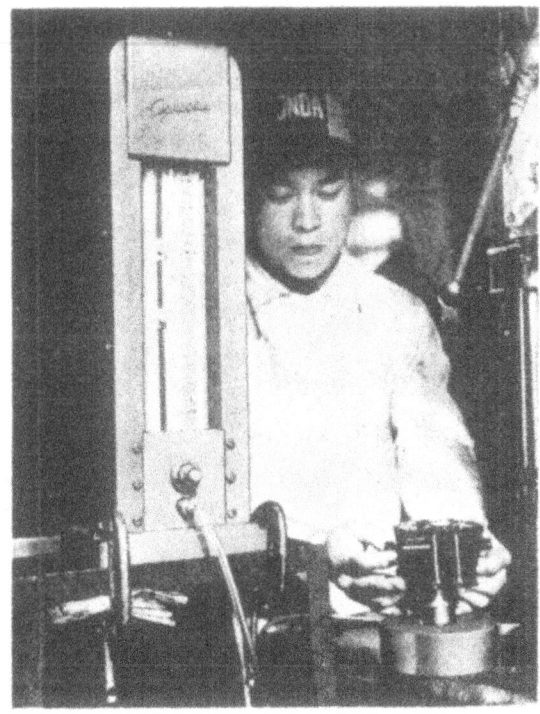

Fig 1.14 Checking the Inside Diameter of Cylinder with an Air-micrometer

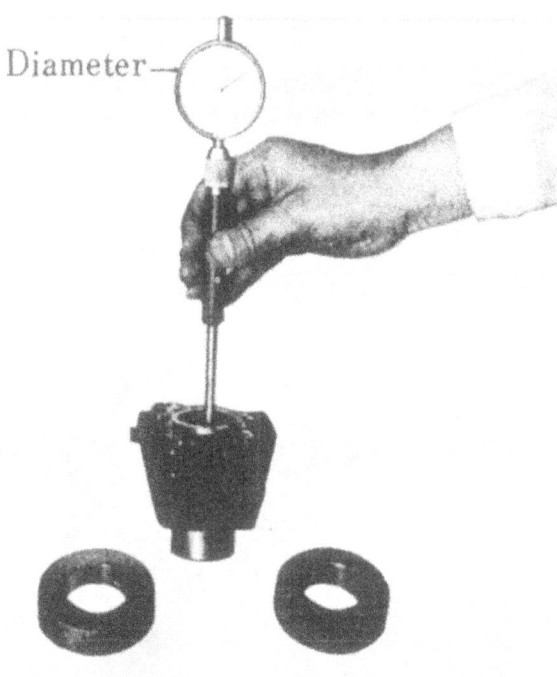

Fig 1.15 Checking Cylinder Inside Diameter with a Dial Gauge

1. ENGINE

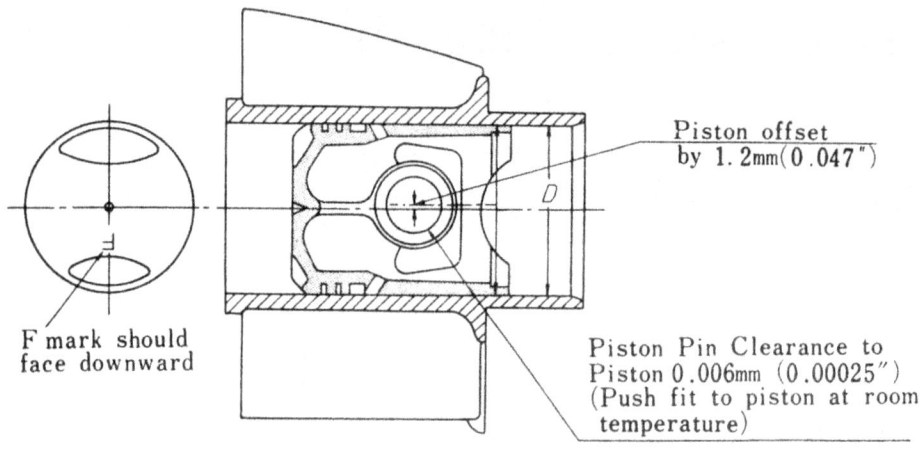

Piston offset by 1.2mm (0.047")

F mark should face downward

Piston Pin Clearance to Piston 0.006mm (0.00025") (Push fit to piston at room temperature)

Specifications

Cylinder inner diameter	40.0~40.1 mm (1.575~1.530")
Cylinder out of round	0.01~0.05 mm (0.0004~0.002")
Cylinder height	63.1~63.4 mm (2.49~2.5")
Piston diameter at skirt	39.0~39.8 mm (1.54~1.57")
Piston clearance to cylinder mfg.std. (at skirt)	0.01~0.03 mm (0.0004~0.000118")

Fig. 1.16 Cylinder & Piston Dimensions

(2) Piston

Check the piston as shown in **fig. 1.15** after carefully removing carbon and other particles. Determine by the spec. shown in **fig 1.16** and replace if found defective.

Special attention must be given to scored surfaces and carbon on both cylinder and piston.

NOTE: On engines numbered after No. 59-935886, the piston offset is 1.5 mm. These new pistons are available for engines previous to the above number.

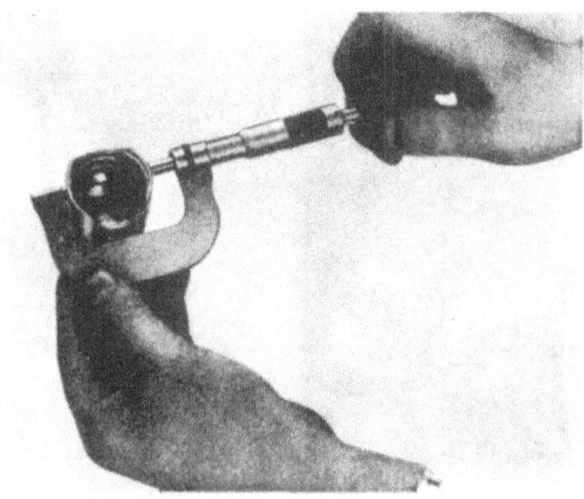

Fig. 1.17 Checking Piston Skirt with Micrometer.

1.3 CYLINDER, PISTON & PISTON RINGS

(3) Piston rings

Piston rings are most related to the cause of low compression and oil pumping up to the combustion chamber.

Ring wear can be determined by checking the opening gap with a feeler gauge, aligning it with the cylinder skirt secton D in **fig. 1.18**.

Tension is checked by using a tester like shown in **fig. 1.19**. Allowable tension of piston rings is as listed is as table 1.19 (**a**).

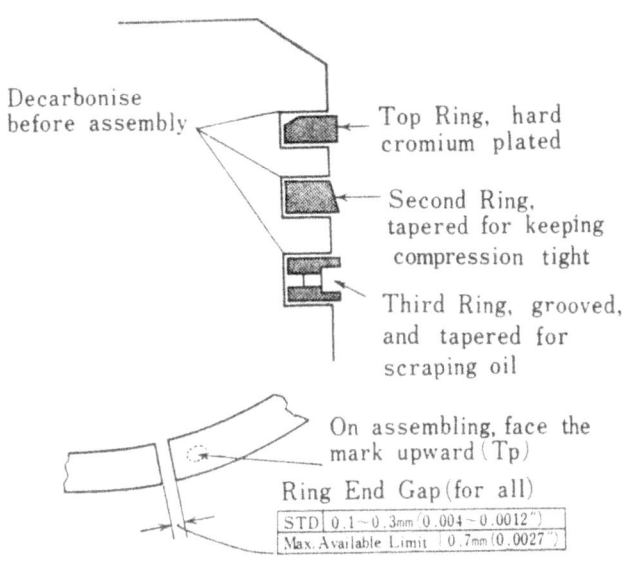

Fig. 1.18 Piston Ring

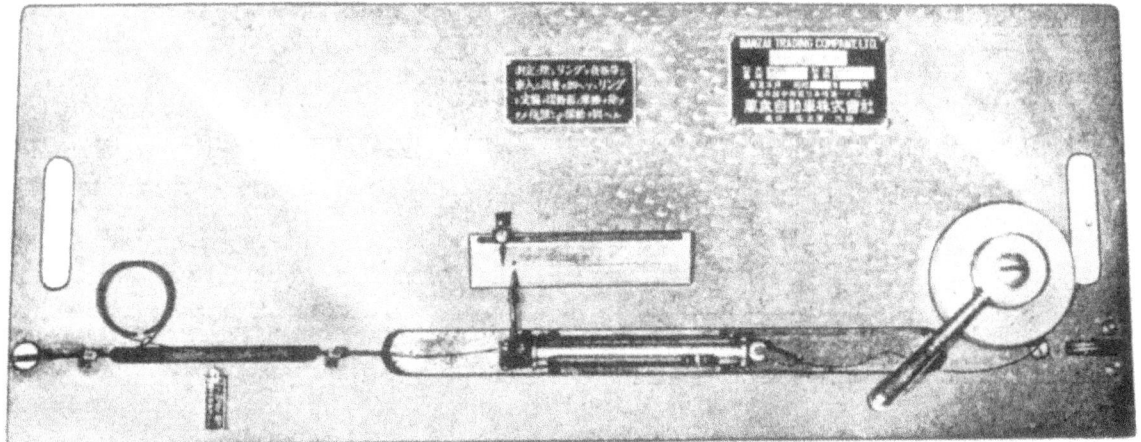

Fig. 1.19 Checking Piston Ring Tension and Its Specification

	Tension [check at the end gap width with 0.2mm (0.002″)]
Top and Second Ring	0.03~0.75 kg (0.66~1.65 lbs)
Oil Ring	0.6~1.11 kg (1.32~2.44 lbs)

Table 1.19 (a)

MEMO

1.4 L Cover & Relative Parts

The work inside the L cover can be accomplished while the engine is installed on chassis. Engine overhall can be done more easily if these are disassembled first.

A. Disassembly

(1) **Flywheel magneto**

Keep the flywheel from turning by using the flywheel holder, remove the nut with 17 mm socket wrench and remove flywheel using flywheel puller as shown in following **fig. 1.20**. During this operation be careful not to damage crankshaft or flywheel and not use unnecessary force.

Stator can be dismantled by removing the two 5×12 mm screws (2 T cross head screw driver). Disconnect wiring harness, high tension terminal, neutral switch and other connections. (refer **fig. 1.21**).

NOTE: Be careful not to damage the 3 mm key (3×5 Woodruff key) and tapered portion of flywheel.

10 mm Flywheel Nut
Torque (2.7-3.0 kg-m) 19~22 ft-lb
Fig. 1.20 Extracting Flywheel

Fig. 1.21 Disassembling Flywheel and Its Coil Base

(2) Drive sprocket

First fold down the 8 mm folding washer, which is holding the clamp bolt from turning, then use drive sprocket holder to keep it from turning and remove clamp bolt with 17 mm socket wrench. There is a 17 mm "O" rubber ring in between the collar, inside the drive sprocket and the oil seal forced into the L crankcase.

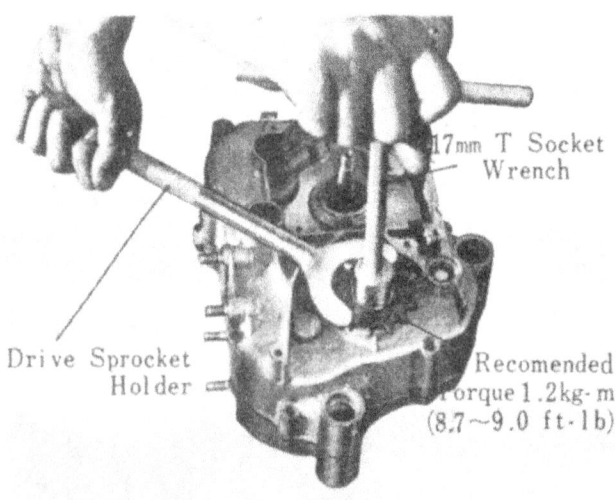

Fig. 1.22 Removing Drive Sprocket Clamp Bolt

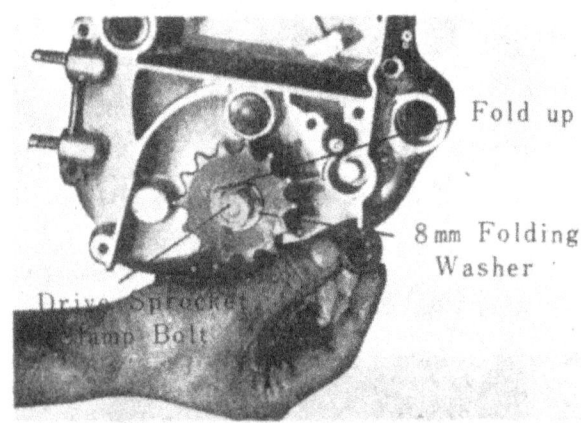

Fig. 1.23 Assemble of Drive Sprocket

B. Reassembly

Reassemble by following the steps for disassembly backwards.
Be careful of connection to flywheel magneto, flywheel taper and 3 mm key and folding up of drive sprocket clamp bolt, etc. while reassembling.

1.5 R Cover & Relative Parts

By removing the kick starter arm and R crankcase cover (Nine 6 mm cross head screws......#3 T-cross screw driver), the interior will be displayed as in **fig**. 1.24. Disassemble this in ① ② ③ ④ ⑤ ⑥ sequence. Follow these steps backwards for reassembling. (Kick starter spindle shaft ⑧ cannot be removed without disassembling left and right side crankcases).

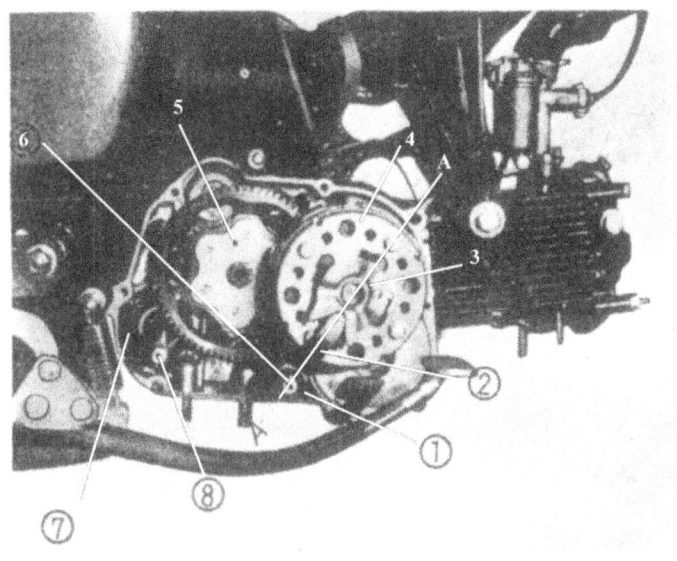

① 10.5 mm flat washer
② Clutch lever
③ Oil through (oil feeding cup)
④ Clutch complete
⑤ Driven gear
⑥ Gear shift spindle shaft
⑦ Kick starter spring
⑧ Kick starter spindle shaft

Fig. 1.24 Disassemly of Right Side Cover

① 10.5 mm Washer
② Clutch Lever
   Align center on A-A' line when reassembling as it is a serration fit.
③ Oil Through (oil feeding cup)
   Clean the oil hole thoroughly when washing as this designed to lubricate the drive gear by the oil coming down from the groove on top.
④ Clutch Unit
   The 14 mm lock nut attaching the clutch complete to the crankshaft has a 14 mm lock washer to prevent it from loosening. Fold down this tongue (screw driver) and remove lock nut with 14 mm pin spanner, holding the clutch in place with the clutch outer holder.
   Lift up the tongue of the lock washer after the lock nut is completely tightened. If the washer tongue and lock nut do meet, do not loosen nut in

1. ENGINE

Fig. 1.25 Dismantling & Installing Clutch Assembly

order to meet the slot of bolt, but always turn the bolt in the direction of tightening before locking.

⑤ Driven Gear

Pull snap ring with snap ring pliers and remove driven gear, which is spline fitted, as shown in **fig. 1.26**.

On assembling, it is necessary make sure that these parts were reset satisfactory and replace set ring if tension is poor.

Fig. 1.26 Removal of Driven Gear Using Snap Ring Pliers

⑥ Gearshift Spindle

First pull out pivot bolt and remove shift drum stopper. Pull the gear-

1.5 R COVER & RELATIVE PARTS

shift spindle towards you while pushing the shift arm tip downward as shown in **fig. 1.27** which is biting with the shift drum, and it will come out as an assembly. Reassembly is the reverse of this, but check the movements at the three points marked ⓐ and also make sure that the shift return spring pin inside of ⓑ is not bent.

Fig. 1.27 Romoval of Gear Shift Arm

⑦ Kick Starter Spring

Same as on the driven gear, remove the snap ring using the snap ring pliers. Remove the kick starter spring with screw driver.

When reassembling hold in place with 22 mm washer, then set.

Fig. 1.28 Remove Kick Starter Spring, Using Snap Ring Pliers

MEMO

1.6 Crankshaft & Connecting Rod

Crankshaft is of constructed type made to endure high revolutions and the large end of connecting rod has roller bearings. There is a dipper on the connecting rod that splashes the oil.

The crankshaft rotates at a maximum of more 10,000 rpm so special care must be taken in press fitting. Also, care must be taken in checking the missalignment at both ends.

A. Disassembly

The crankcases can be split in half after removing cylinder and the parts covered with right and left cover, such as A. C. dynamo, drive sprocket, clutch and changing device.

After finishing each disassembling procedure until the comment stated on chapter 1.5., crankcase can be split in half by unscrewing 5 cross screws, one bolt (6 mm) and two stud nuts in L crankcase. If the fitting of crankshaft bearings are so tight as they can not be separated by hand, tap slightly straight on left end of crankshaft with wooden block hammer.

When the crankcase is disassembled in half, the crankshaft is assembled to the R crankcase. In order to seperate this crankshaft, pull out timing gear with the timing gear puller and pull out the timing knock pin with a plier as shown in **fig. 1.29.**

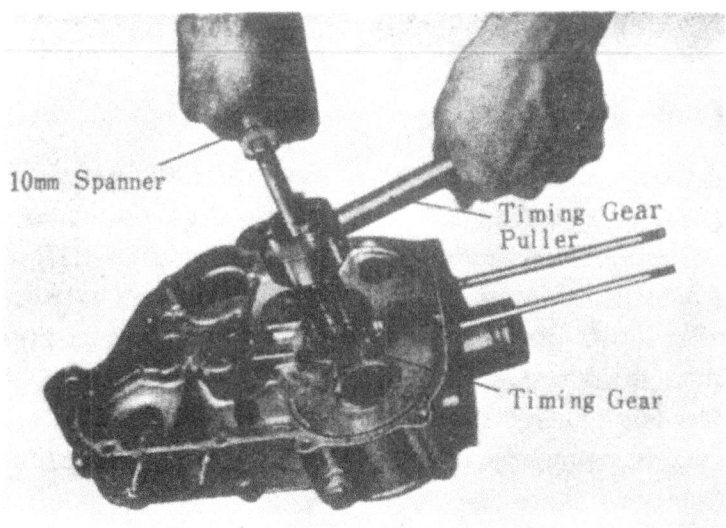

Fig. 1.29 Taking out the Timing Gear with Timing Gear Puller

The crankshaft and crank pin have been modified from the Engine Serial Number C 100 E-948004. The modification is as seen below.

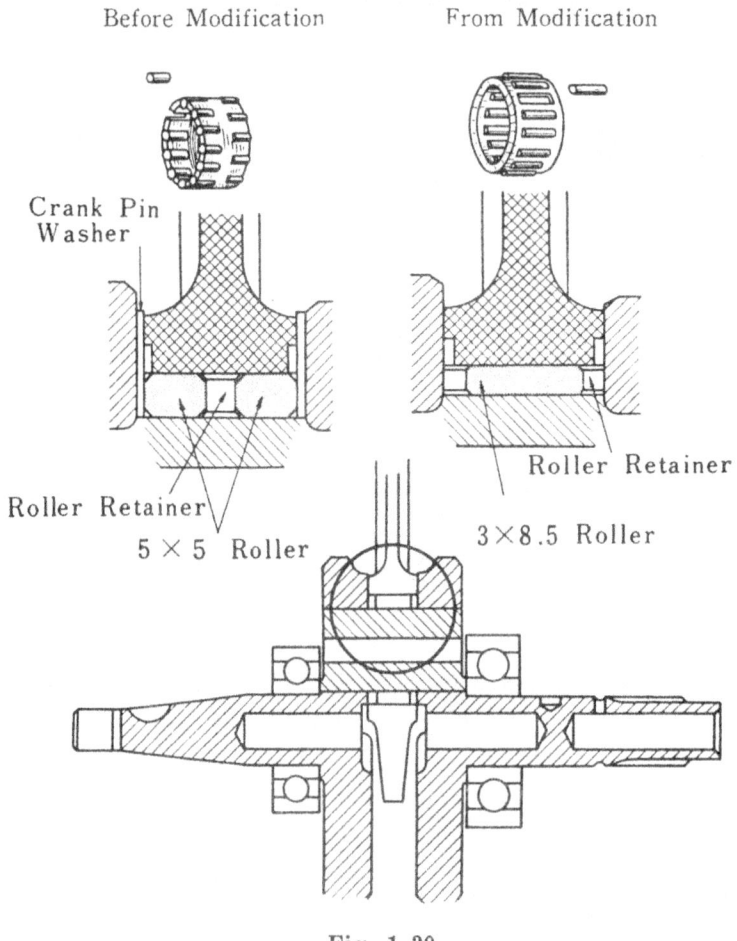

Fig. 1.30

B. Inspection & Servicing

As crankshaft and connecting rod is assembled by press fitting crank pin. Check the play at the small end of connecting rod, the wear at the large end of rod and the alignment at both ends of crankshaft. If found faulty, disassemble the crankshaft and replace with new parts if necessary.

As shown in **fig. 1.30**, check alignment with dial gauge and measure the out side diameter with micrometer. Also, check alignment at small end of connecting rod as shown in **fig. 1.31** and check wear at large end.

During this inspection correct any faults and when having work done through sources other than own shop, be sure to order work to shop where high precision work can be done. Because special jig is needed for fitting crank pin pressing machine. If it cannot be repaired replace the crankshaft in complete.

The ball bearings supporting both ends of crankshaft are 6303 at R crankshaft and 6203 at L Crakshaft and are both inserted into R. and L crankcases.

Check if these bearings can run smoothly without any noise after cleaning with solvent. Faulty bearings must be replaced.

1.6 CRANKSHAFT & CONNECTING ROD

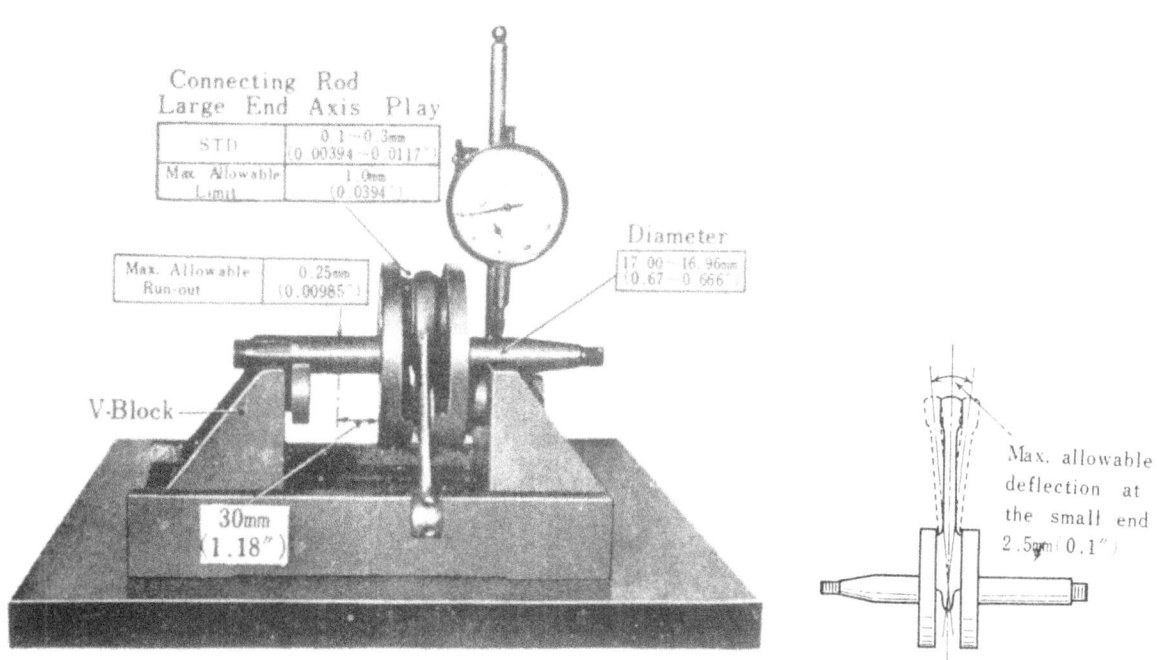

Fig. 1.31 Checking Crankshaft Alignment   Fig. 1.32

C. Installation of Timing Gear

Set crankshaft to bearing 6303, pressed into R crankcase, drive in timing knock pin and drive in timing gear with timing gear driver. During this operation use hand or jig to hold middle of balance weight of crankshaft, in other words the large end of connecting rod, so as not to distort crankshaft.

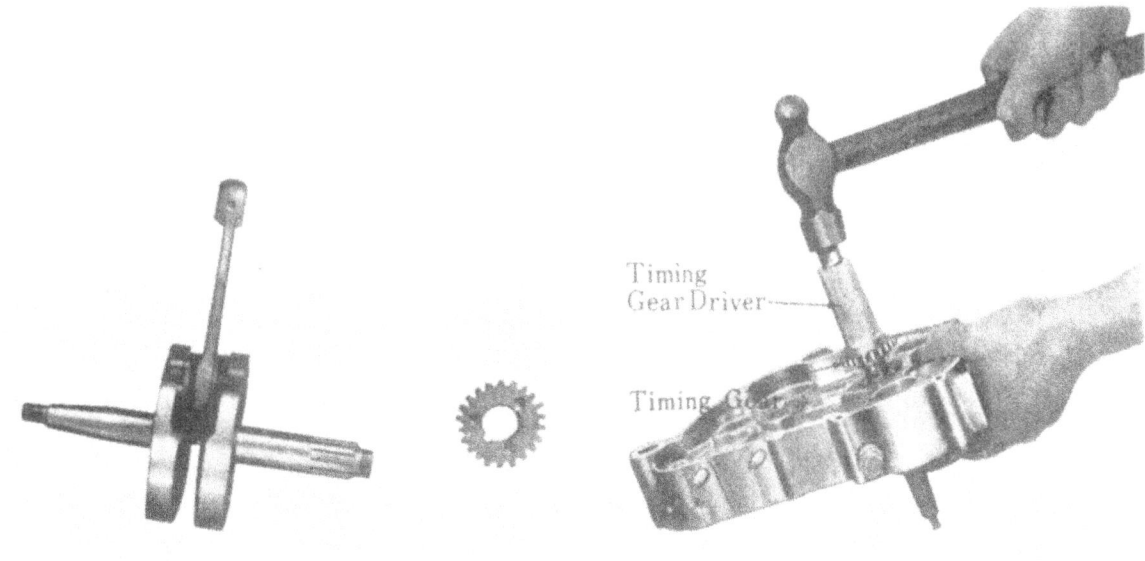

Fig. 1.33 Crankshaft & Timing Gear   Fig. 1.34 Driving in Timing Gear

1.7 Lubrication System

Lubricating system is wet sump type without oil pump. Oil is distributed to the crank parts from the oil sump by cam gear and dipper on large end of connecting rod which splashes oil to the piston pin and cylinder (**fig. 1.35**)

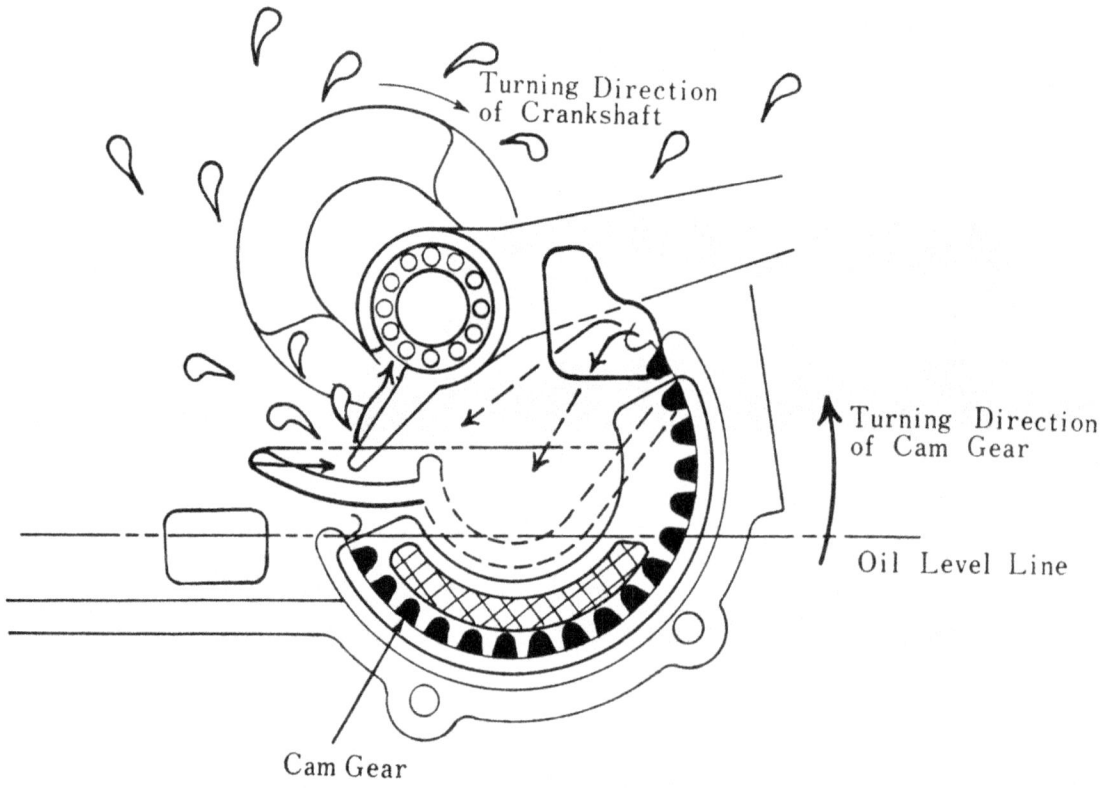

Fig. 1.35 Lubrication of Crank Parts

Oil is forced through the screw type groove machined in the camshaft bearing, by the revolution of the camshaft and sent to the top of the head-cover through the oil pipe. Oil returns to the crankcase through the hole below the cylinder.

Lubrication of transmission and clutch is performed by oil splashed by the revolution of each gear.

Inspect the circulation of oil while engine is running. An inspection can be made by removing the oil pipe clamp bolt ① and see if oil flows out from the pipe. When oil does not happen to come out at idling blow oil lines through with air. Check wear on cam shaft journal or crankcase bushing when disassembled and if they are in bad condition, replace.

1.7 LUBRICATION SYSTEM 21

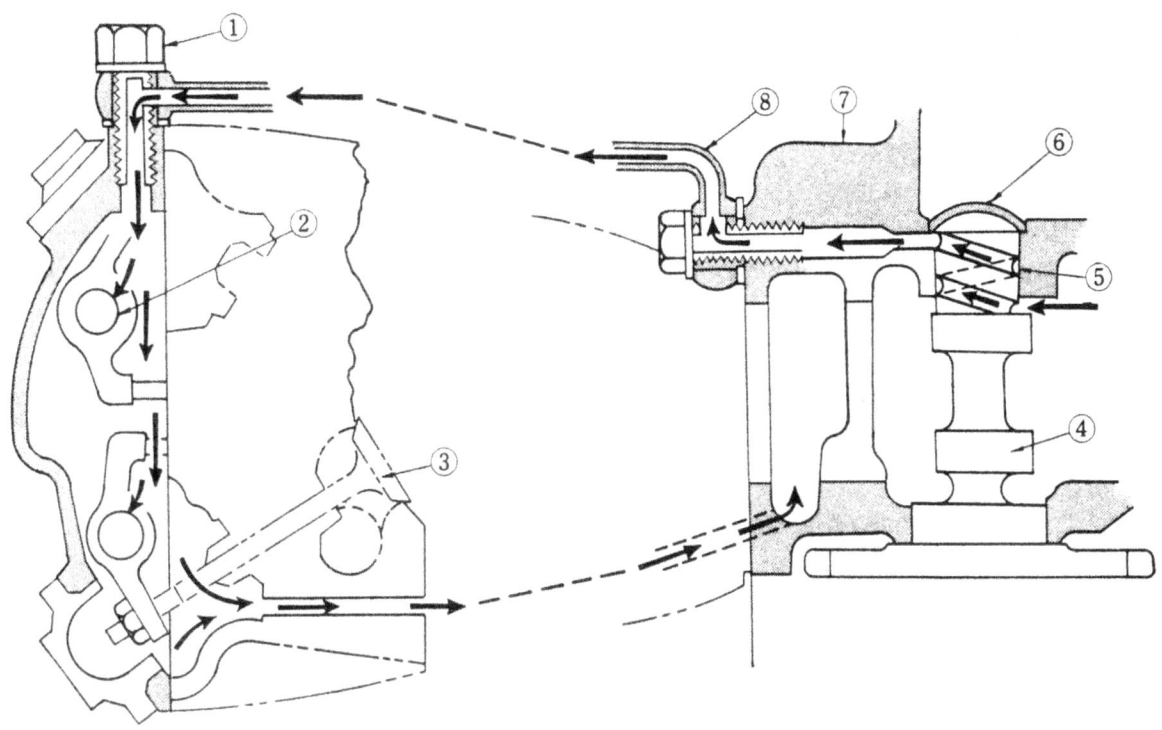

① Oil pipe clamp bolt.
② Rocker arm
③ Valve
④ Camshaft
⑤ Max. allowable clearance
⑥ Blind cap
⑦ Left side of engine
⑧ Oil pipe

Fig. 1.36 Circulation of Lubricant to the Head

MEMO

1.8 Cam and Valve Mechanism

The movement of the intake and exhaust valves, angled oppositely towards the dome shaped combustion chamber, is transmitted from the cam gear to the valve lifter, the push rod and to rocker arm.

This mechanism, constituting the basis of the 4 cycle engine, is constructed to endure the high speed revolution by smooth operation and efficient lubrication. See page 103 for tappet clearance adjustment.

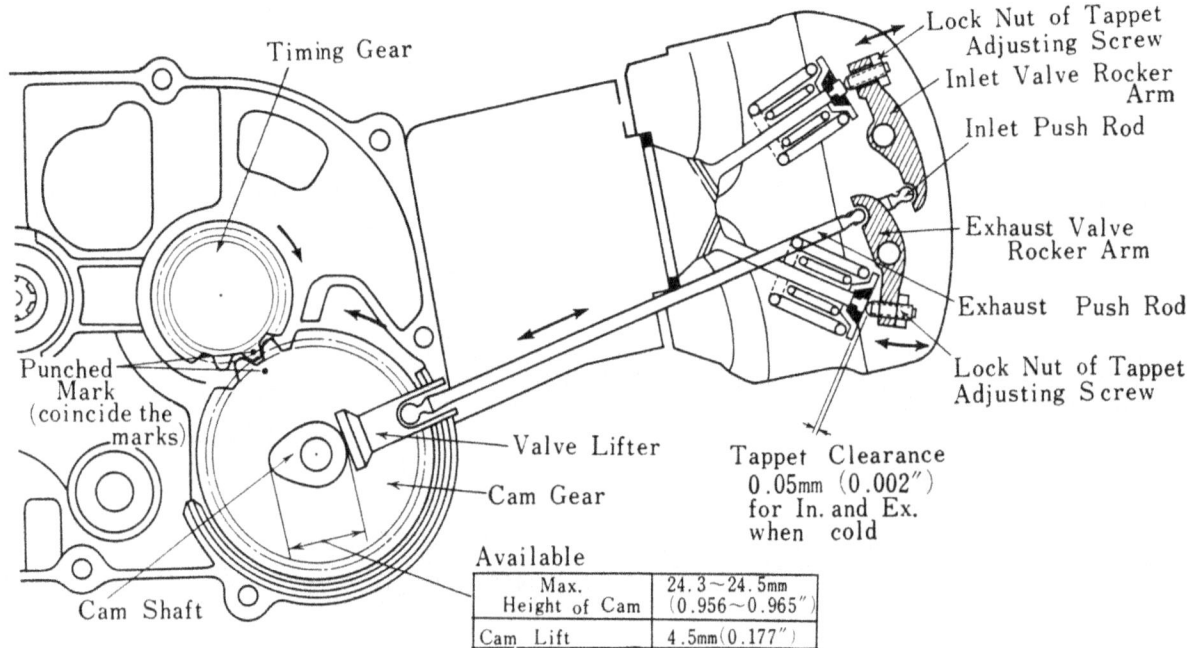

Available	
Max. Height of Cam	24.3~24.5mm (0.956~0.965")
Cam Lift	4.5mm (0.177")

Fig. 1.37 Cam & Valve Mechanism

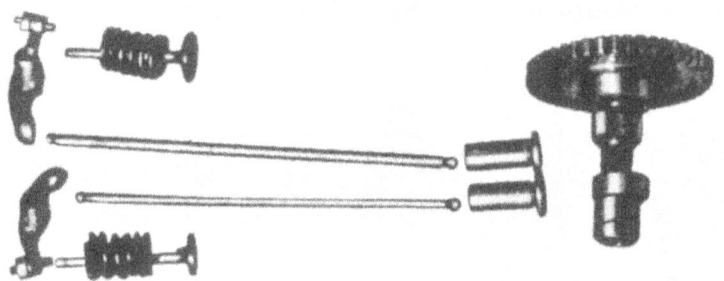

Fig. 1.38 Cam & Valve Parts

A. Disassembly

As the rocker arms are attached on the cylinder head cover, firstly remove the head cover, then unscrew the rocker arm shaft. (refer to p. 4)

Pull out the push rods from the head.

The valves are disassembled with the special tool-valve lifter (P-2) after removing cylinder head. It is used to compress the valve springs down in order to take valve cotters off.

Extract the cam shaft and tappets after disassembling clutch assembly.

1.8 CAM & VALVE MECHANISM

B. Inspection

(1) Check wear or blow-by around the valve face.

If flaws are slight, or depth of wear is within 0.2 mm (0.007"), grind minimum amount of metal to diminish the flaw with valve refacer.

Complete it to the angle 45° on both exhaust and inlet.

If the depth of flaw is more than 0.2 mm (0.007") replace the valve.

(2) Check valve stem with micrometer, if it is out of the specification, replace. (refer to p. 132)

(3) Replace the cam, tappets and cam gear if worn excessively.

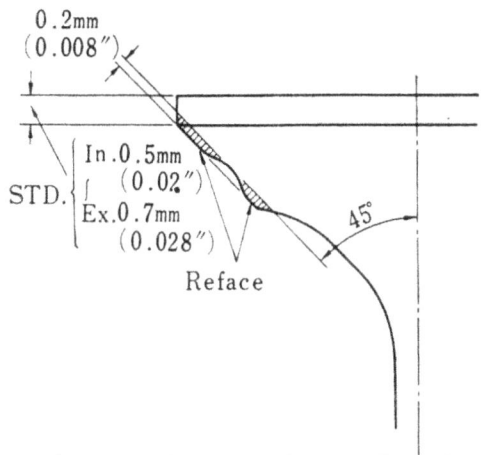

Fig. 1.39 Measurement on Valve Refacing

C. Assembly

Install the tappets to the hole in crankcase and push them home. Then insert the cam shaft with its cam gear assembled back to crankcase.

In order to coordinate valve timing, line up punch mark on both gears when meshing timing and cam gear.

> NOTE: Cam shaft and cam gear were one cast iron body, but on engines numbered No. C 100 59-920706 and after the cam shaft is of forged-steel and separated, and bolted together by 8 mm bolt.

After tightening cylinder head stud nuts, insert the longer push rod in left side hole, and the other in the right side hole of engine.

Replace the cylinder head cover assembled with rocker arms, taking special care to fix push rod ends on rocker arm bowls.

Tighten bolts and nuts to required torque.

1. ENGINE

1.9 Transmission and Kick Starter

The three forward-speed syncromesh transmission is designed to fully display ascending and accelerating ability according to the engine output. With a light load on level ground, second gear is sufficient for starting out and low gear is used only for steep inclines. Therefore, neutral is placed between low and second.

The 8 mm bolt tightening the drive sprocket is hollowed, acting as a breather, expelling the pressure inside the crankcase out through the countershaft.

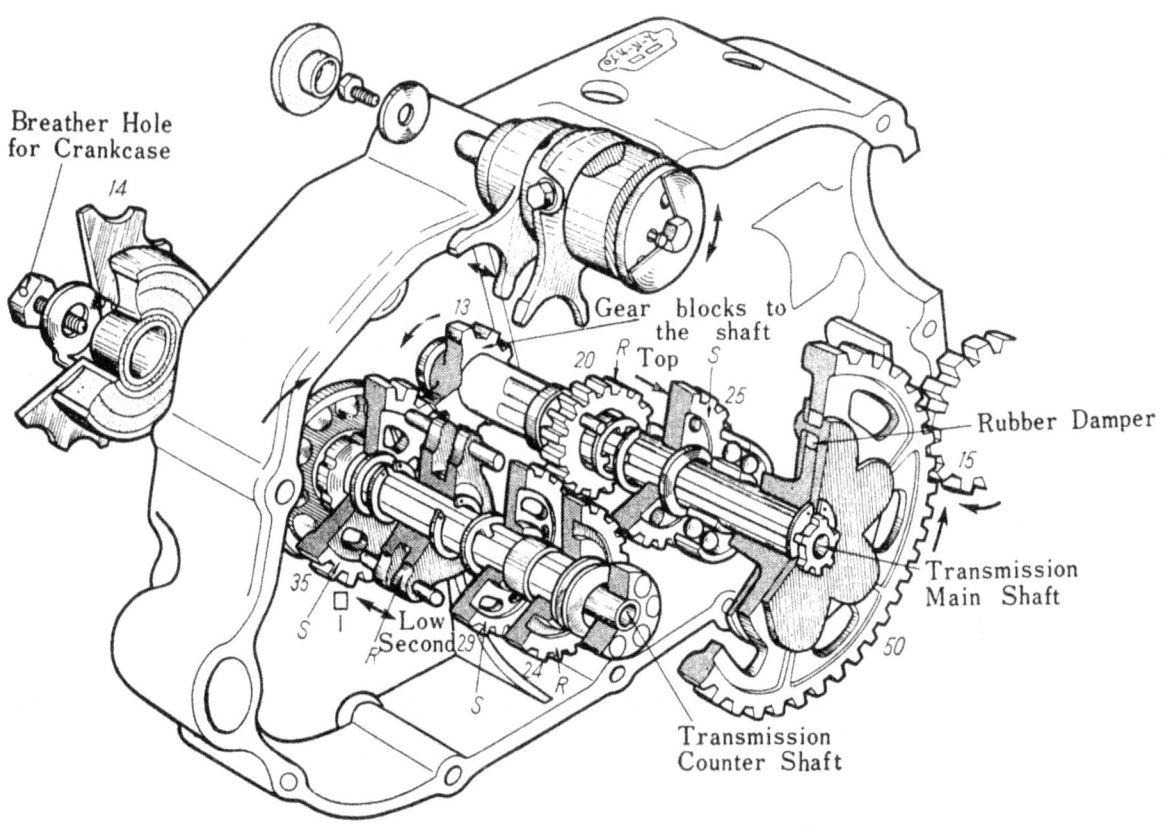

Fig. 1.40 Construction View of Transmission

This type, meshing kick starter pinion into the low gear makes kick starting easy and light and by utilizing the transmission gear causes very little trouble.

fig. 1.41 shows the gear train from crankshaft and the direction of rotation and shaft position.

1.9 TRANSMISSION AND KICK STARTER 25

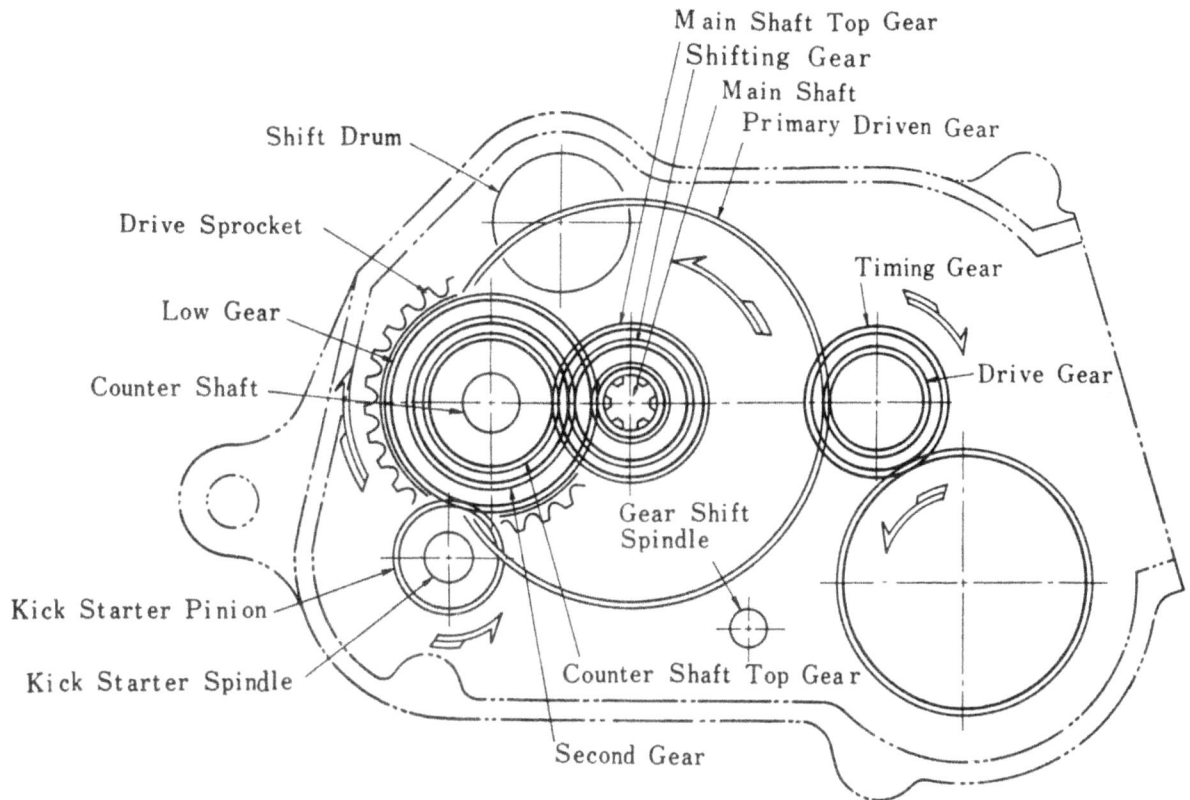

Fig. 1.41 Gear Train

The 5 gears set on the mainshaft and countershaft consist of those whose rotation is fixed by the spline (marked R in **fig. 1.40**) and those whose shaft run is fixed by snap ring (marked S). The former should be checked for fit with spline grooves and the latter to see that thrust washer (with tongue) is inserted and rotates smoothly when set with snap ring.

A. Disassembly

Transmission gears and shafts are disassembled after splitting crankcase in half.

Transmission gear complete is left in the L crankcase as **fig 1.42** when R crankcase and crankshaft has been removed. Remove kick starter shaft with ratchet and pinion gear. Pull out the countershaft, transmission shaft and shift drum altogether, as the manner composed the gear train with two hands. Then separate each gear or shift fork from the shafts.

B. Inspection

First check wear or damage on gear or shaft. Replace the parts in bad condition.

C. Assembly

Fix gear snap rings exactly in their shaft grooves.

Fig. 1.42 Structure of Transmission Gear

Fig. 1.43-a Transmission and Kick Starting Component Parts

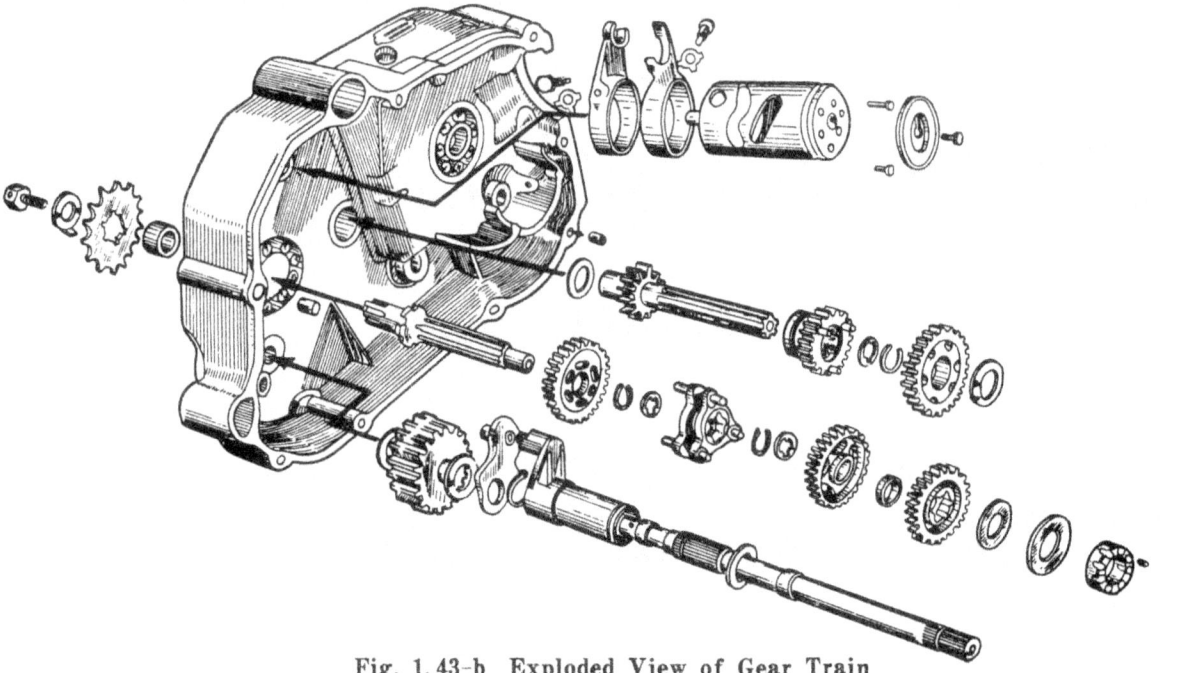

Fig. 1.43-b Exploded View of Gear Train

Insert the shift fork to the shift drum and fix with guide pin, never forget to fold up the washer.

Compose adequate gears and washers in each shaft (main shaft and counter shaft) as seen in **fig. 1.43-a**.

Hold main shaft gears and counter shaft gears in one hand such that they are meshed each other (as in **fig 1.43-a.** except kick shaft), and place the shift drum on them such as the shift forks encounter to each shifter and shift gear.

1.9 TRANSMISSION AND KICK STARTER 27

Now, three journals to their correspondent bearings in the L. crankcase at same time.

Install kick shaft with pinion gear and ratchet.

While proceeding installing, take care so that the thrust washers seat properly.

Install crankshaft and replace right crankcase tight with screws.

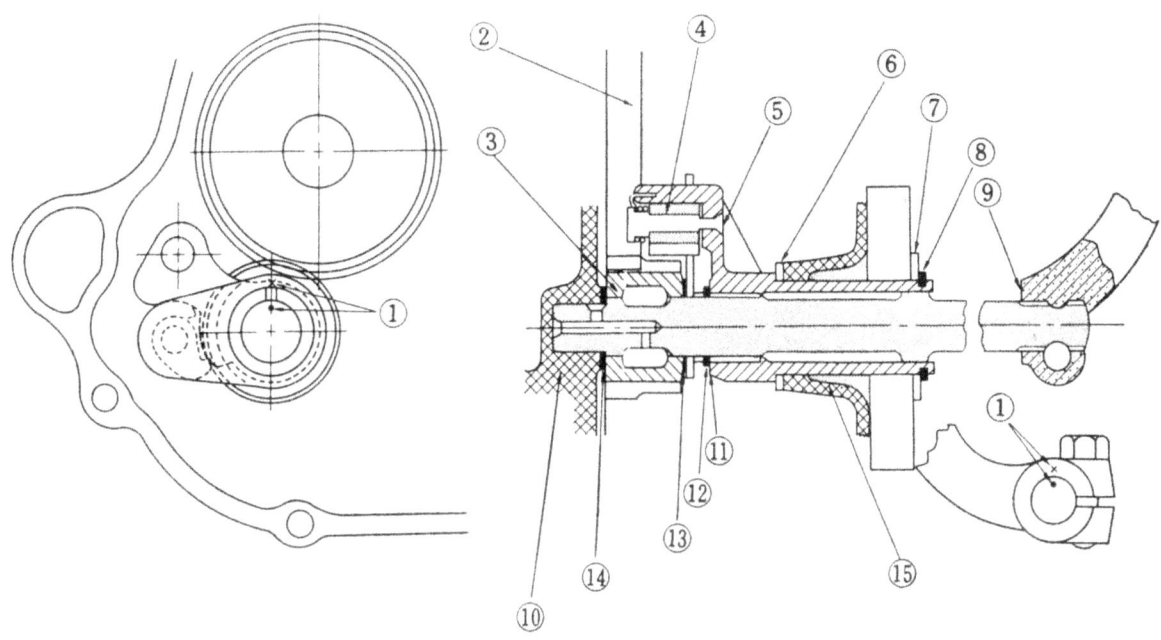

① Coincide the punched mark
② Low gear
③ Kick starter pinion
④ Kick starter ratchet
⑤ Rivetted
⑥ Kick ratchet flange washer
⑦ Washer, 22 mm
⑧ Snap ring, 23 mm
⑨ Punched mark
⑩ L. crankcase
⑪ Punched mark
⑫ Snap ring, 17 mm
⑬ Thrust washer, 14 mm
⑭ Starter pinion washer
⑮ R. crank case

Fig. 1.44 Sectional View of Kick Starter

Furthermore, the stopper of the kick starter ratchet has been attached from Engine Serial Number C100 E-952932. In relation with this modification the shape of ratchet and R. crankcase are changed.

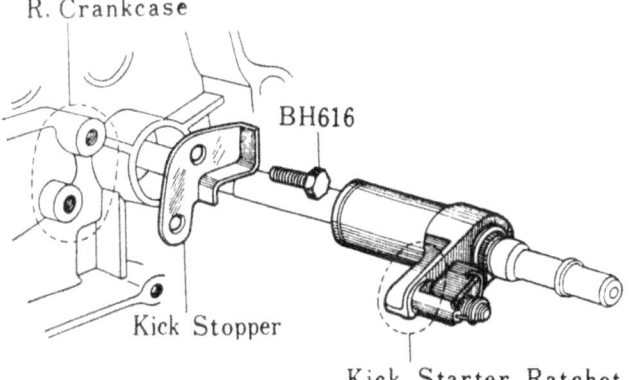

Fig. 1.45 Kick Ratchet Stopper

Fig. 1.44 is sectional view of kick starter mechanism. Be careful of washers and snap ring of the various parts and always align the punched marks of kick starter spindle and kick starter ratchet and kick arm serration fit when disassembling and reassembling.

NOTE: There are no marks on kick arms with frame serial numbers pre C 100 59-24473. In this case for install kick arm so that it is within of 45° degrees to horizontal line.

MEMO

1.10 R. Crankcase and L. Crankcase

Crankshaft 6303 ball bearing and transmission mainshaft bearing #6303 are tight fitted in R. crankcase. To the L. crankcase ball bearing #6203 for left crankshaft, SI 7347 oil seal, counter shaft ball bearing #6023, S 22347 oil seal and main shaft bronze bushing are press fitted.

Therefore, if pressing machine is unavailable, use correct driver and hammer to fit those bearings and oil seals into the crankcase.

Check all these parts whether they are in good condition. Care must be taken not to injure the face of crankcase which the gaskets are seated while disassembling.

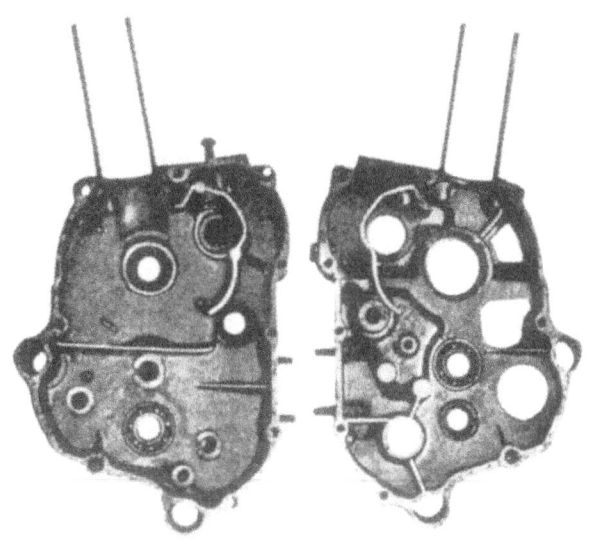

Fig. 1.46

MEMO

1.11 Clutch

Although this is a centrifugal type automatic clutch, the clutch can be disengaged and engaged by operation of the change pedal. This is also connected to the transmission for shifting gears. The clutch assembly can be broken down into three sections, described below.

(1) Clutch center & drive gear

These serve to hold clutch stationary when using kick starter and when engine-braking, and has screw-spline type operation in order to disengage clutch when engine is revolving at low speed (when centrifugal force is small).

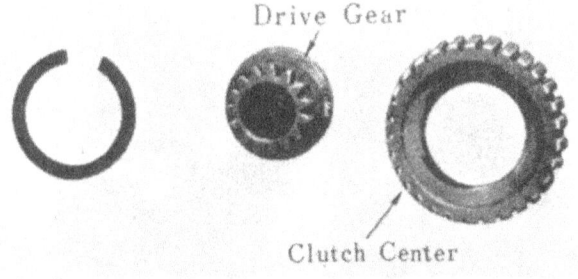

Fig. 1.47 Drive Gear & Clutch Center

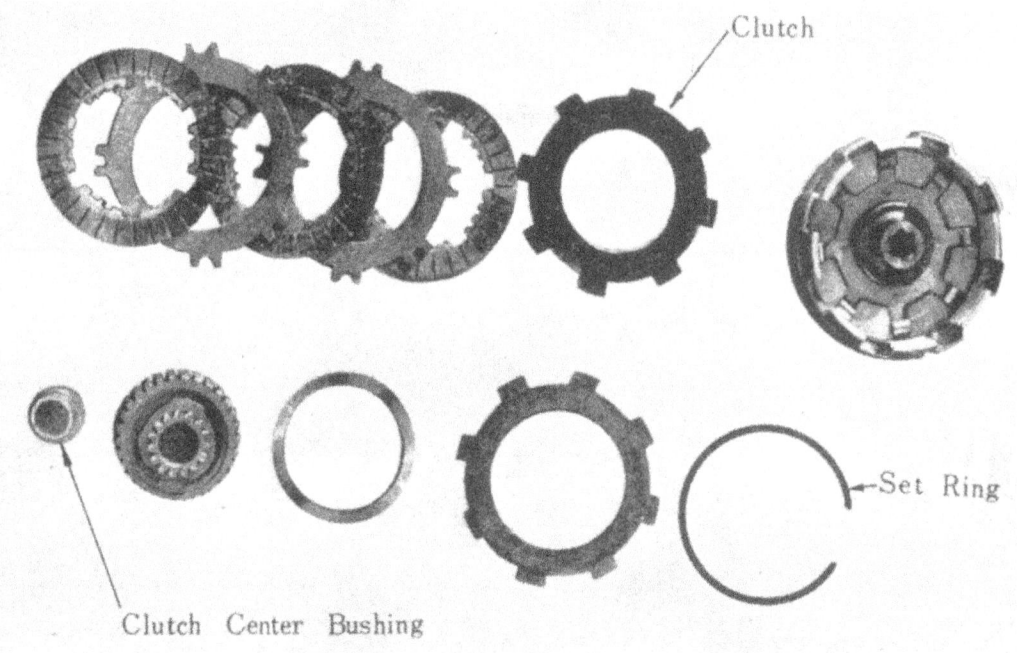

Fig. 1.48 Clutch Assembly Parts

1.11 CLUTCH

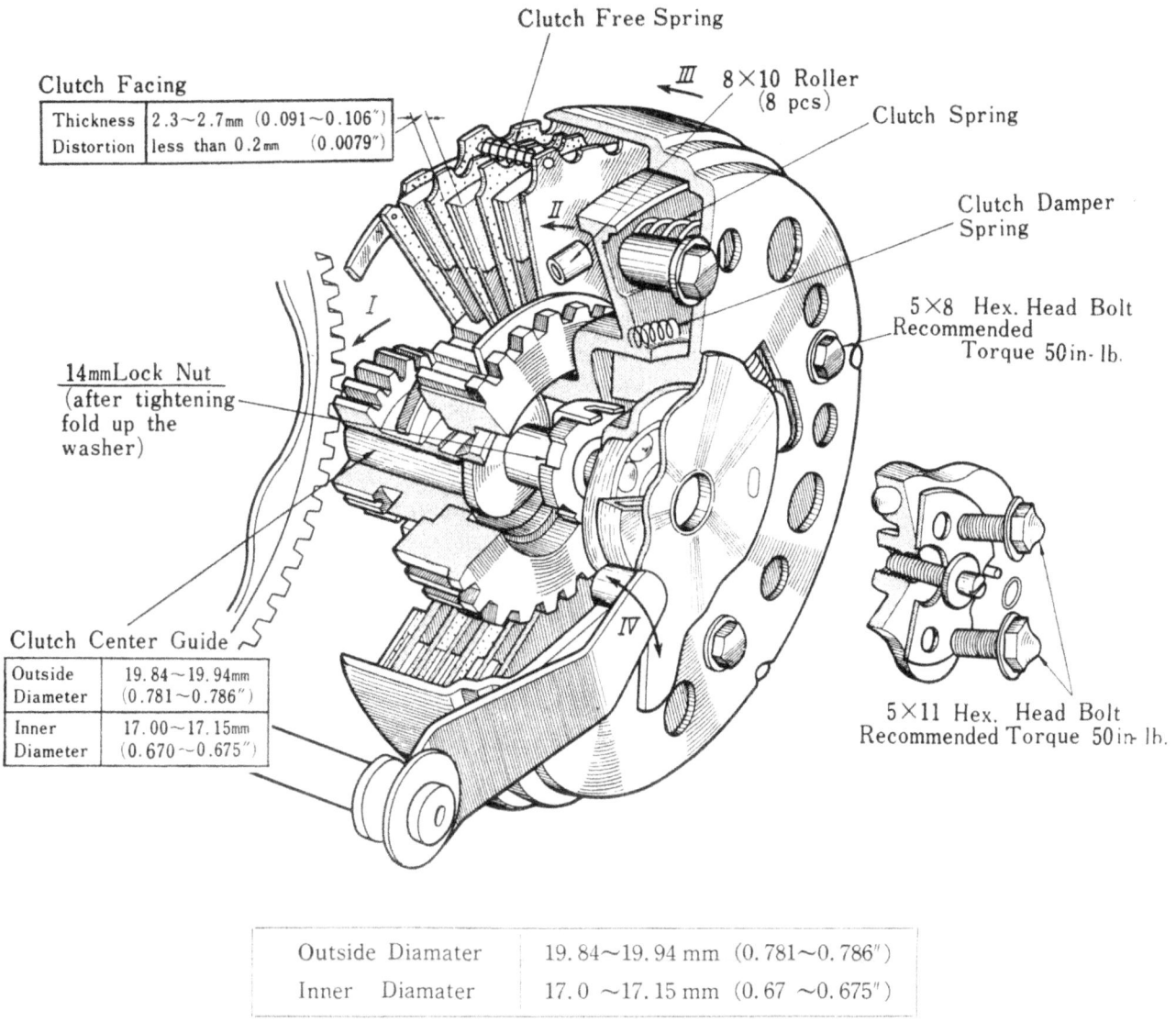

Outside Diamater	19.84~19.94 mm (0.781~0.786")
Inner Diamater	17.0 ~17.15 mm (0.67 ~0.675")

Fig. 1.49 Automatic Centrifugal Clutch

NOTE: When clutch is in engaged position, check to see that drive gear will turn easily when turned in direction of arrow I in fig. 1.49 and will stick when turned suddenly in the opposite direction. The moving parts of clutch center and drive gear should be oiled well before reassembling.

(2) **Centrifugally operated parts & clutch free spring**

The special feature of this clutch is that when it rotates faster than a certain speed, the mechanism transmitting the power is made up by 8 rollers and free spring.

The 8×10 roller pushed out by centrifugal force, move in the direction of arrow II along the tapered face of drive plate and press against the clutch plate. This centrifugal force action is stronger than the spring of clutch springs and furthermore the faster the revolution the stronger this force gets.

Something is needed to resist this centrifugal force in order to disengage clutch at low speed revolutions, as this centrifugal force operates

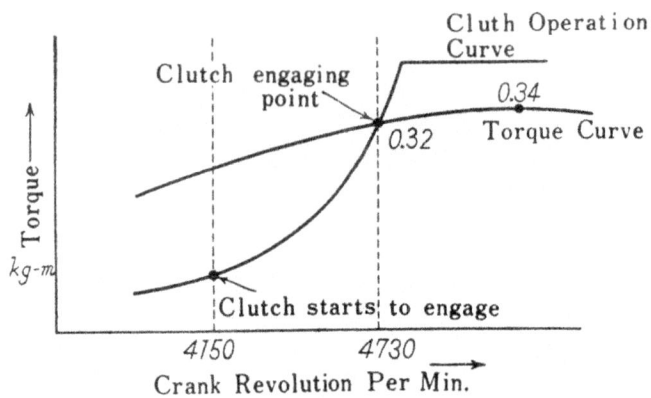

Fig. 1.50 Centrifugal Clutch Operation

as soon as the crankshaft rotates. The clutch spring does this operation. The operation diagram, concerning to the engine r.p.m. torque and centrifugal clutch is shown in **fig. 1.50**.

(3) **Clutch outer & drive plate**

The drive plate, fixed to the crankshaft, is the main component of the clutch assembly.

The clutch arm, which is attached to the drive plate through the clutch spring by four 5×8 hex. head bolts, is connected to the shift arm which operates by the change pedal when pushed in the direction of arrow III in **fig. 1.49** this disengages the clutch, regardless of the relations described in previous paragraphs A and B. In this case the clutch lever can be moved up or down in the direction of arrow IV, and the changing of transmission

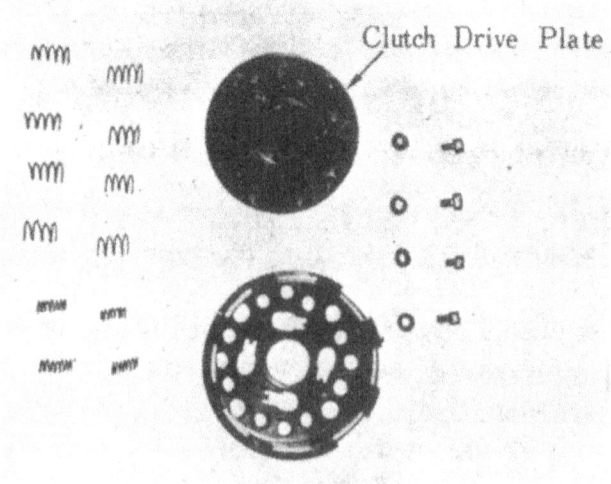

Fig. 1.51 Clutch Outer Parts

1.11 CLUTCH

gears is therefore done by always disengaging the clutch, without causing undue strain during operation.

NOTE: The specification for the 3 springs in the clutch assembly is as follows. Check them before using — as for valve springs.

Table 1.51 (a) Specification of Clutch Springs

	Test Length	Compression
Clutch Spring	21.5~23.2 (0.846~0.912)	0 (free length)
	12.0 (0.473)	1.04~3.04 kg (2.28~6.68 lbs)
Clutch Free Spring	13.9~15.2 (0.548~0.598)	0 (free length)
	12.3 (0.485)	1.7~1.9 kg (3.74~4.18 lbs)
Damper Spring	18.5~19.8 (0.728~0.78)	0 (free length)

A. Disassemble

Clutch assembly can be removed by following the procedure on p. 13 ④.

Place inside of the clutch assy up and remove the 101 mm (3.98″) set ring forcing with driver.

Then it is disassembled as shown in **fig. 1.48**.

Remove the 37 mm (1.46″) clip ring from the drive gear and dsassemble the clutch center as in **fig. 1.47**.

Removing four 5×8 mm (0.2×0.31″) bolt from outside of clutch outer, the parts are disassembled such as **fig 1.51**.

B. Inspection and Assembly

Check thickness of clutch facing with gage. Check strength or free length of clutch spring with spring tester.

And dispose of them in refer to the specifications of **fig 1.49**.

If exessive wear seen in 8×10 mm clutch roller or clutch plate roller leading groove, replace.

Check clutch center guide and dispose of it in refer to the specification described in **table 1.51 (a)**. Assembly can made by following reverse the disassembling procedure.

MEMO

1.12 Shift Mechanism

This mechanism, by the use of one change pedal, operates the clutch and gear shift of transmission and combines straight line and rotating motion. The procedure or disassembly is shown p. 14 ⑥. The main point in servicing is to see that there is no excessive play in the operating angles. In other words, check for excessive wear on moving parts, spring tension, and the operation of the shift drum stopper.

Fig. 1.52 shows the operation of this mechanism.

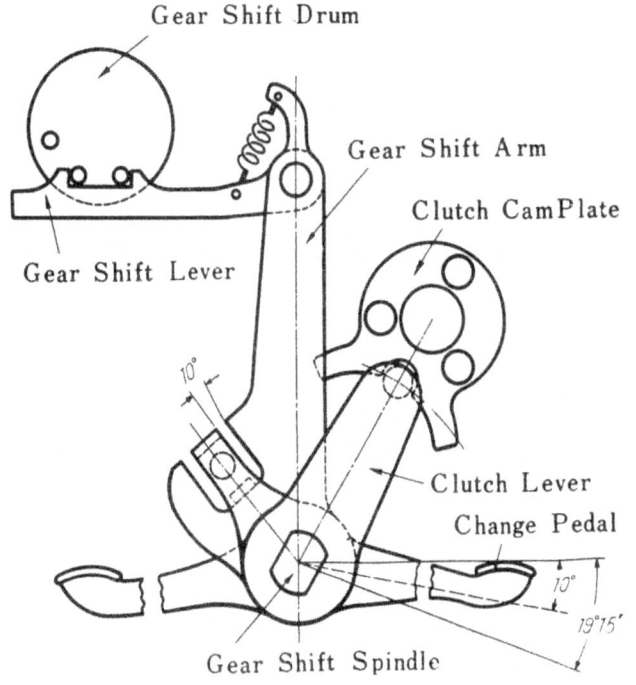

Fig. 1.52 Shift Mechanism

Fig. 1.53 Gear Shift Arm in Assembled Position

1.13 Neutral Switch

On models with engine serial numbers after C 100 E-926506 a neutral switch is installed as shown in **fig. 1.54**. This enables checking if the changing gear is in the neutral position or not, because the lamp lights when the gear is in neutral. (refer to the p. 93)

Fig. 1.55 shows this device in installed position.

Neutral switch contact can be removed by unscrewing 6×16 forhead screw. Check if the contact face of the central electrode and neutral switch rotor are not pitted or burnt and the 7.2×16 O-ring is in good condition, otherwise it causes oil leak.

Fig. 1.54 Neutral Switch

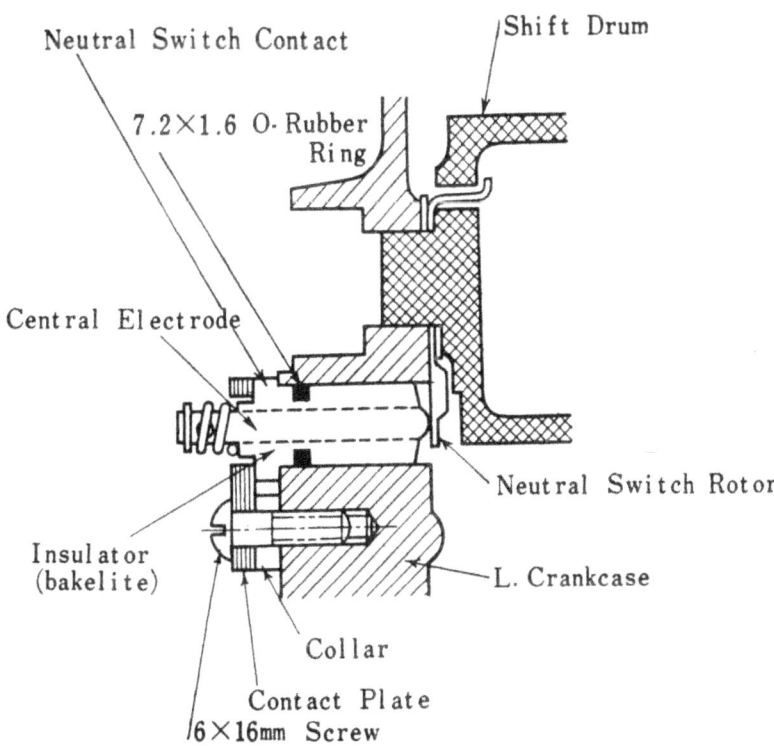

Fig. 1.55 Installation of Neutral Switch

1. ENGINE

1.14 Carburetor

This is a downdraft type carburetor, which draws down towards the horizontal type cylinder and the venturi is of unique elliptical shape, increasing stability at low speed and high speed performance.

The carburetor is installed onto the cylinder intake through the carburetor insulator, with packing and a "O" ring between the insulator and carburetor, which prevents intake air leakage.

The air travels at speeds of about 15 mm per second through carburetor at 5,000 rpm and as this is delicately constructed to insure proper air-fuel mixtures, special care is required in handling.

A. Disassembly and Servicing

To make operation easier, dismantle the front cover removing air cleaner cover and six mounting bolts.

Procedure of disassembly is done by removing those parts following the number in **fig. 1.56**. Then the fuel feed tube should be clipped so that the gasoline contained in tank might not flow out.

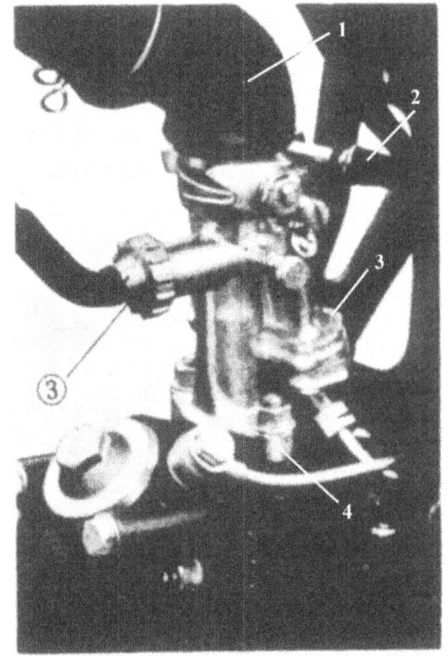

① Air connecting tube
② Fuel feed tube
③ Throttle top cap
④ Over flow pipe connector
⑤ Carburetor mounting

Fig. 1.56 Carburetor

(1) Fuel cock assembly

Removing the float chamber cover screws, the fuel cock ass'y can be split from the float chamber.

Connect the fuel feed tube to the fuel cock joint pipe, feed gasoline to the cock and check if it functions properly. When the cock tap positioned closed, there should not be any symptoms of seepage.

(2) Float chamber

Disassemble the float chamber from the carburetor body removing two flat head screws and clean and check inside float chamber.

(3) Carburetor main body

Remove main jet, slow jet and needle jet and blow all holes through by compressed air. Do not use any stick to take off dust.

1.14 CARBURETOR

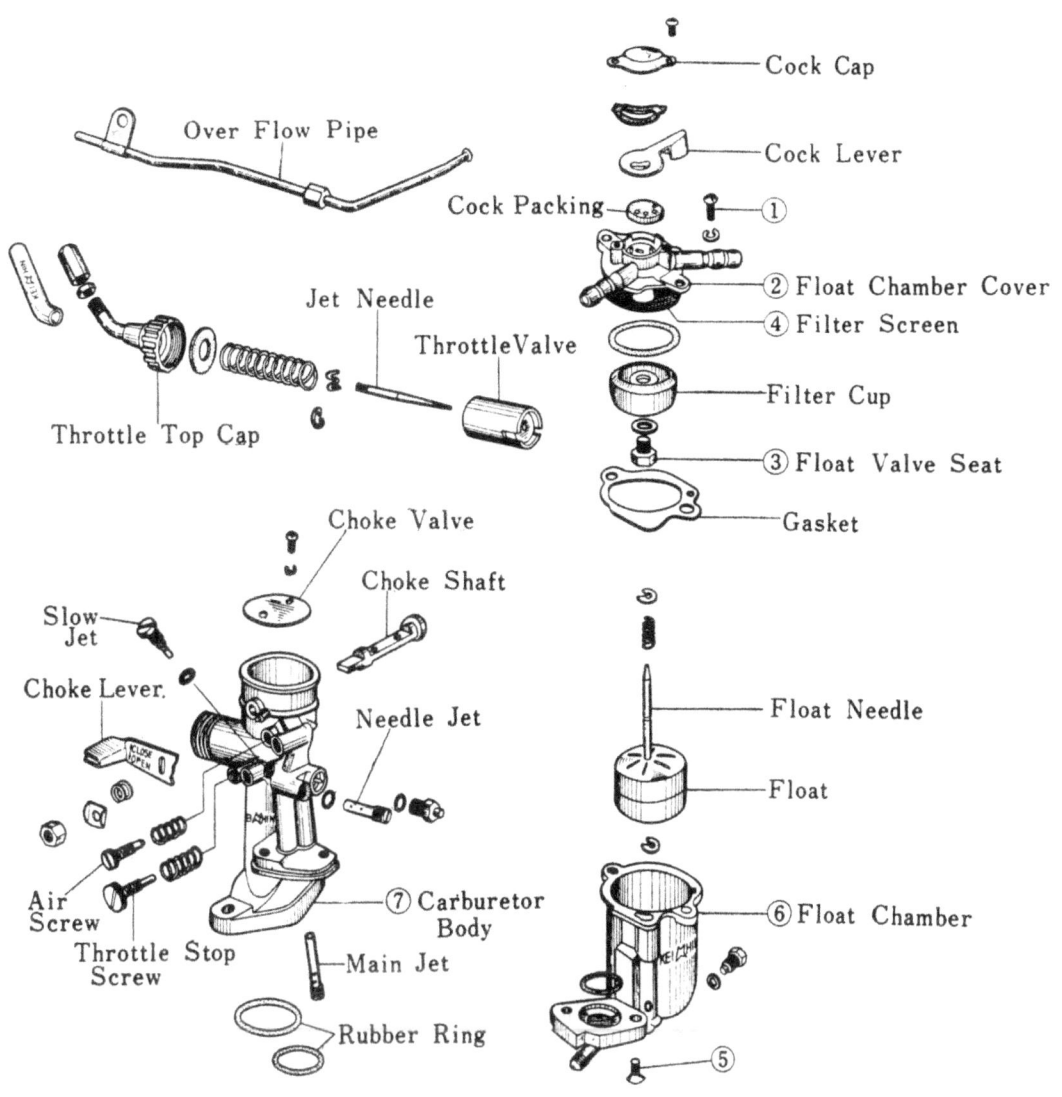

Fig. 1.57 Exploded View of Carburetor

B. Reassembly

Special care must be paid on assembling all jets so that the openings and holes of jets may not be distorted or damaged.

Always use new gaskets and packings when assembling.

After assembling the C type carburetor (refer to the item E) never forget to connect and insert the air vent tube into the frame with fuel feed tube.

C. Adjustment

(1) Throttle opening adjustment

Fig. 1.58 illustrates crank revolutions and carburetor operating parts in proportion to the throttle opening, against venturi, which is most important

1. ENGINE

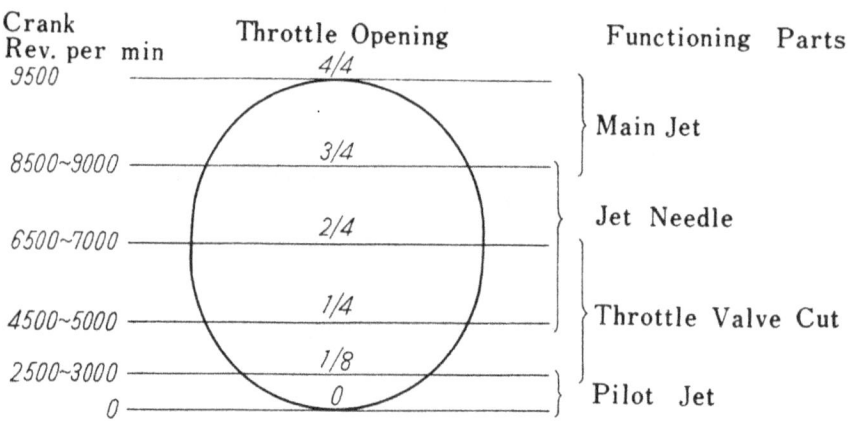

Fig. 1.58 Throttle Opening and Its Function

in developing fuel/air mixture.

Adjust the operating part, according to rpm when revolution is not smooth.

(2) **Idle speed adjustment**

Fig. 1.60(2) illustrates the necessary functions to stabilize idling (up to 2,000 rpm). This is adjusted by the air screw and throttle stop screw shown in **fig. 1.57**.

As seen in the **fig. 1.58**, until the throttle openning to 1/8, the fuel/air mixture is mainly controled by means of the pilot air screw.

Turning it in the mixture will be richer and out will be weaker.

Keeping the throttle at idling opening, turn the screw to find out the point where the engine does neither stall nor stop when the machine is leaned to both side about 10 degrees off from vertical position.

Usual opening of air screw is 1~1 1/4 turn from shut.

Then slow down the engine revolution to the 800~1,000 rpm.

(3) **Intermediate speed and accelerating adjustment**

Engine trouble during acceleration is caused more in the ignition and valve system and it is wrong to attribute this only to the carburetor. When the trouble is in the carburetor, adjust this by throttle valve cut-away and jet needle and needle jet.

From the throttle opening 1/8 to 3/4, the mixture is regulated by the height of throttle cut-away and jet needle (**fig 1.60(1)**)

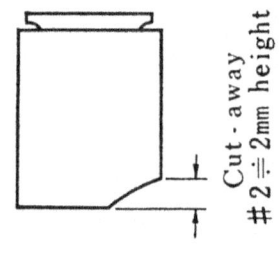

Fig. 1.59

If the machine does not respond in normal manner when the throttle is opened from 1/4 ~ 1/2 way, or the engine miss fires at constant opening of throttle in normal cruising, the mixture is too weak, and the jet needle should be raised one notch.

On the contraly, if the engine shows any tendency that the fuel consumption is too much or spark plug electrodes get sooty too early, it is being supplied with too rich mixture, then lower the jet needle by one notch.

1.14 CARBURETOR

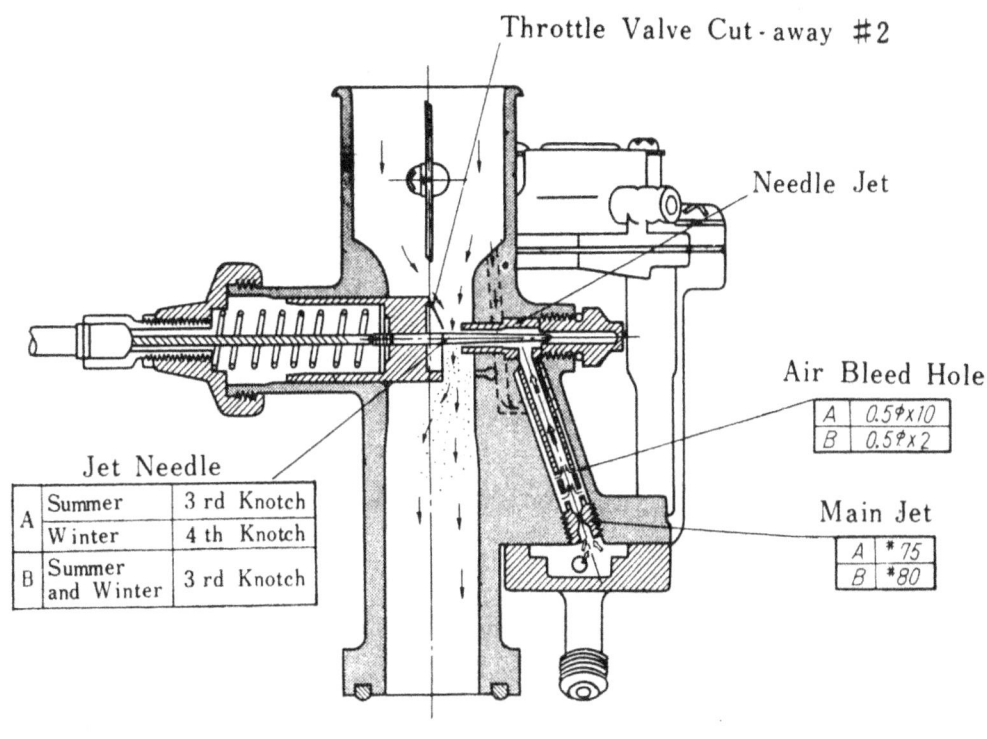

(1) Main System

→ Course of Air
⇒ Course of Gasoline

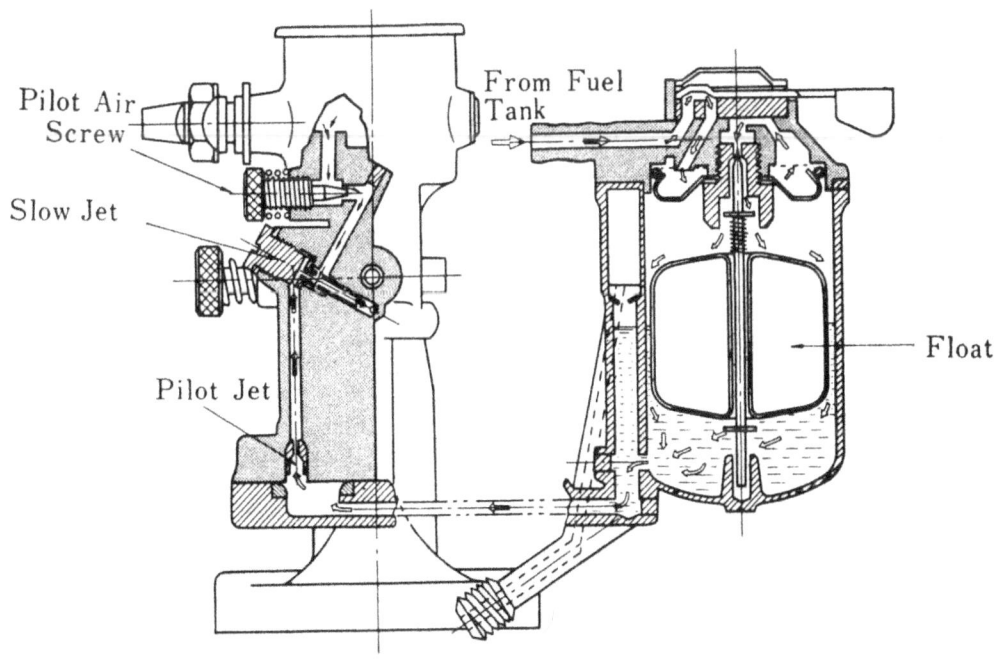

(2) Slow System

Fig. 1.60 Sectional View and Function of Carburetor

1. ENGINE

(4) High speed adjustment

Almost all the trouble at high speed is caused by the main jet. Check ignition and valve systems first before adjusting, as in the case of acceleration.

Adjustment of the throttle opening from ¾ to full (4/4) is determined by main jet.

So, in case of determining the optimum size of main jet, speed test should be done on a straight level road in order to find out the main jet which is able to output the fastest speed.

However, if it is found that the speed can increase by closing the choke valve about a quarter way or so on full throttle running fit a jet one or two size larger.

D. Setting and Function of Carburetor

Initial setting of the carburetor is as follows.

Table 1.60 (a)　The Various Settings of Carburetor

Engine Number	100E-946464~949850	949851~956535	956536~
Main Jet	#95	#93	#88
Air Head Hole (dia×number)	0.5φ×12	0.5φ×12	0.5φ×12
Jet Needle	13321-3	13321-3	13321-3
Fuel Level (from the center of throttle valve)	−12mm	−12mm	−10mm
Cab. Punched Mark	A	B	C

From the Engine Serial Number C 100 E-956536, in order to reduce the variation of atmospheric pressure in the float chamber, air vent tube has been equipped.

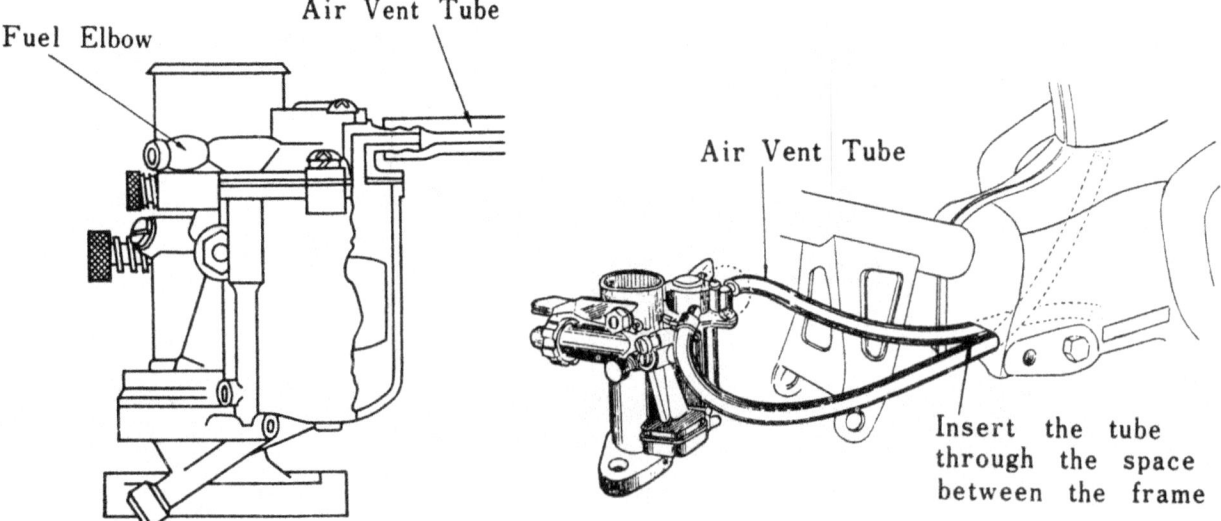

Fig. 1.61　Air Vent Tube　　　　Fig. 1.62　Air Vent Tube

MEMO

MEMO

2. CHASSIS

A vehicle is only good for practical use after the energy created by the engine is transmitted to the drive wheel and becomes power to run it along the ground, and only when anybody can operate it safely.

The frame construction of Super Cub is illustrated in **fig.** 2.1. The following sections explain this construction.

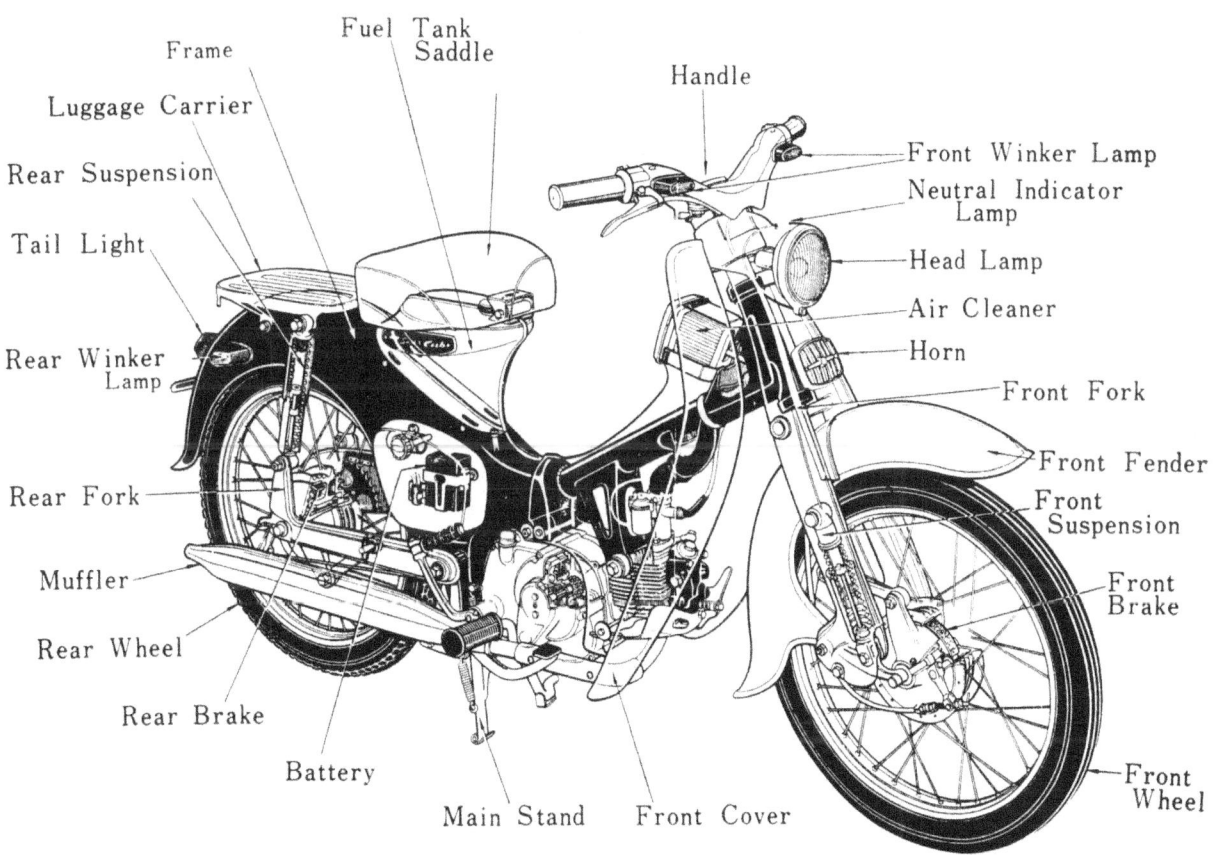

Fig. 2.1

2. CHASSIS

2.1 Steering Handle and Various Wires & Cables

The handle assembly is made of pipe and steel-sheet-metal.   All wiring is passed through the inside of these.   The wires and cables are part of the locomotion convey mechanism.

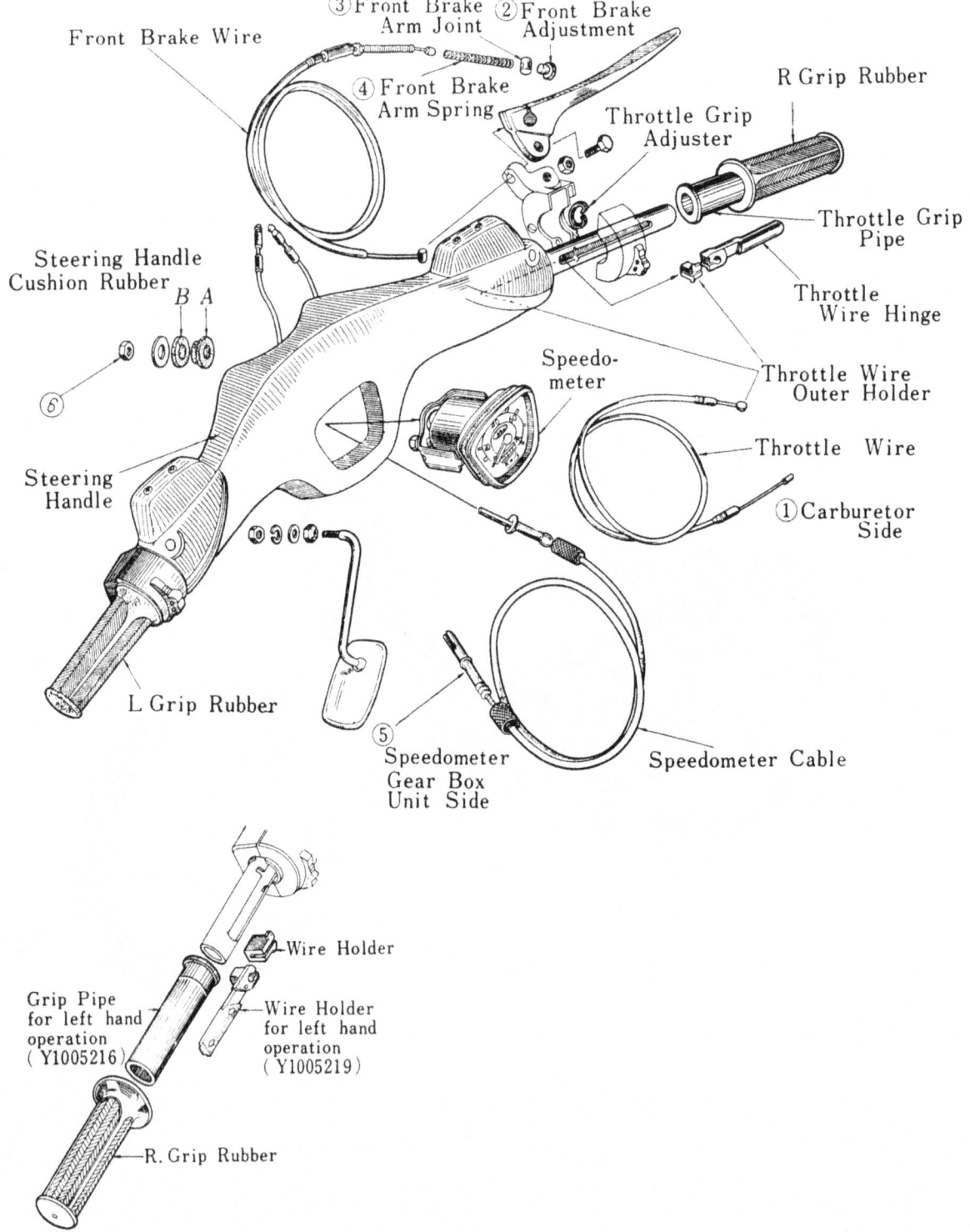

Fig. 2.2

2.1 STEERING HANDLE AND VARIOUS WIRES & CABLES

The engine is installed to the front fork through a rubber cushions so engine vibration will not be transmitted directly to the hands.

Throttle grip is normally on the right side, but may be changed to the left side, due to use of accessories.

A. Disassembly

Remove throttle, front brake wire and speedometer cable in sequence of ① ~ ⑤, remove left and right handle mounting nuts ⑥, take off head lamp and disconnect the each cord-connectors. The handle will come off as assembly with various wirings.

Further disassembly is as follows.
(1) Speedometer will come off by removing cable and taking off clamp on the back.
(2) Front brake wiring is removed by taking off handle lever.
(3) Throttle wiring is taken out by first disassembling right grip metal plate (remove front and rear screws) and twisting out grip pipe. Then remove wire holder and hinge and pull out wiring from handle pipe.

B. Inspection & Reassembly

(1) If the covering on the throttle wire and brake wiring outer is torn or worn, repair with taping or replace.

(2) On the above wiring, if the outer is excessively bent or broken causing faulty operation of inner, replace wiring.

(3) If the outer covering of speedometer cable is torn, excessively bent or damaged, repair or replace outer. Replace inner even if only partial damaged.

Before reassembling, replenish inner of wiring and cables well with oil for easy movement of parts.

Grease throttle hinge and inside of throttle grip pipe and reassemble.

Reassemble handle following steps for disassembling backwards. All wirings must be passed through the place originally designated.

NOTE: (1) In case of left grip, install left hand parts installing as in the case of right hand parts.
(2) Be sure to pass cables and wirings correctly and clip securely. Be specially careful of clips for throttle wire and brake wiring.

MEMO

2.2 Front Fork

The steering stem is welded to the pressed metal front fork. The stem incorporates a ball bearing cone on which this turns, with the head pipe in center, and is an important part of steering system. **Fig. 2.3 (b)** illustrates the layout. Polyethylene made headlamp case, and front fender, and handle lock, to prevent pilferage, are attached.

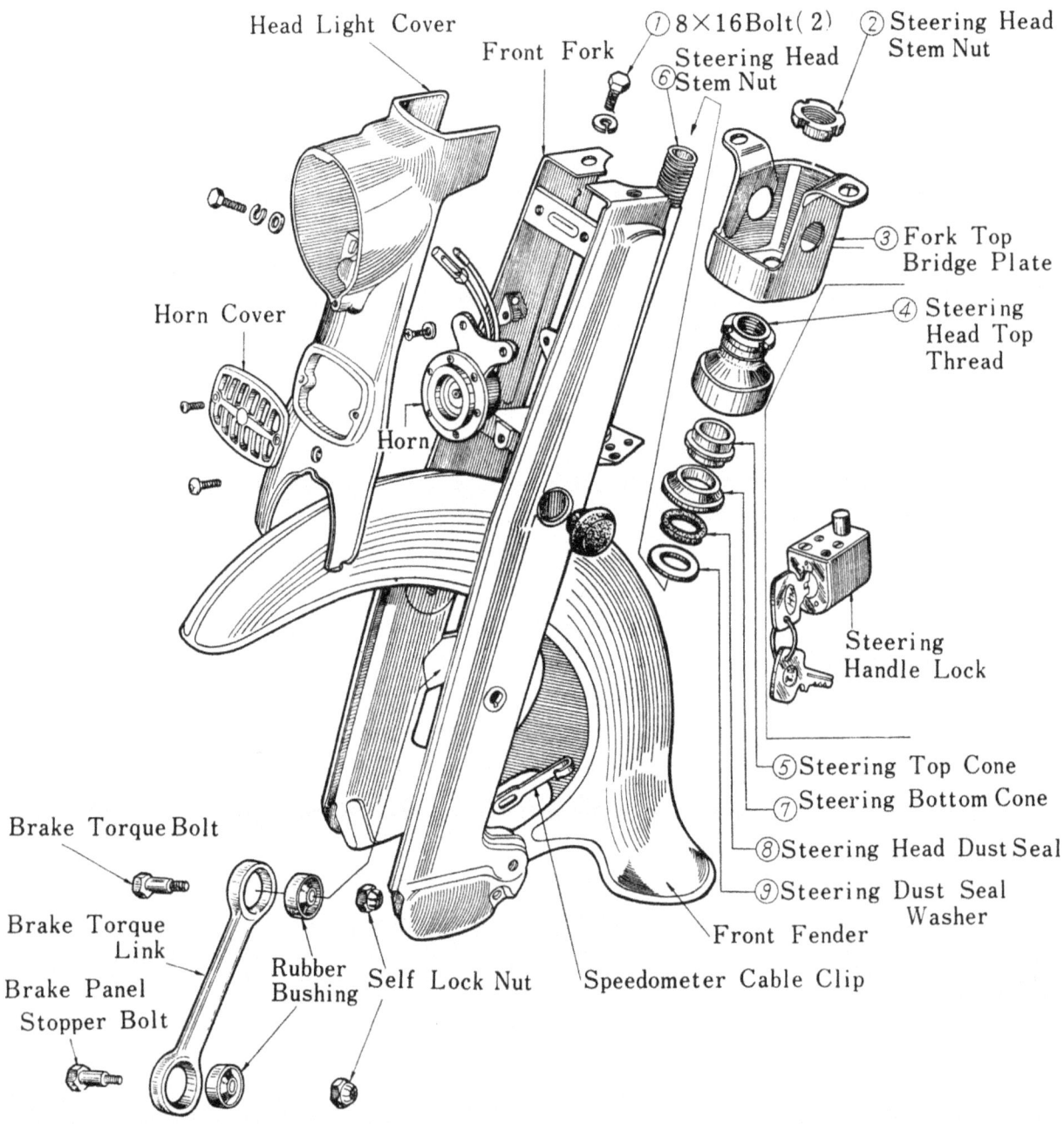

Fig. 2.3 (a)

2.2 FRONT FORK   47

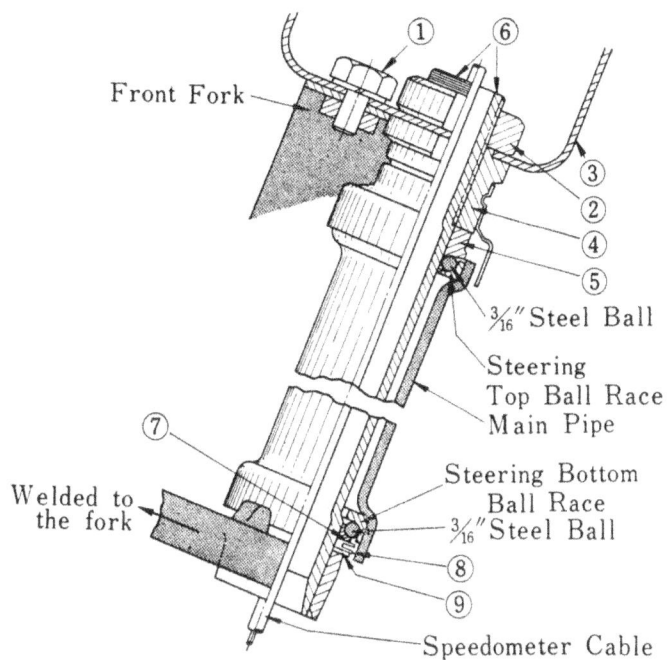

Fig. 2.3 (b) Section View of Steering Head

Fig. 2.3 (c) System Nut Box Wrench   Fig. 2.3 (d) 36 mm Spanner Hook

A. Disassembly

Remove front wheel p. 60. Remove steering handle in manner described in previous clause and disconnect horn, then follow steps ① ~ ⑥ in **fig. 2.3 (a)** for disassembling and the frame and fork parts will come apart. Loosen stem nut ① with box wrench (**fig. 2.3 (c)**). In this case take hook spanner wrench (**fig 2.3 (d)**) and slightly tighten top thread ④ and stem nut will loosen quite easily. Handle lock cannot be removed until fork is taken off. Loosen attaching bolts and remove headlamp case and front fender.

B. Inspection

(1) Replace damaged or worn steel balls.
(2) Replace top and bottom cone races if faces are damaged or have worn marking.
(3) Replace worn or damaged head dust shield.
(4) Replace excessively twisted front fork and stem. (Special jig is required

for measuring. Use surface gauge and measure for rough checking.)
(5) Replace damaged or old worn rubber bushing of brake torque link. Bushing is pressed in, so use press or drive in with a driver and hammer, evenly.

C. Reassembly

Install attaching parts to fork and follow steps ① ~ ⑥.

In this case tightening of top thread ④ requires experience. Tighten steering head top thread with hook spanner wrench so that handle steers a little harder than usual. Tighten head nut ② and fork nut ①, then turn back ④ all the way, which will enable you to tighten steering stem without play and also snugly. The handle should turn both ways by its own weight with slight push, with the front wheels clear off ground and must not have any play in the cone race when front wheel is shook back and forth.

NOTE: (1) When reassembling clean off dirty grease of ball race and repack with new grease.
(2) Do not tighten polyethylene made parts too tight.
(3) Tighten handle lock before installing fork.
(4) On models before No. F-58-10706, when passing stem through frame to tighten, be careful of steel balls between stem and head pipe.
(On models after above number this will not happen.)

FOR REFERENCE: On assembled vehicles the angle between line extended down through center of stem and ground is the caster. Trail is the distance on ground between vertical line extended down center of wheel axle and line extended down center of stem.

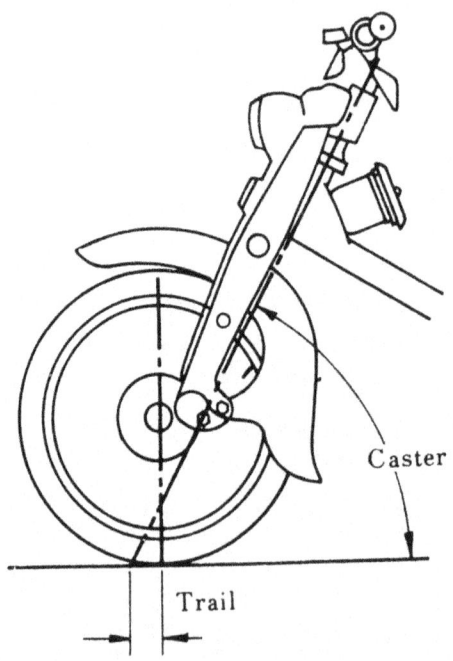

Fig. 2.3 (e) Relation betwen Caster and Trail

2.3 Front Suspension (Cushion)

This has bottom link type arm and the oil damper shock absorber and cushion spring is one piece and installed inside the front fork.

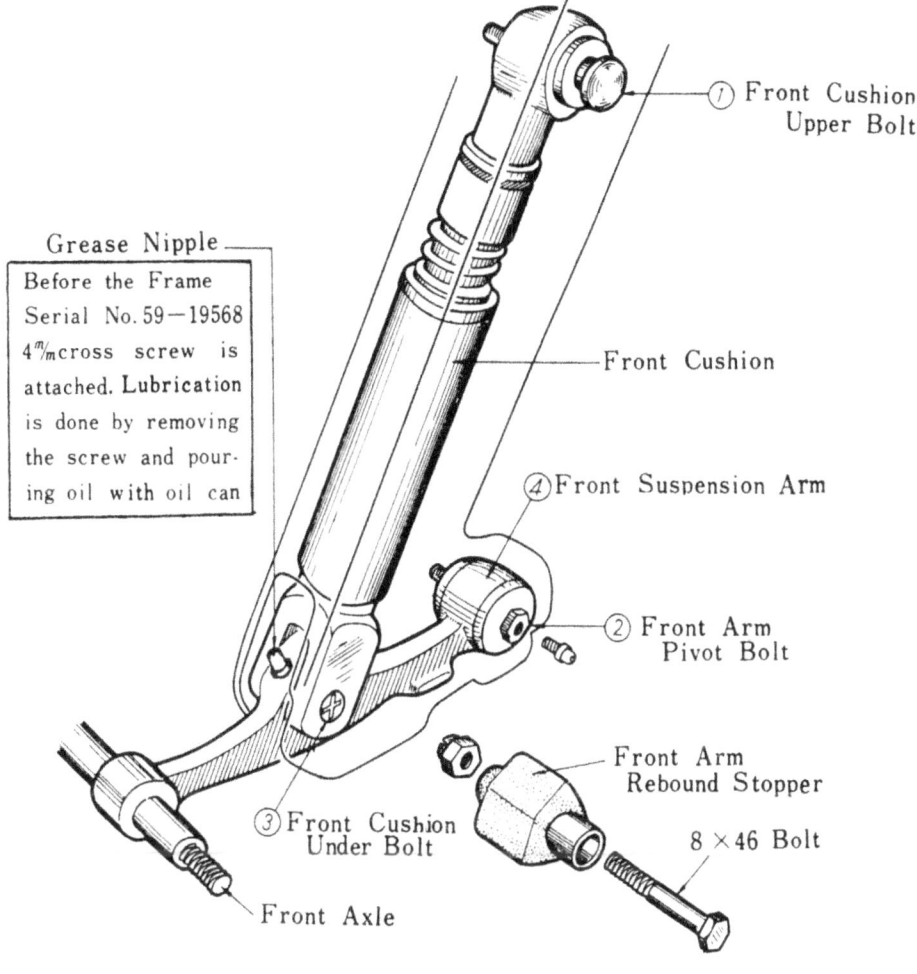

Fig. 2.4 (a) Front Suspension Component

A. Front Arm

(1) Disassembly

Front arm and front cushion are taken out as an assembly by removing front wheel (p. 60), then removing front arm pivot bolt ② and rebound stopper bolt shown in **fig. 2.4 (a)** and removing front cushion upper bolt ①. Front arm is disconnected by loosening front cushion under bolt ③ with cross head ④ driver.

Dust seal, cap and collar are inside front arm and these are disassembled as illustrated in **fig. 2.4 (b)**.

2. CHASSIS

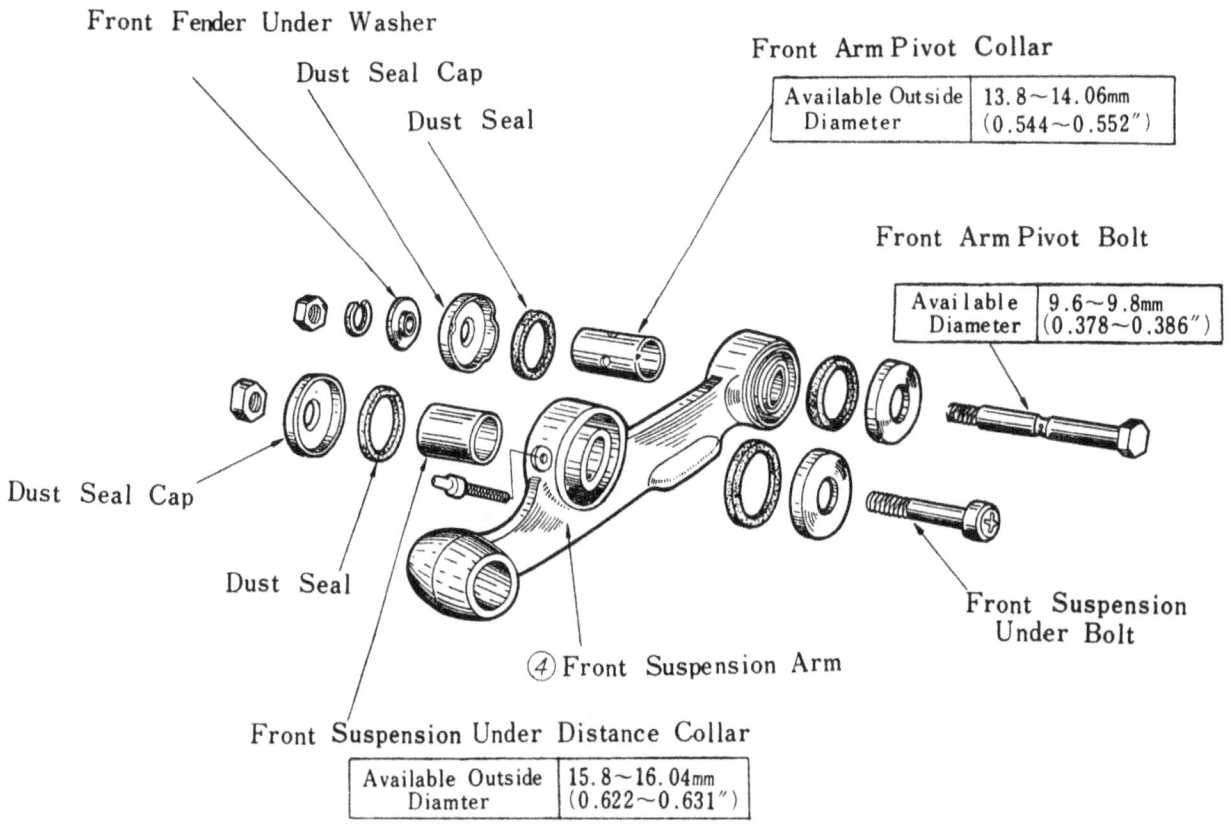

Fig. 2.4 (b) Specifications of Front Suspension Arm

(2) Inspection & Reassembly

i. If there is too much clearance between front arm pivot collar and pivot arm bolt, measure outside diameter of bolt and replace if it is worn beyond the specified limit.

ii. If there is excessive clearance between pivot collar and suspension arm, replace collar.

iii. If there is excessive clearance between front cushion under distance collar and suspension arm, replace collar.

iv. Replace damaged or defective dust seals.

v. Replace distorted or damaged rubber of front arm rebound stopper.

Reassembling is as illustrated in **fig. 2.4 (a)** and is simple, but do not forget to grease after reassembling.

B. Front Cushion

Coil springs are inserted around the oil damper and under-case protects the springs, which make up the front wheel shock absorber apparatus.

There is 23cc of white spindle oil No. 60 inside the front cushion damper and the vibration is dampened by the action of damper piston with valve. Oil

2.3 FRONT SUSPENSION (CUSHION) — 51

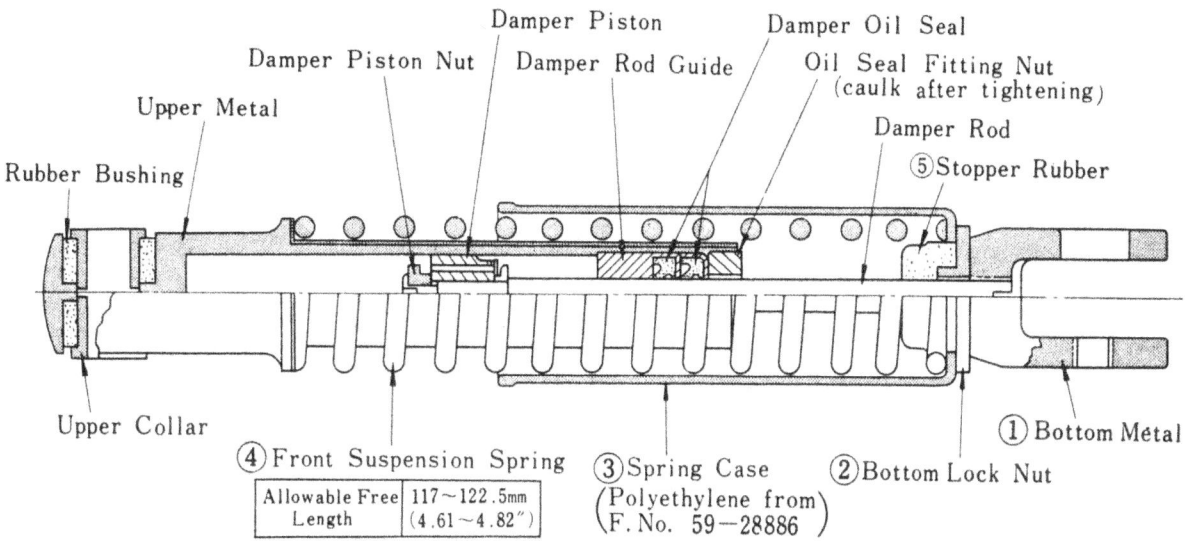

Fig. 2.5 Section View of Front Cushion

leakage is prevented by the chrome plated and smooth finishing piston rod facing and oil seal with double lip.

(1) **Disassembling**

Disassemble by following steps ① ~ ⑤ in illustration **fig. 2.5**. To take out spring, first lift up caulk as piston rod end and bottom metal are caulked, then hold bottom lock nut ② using adjustable end wrench, loosen and remove bottom metal ①, hold groove of damper rod end with driver, loosen and remove bottom lock nut ② and then take off spring case.

Be sure not to mar or damage rod when holding.

(2) **Inspection & reassembling**

i. Check spring free length, distortion and tension and if over specified limit, replace.
ii. Check for oil leakage in oil damper and if leaking replace damper.
iii. Replace damper rod if marred or distorted.
iv. Replace stopper rubber ⑤ if damaged or worn.
v. Replace rubber bushing of upper metal if damaged or distorted.

Check and replace all parts before reassembling. Then pull out damper rod fully and cover with spring case, insert bottom lock nut while pressing spring and hold rod with driver and then tighten lock nut all the way. Tighten bottom metal all around and caulk end of rod and bottom metal with chisel.

> NOTE: Replace damper as complete assemble when damper rod is damaged or distorted or leaks oil. As special jigs are required for disassembling inside of damper and inside parts are not available as service parts.

MEMO

2.4 Rear Fork & Rear Suspension (Cushion)

This has a fork with swing arm that can swing on the center pivot shaft. Rear end of fork is supported to the frame by rear cushion.

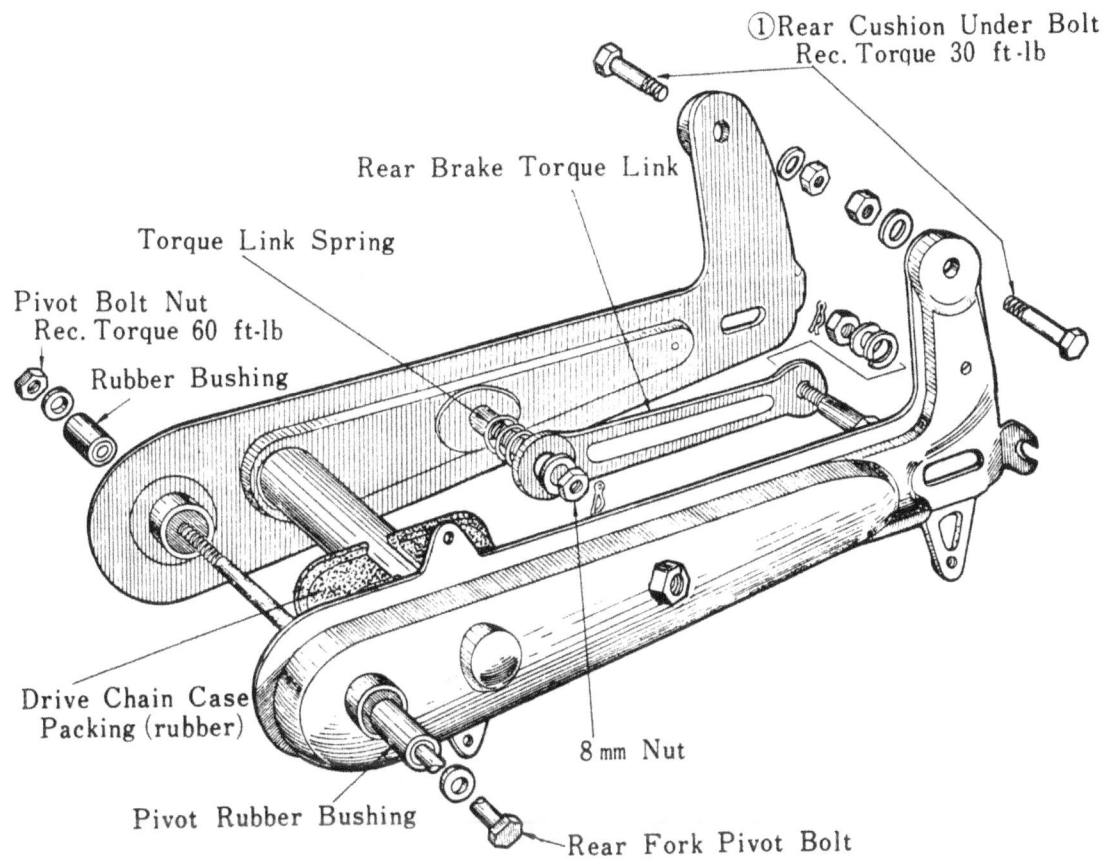

Fig. 2.6 Exploded View of Rear Fork

A. Rear Fork

(1) Disassembling

  i. Remove rear wheel and flange. (p. 61)
  ii. Remove top and bottom chain case and chain. (p. 56)
  iv. Remove rear cushion lower mounting bolts ①, loosen pivot bolt nut in **fig. 2.6**, pull pivot bolt and take off rear fork.

(2) Inspection & reassembling

  i. Replace drive chain case packing if damaged or worn.
  ii. Replace rear fork pivot rubber bushing if rubber is damaged or too worn to act as bushing. Bushings are pressed in so use press to insert each side seperately. (If press is not available drive in with hammer).

iii. Check visible distortion and twist of rear fork and if found defective replace.
   Conventional way of checking twist is to use inspection jig or insert gage.
iv. Replace brake torque link if hole is worn and enlarged.

To reassemble insert pivot bolt to pipe on frame, where pivot is passed through, and tighten with nut to the recommended torque. Install onto rear cushion before attaching chain case. Be careful not to forget chain case packing.

B. Rear Cushion

This connects the rear fork and body and acts as a cushion in between. Cushion consists of uneven pitch coil spring inside, which is covered by metal bottom case and polyethylene made upper case, and damper piston runs up and down inside the main pipe. Shocks are absorbed by rebound spring, piston friction and resistance of air pressure built up in the chamber.

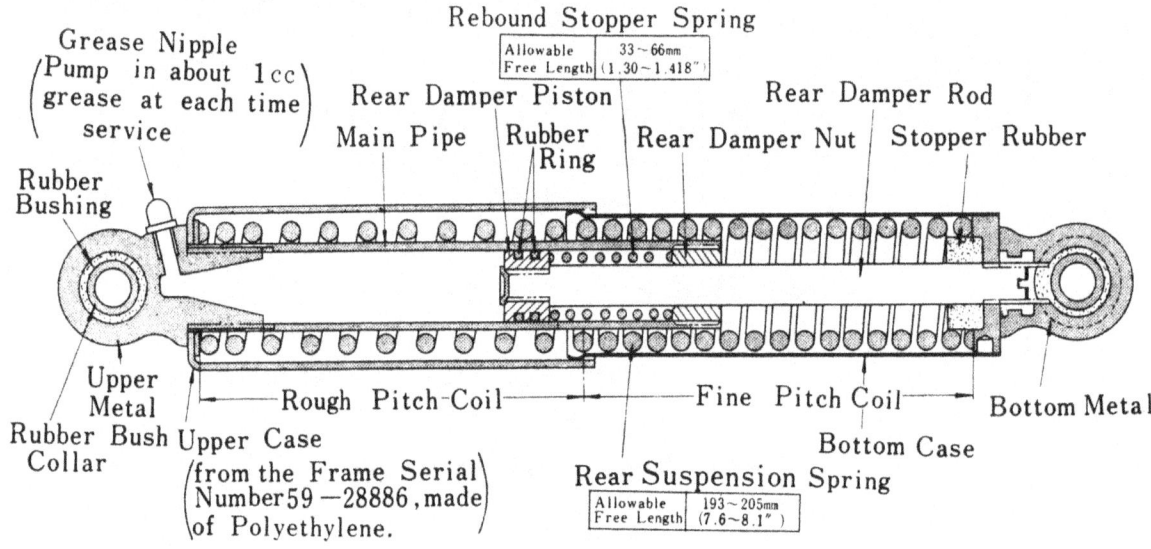

Fig. 2.7 Section View of Rear Cushion

(1) Disassembling

i. Remove cap nut securing rear cushion top, then remove bottom support nut.
ii. Remove knock screw of bottom metal, then loosen bottom metal.
iii. Bottom case and spring will come off.

(2) Inspection & reassembling

i. Check rear suspension spring and dispose according to maintenance specification.

2.4 REAR FORK & REAR SUSPENSION

ii. Replace damper as complete assembly if damper rod is damaged or distorted and if grease leaks excessively from the rod.
iii. Replace stopper rubber if damaged or distorted.
iv. If knocking noise occurs when main spring is stretched all out, while riding, this would mean that main spring is defective and should be replaced.
v. If rubber bushing of upper and bottom metal is found damaged or distorted, replace.

To reassemble follow steps for disassembling backwards. First pull out piston rod all the way and install bottom case, compress spring as much as possible and insert nut of case, then screw in piston rod all the way with driver, and attach bottom metal. Be sure not to forget knock screw after installing bottom metal.

Insert only about 1cc of grease through nipple of upper metal with a pump.

NOTE: Too much grease will harden cushion and impair riding comfort. In case too much is inserted take out by unscrewing grease nipples and depressing rear cushions (excess grease will pump out).

MEMO

2.5 Drive Chain System

Engine power is transmitted to the driven sprocket of the rear wheel by the drive sprocket and drive chain. The driven sprocket acts as shock absorber through cushion damper and transmits power to the rear wheel. The section from drive sprocket to driven sprocket is enclosed by the chain case and prevents early wear from dirt and dust.

A. Drive Chain Case

Chain case is disassembled by removing the four 6 mm bolts from ① to ④ in **fig. 2.8 (a)**. After disassembling, wash out the dirt and dust, then reassemble.

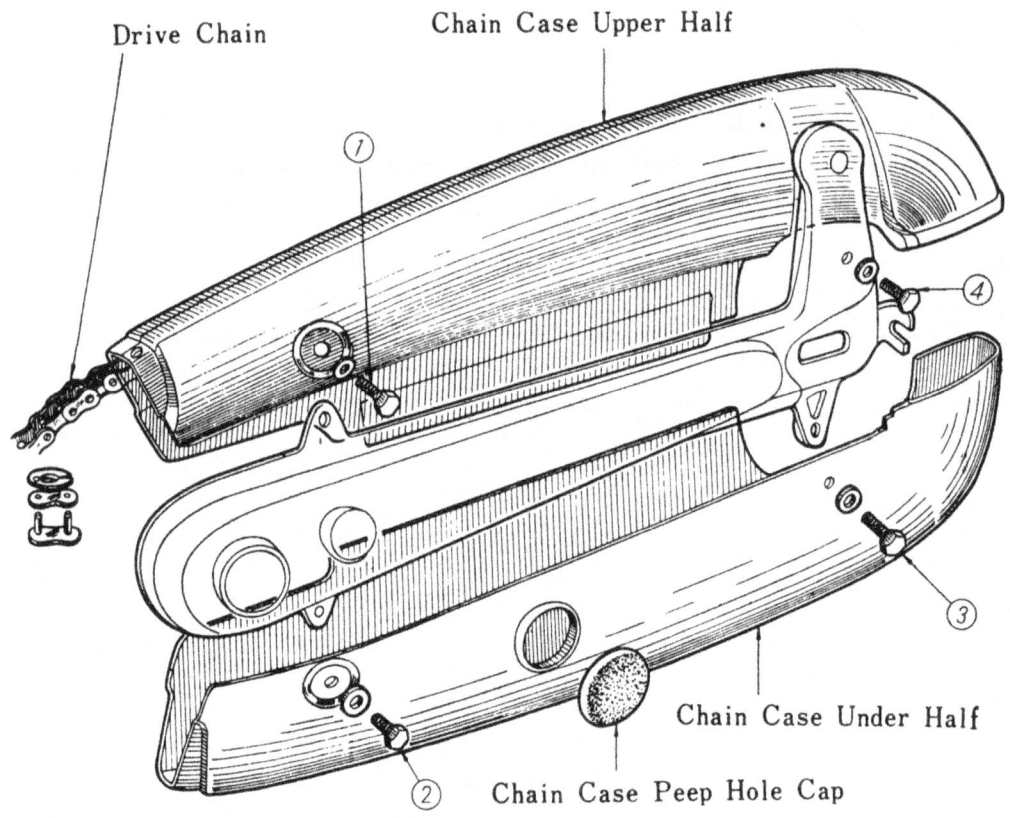

Fig. 2.8 (a) Chain Case Disassembly

B. Drive Chain

The chain size is DK 420 and is made up of 100 links. This is usually taken off by removing cover on left side of engine and removing chain joint clip. If difficulty is encountered remove chain case underhalf and work can be readily done.

When chain stretches beyond limit of chain adjuster, this can be adjusted once by cutting a piece of the chain, but if this is required again the chain must be replaced.

2.1 DRIVE CHAIN SYSTEM 57

When replacing chain, check the drive and driven sprocket and if found excessively worn replace at the same time.

When installing clip onto joint be sure opening of clip faces opposite direction of chain rotation. (**fig. 2.8 (b)**).

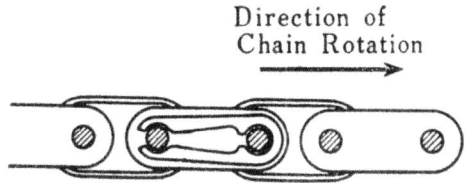

Fig. 2.8 (b) How to Clip Chain Joint

C. Final Drive Flange Mechanism

Driven sprocket is bolted to the flange. The flange claws interlock with the 4 rubber couplings inserted into the wheel and transmit the power. Elasticity of the rubber couplings prevent chain knocking.

On models before No. F 58-11510 there are three rubber dampers.

Fig. 2.8 (c) Removal of Rear Wheel

(1) Disassembling

Take off chain case and remove drive chain. Drive flange assembly will come off by removing rear axle sleeve nut and pulling out axle sleeve.

Oil seal, bearing and collar are located inside flange. Take these out and clean. Driven sprocket is removed by taking off setting bolt.

2. CHASSIS

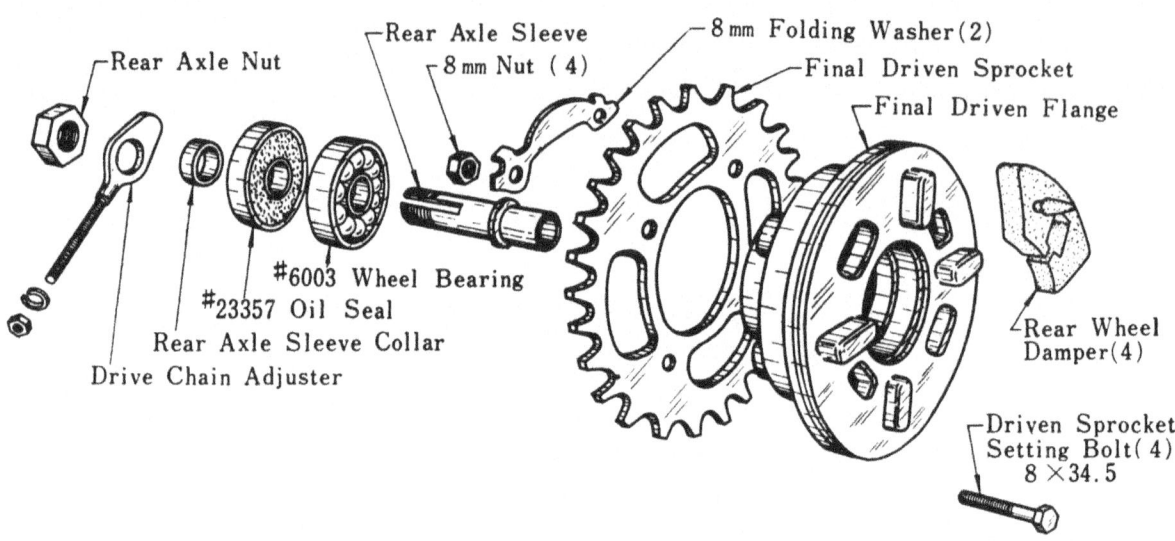

Fig. 2.9

(2) Inspection & reassembling

i. Take cleaned washed ball bearing 6003 in hand and rotate outer race. If this catches excessively or does not turn completely or there is too much axial play, replace.

ii. If lip of oil seal 23357 is distorted or excessivly worn, replace.

iii. Replace driven sprocket if cog facing is worn or if cog thickness and cog bottom diameter is excessively worn. Upon reassembling, grease bearing well.

iv. Replace damper rubber on wheel hub side if found damaged or distorted.

Pack grease well around balls in bearings, insert bearing into flange hub, hammer in oil seal evenly, using guide. Tighten sprocket to flange with setting bolt tightly. Prevent loosening by securely bending folding washer. Do not bend this on corner of bolt such as seen in **fig. 2.11**.

When flange is set, do not forget to insert collar through sleeve. Install this lightly on rear fork and tighten while expanding chain.

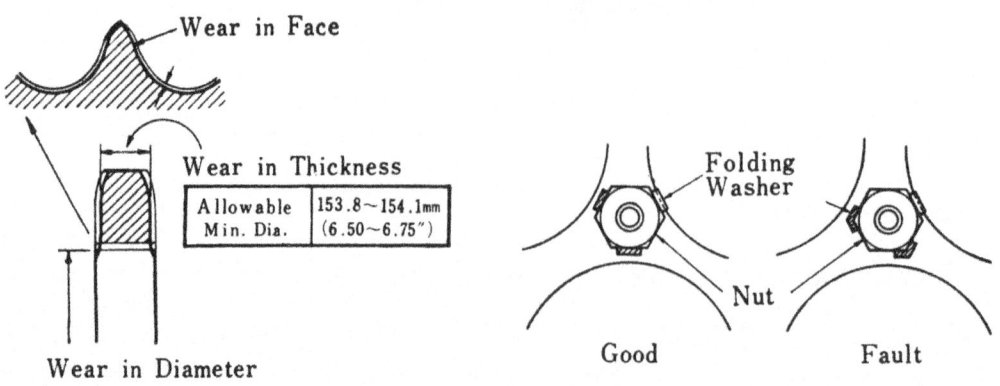

Fig. 2.10   Fig. 2.11

2.6 Front & Rear Wheel

Front and rear tire size is 2.25-17-4 ply **Fig. 2.12** is a sectional diagram of tire. Rim is made of steel. Spokes are fastened onto bottom of rim with nipples and are all balanced for even tension and tightened. Front spokes consist of 36 pieces straight #12, rear spokes 36 pieces one end thickened #10 and #11. To increase tightening of spokes, use nipple spanner and tighten so that tension is same as all other spokes, by hand feel.

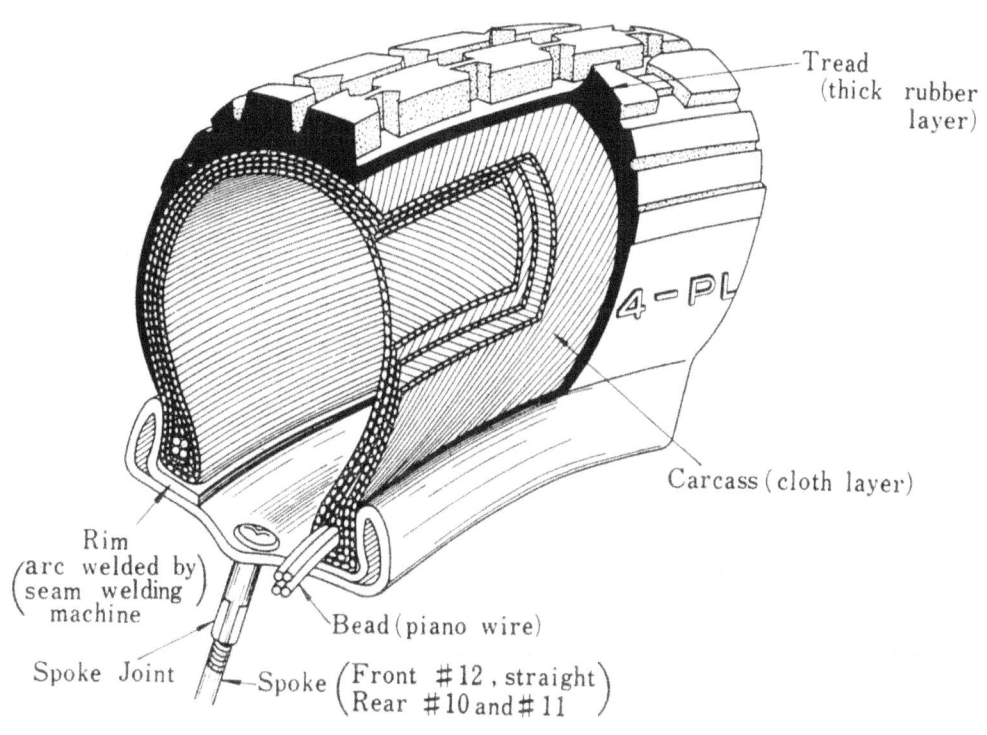

Fig. 2.12

MEMO

60   2. CHASSIS

A. Front Wheel

(1) Dismantling

Place stand under engine and lift front wheels off ground, remove each bolt and nut following steps ① to ⑤ as in **fig. 2.13 (a)**, pull out axle ⑥ and front wheel will come off with front panel. In this case only the wheel itself can be removed without loosening front brake wire ④ by pulling out front wheel slightly forward and separating with panel. When wheel is disassembled be careful not to drop bearing inside hub, on ground as dirt will get into grease. Ball bearing 6201 can be removed by hand and if it is tight, remove it by hitting lightly from the inner side.

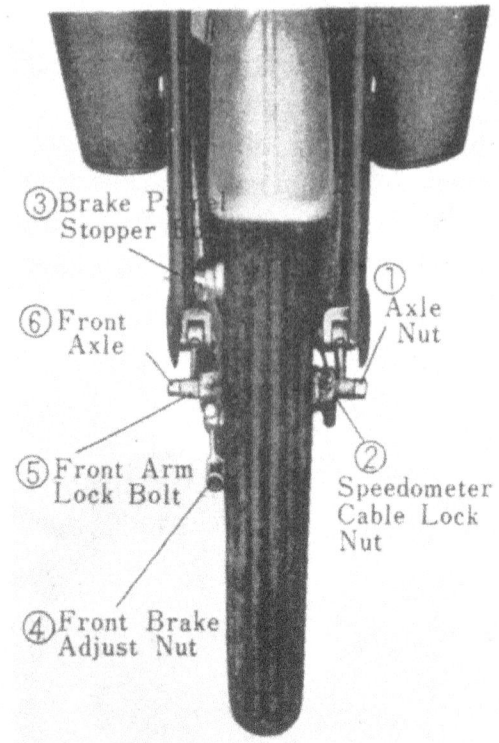

Fig. 2.13 (a) **Procedure on Disassembling Front Wheel**

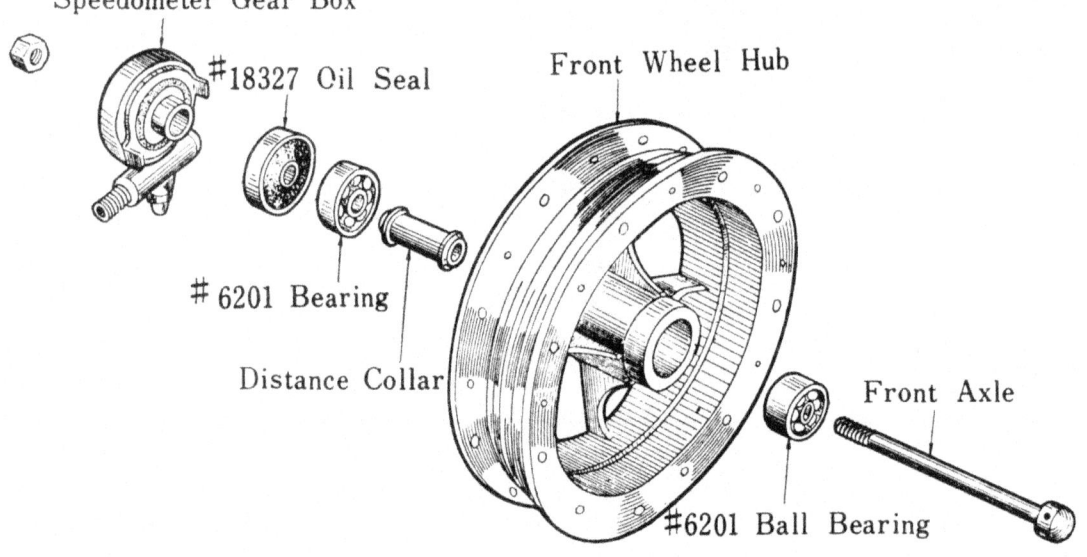

Fig. 2.13 (b)

(2) Inspection & reassembling

i. As illustrated in **fig. 2.14**, pass axle through bearings and hold axle stationary, set a dial gage on the face of rim Ⓐ or drum Ⓑ, then turn wheel easily reading run out of their dimensions. If rim is bent

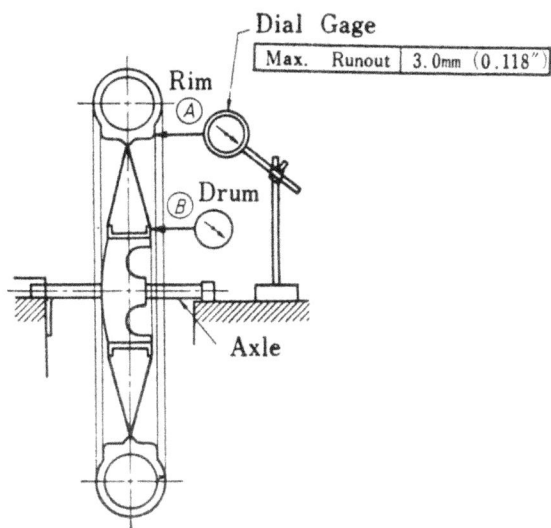

Fig. 2.14 Cheking Run-out of Wheel

or distorted beyond limit, replace.

ii. Check for slack of spokes and tighten where necessary.
iii. Check tires for marrs and nails and repair accordingly.
iv. Wash ball bearing 6201, inside hub, thoroughly and check for excessive play and roughness while turning. Replace if not in good condition.
v. Check oil seal lip for damage or distortion. Replace if not in good condition.
vi. Replace axle if bent or damaged.
vii. Turn drive plate of speedometer gear box lightly and if hard to turn check and grease.

When installing, grease ball bearing well, greasing inside of hub slightly, and install oil seal following disassembling steps backwards. Tightening torques are as follows.

Axle Nut	25~35 ft·lb (3.5~4.5 kg-m)
Stopper Bolt	20~25 ft·lb (3.0~3.5 kg-m)
Front Arm Lock Bolt	20~25 ft·lb (3.0~3.5 kg-m)

B. Rear Wheel

(1) Disassembling

With the stand in the standing position, remove ①~② in **fig. 2.15 (b)**, take off rear axle nut and pull out rear axle ③ together with adjuster ⑤, remove side collar ④, and while tilting vehicle, shift wheel to the right and remove wheel from drive flange. Then remove bearing 6301 from inside wheel hub and take out oil seal. Bearing will come out by hand, but if hard, tap lightly from inner side and remove. Oil seal will come off at the same time.

2. CHASSIS

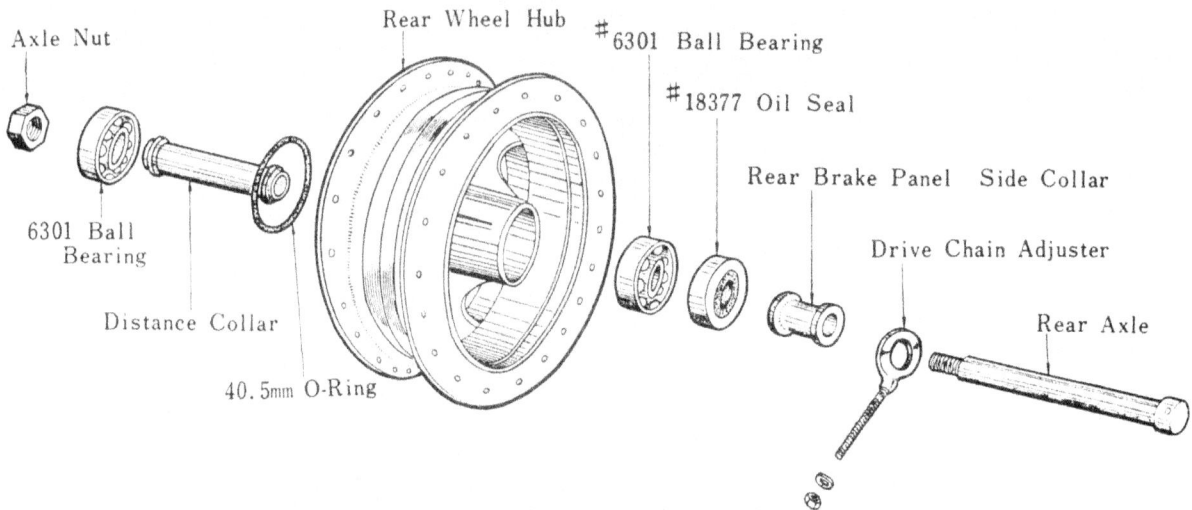

Fig. 2.15 (a) Exploded View of Rear Wheel Hub

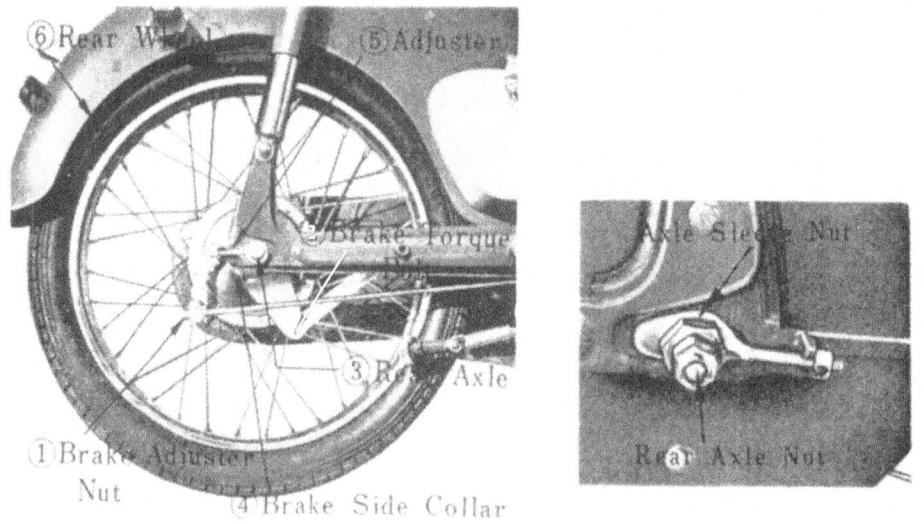

Fig. 2.15 (b) Procedure on Disassembling Rear Wheel

(2) Inspection & reassembling

i. Check rim for twist as on front wheel and determine according to same limit as front wheel.

ii. Check spokes for slack as on front and tighten where required.

iii. Check tire for marrs and nails and repair accordingly.

iv. Check 40.5 mm 0 ring (rubber) on drum boss for damage or wear. If not in good condition replace.

v. Check ball bearing 6301 for play and roughness, when rotating, after washing thoroughly. If not in good condition replace.

vi. Check lip of oil seal 18377 for marring or distortion. If not in good condition replace.

Upon installing, pack grease well into ball bearing #6301, greasing inside

2.6 FRONT & REAR WHEEL

of hub slightly, insert oil seal and reassemble according to steps for disassembling, backwards. Do not forget cotter pin after tightening nut on brake torque bolt.

When tightening rear axle nut be sure to align drive chain adjuster mark, on top of fork, with left hand adjuster mark.

Tightening torque is 25~35 ft-lb (4.0~4.5 kg-m)

After securing this nut tighten adjuster nut.

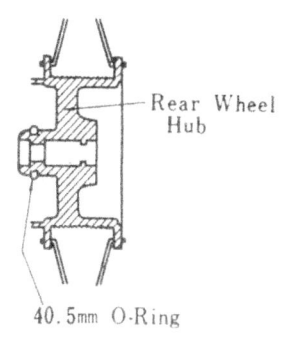

Fig. 2.16

NOTE: (1) After securing all nuts check tension of drive chain.
(2) It is not necessary to loosen axle sleeve nut when disassembling.
(3) Do not forget or damage "O" ring on drum boss.

C. Tire & Tube

Disassembling

To disassemble tire to fix flats or for other repairs (burst), remove tube valve cap and lock nut, then remove rubber of cap, and deflate tube of air by loosening valve stem with the tip of the cap. Lay tire on ground as in **fig. 2.17** and pull bead from rim. Insert tire lever between rim and tire bead, and while lifting lever up, pull tire out and away from rim. Using two tire levers makes this operation easier. When bead of tire on one side is completely separated from rim, push stem of tube valve into rim and pull out tube. After repairing tube, push back into tire and rim, aligning tube valve with hole in rim and making sure that tube is not twisted.

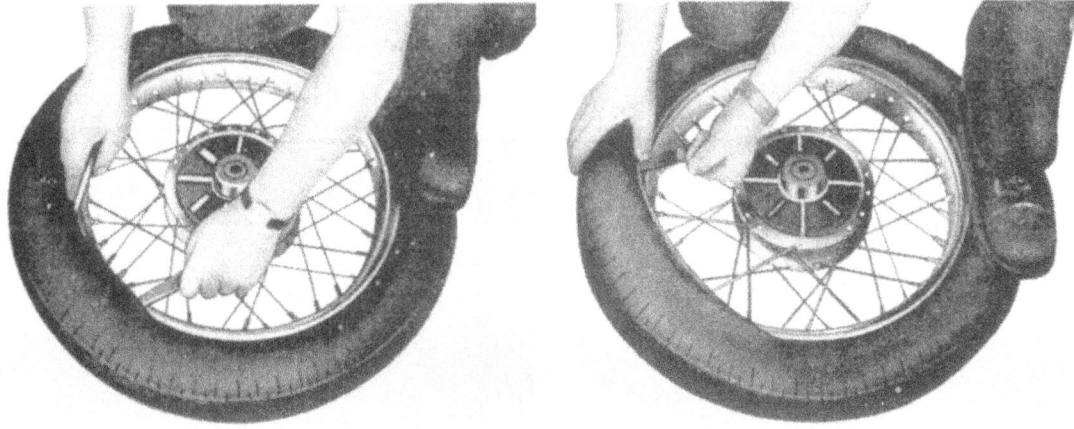

Fig. 2.17

To reinstall tire onto rim, place lever on tire bead and push under rim, following this operation all around until bead is completely in place.

NOTE: (1) Be careful not to force as tire bead is very tight. When assembled insert stem into valve and inflate with air. Inflate tire slowly knocking tire all around to get tube in place. Tighten lock nut onto valve and

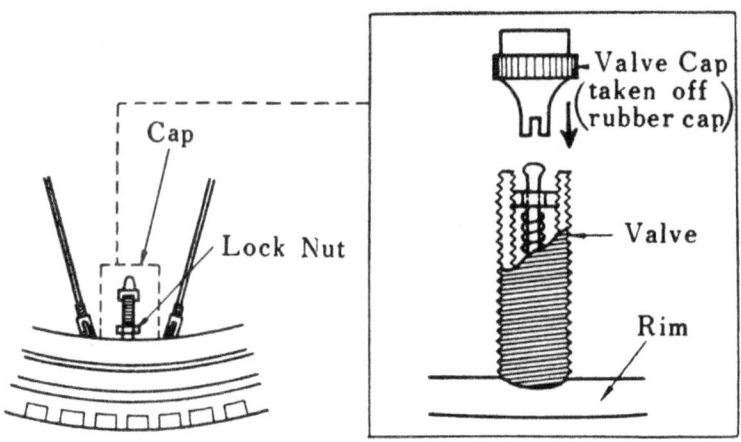

Fig. 2.18

recap. When the tire gets flat check and pull out the sticking nail from tire, after tube is removed.
(2) When replacing tires or tubes always use the same sizes.
(3) Standard tire pressures are;
Front   22 lb-in^2
Rear   28 lb-in^2
(4) When inflating tire be sure to maintain tube valve at right angle to rim.
(5) After inflating tire make sure valve does not leak. Tighten valve if leaking and replace if leakage does not stop.
(6) When disassembling and reassembling tube be sure not to damage thread of valve.
(7) Use tire lever for tire size 2.25-17. Be careful not to use other object and damage rim or tube.
(8) It is best to have tire repaired at regular tire shop.

MEMO

2.7 Brakes

Brake system is illustrated in **fig. 2.19**. Both brakes are inner expanding type shoe and drum designed to contact mechanically by the rotation of brake cam. Resin mold lining is glued to shoe with a special glue.
Brake shoes come off as an assembly with brake panel, after removing wheel in manner explained in section 2.6.

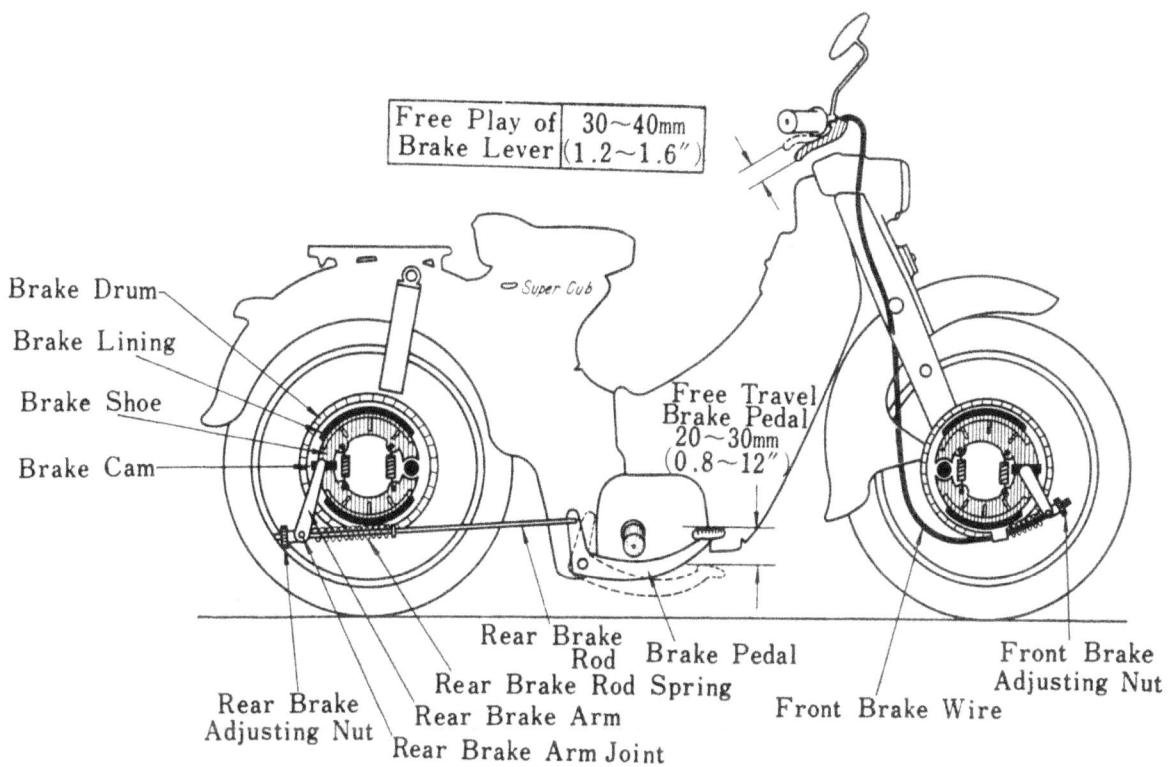

Fig. 2.19 Brake System

A. Front Brake

(1) Disassembling

By removing brake shoe spring, following steps ① ~ ⑤ in **fig. 2.21**, the shoe will come off. Also, while pulling one side of shoe and lifting it over head of cam, the other will come off.

After removing shoe, remove brake arm and take off cam.

From the Frame Serial Number 59·40346. In order to prevent invasion of mud into brake drum, shape

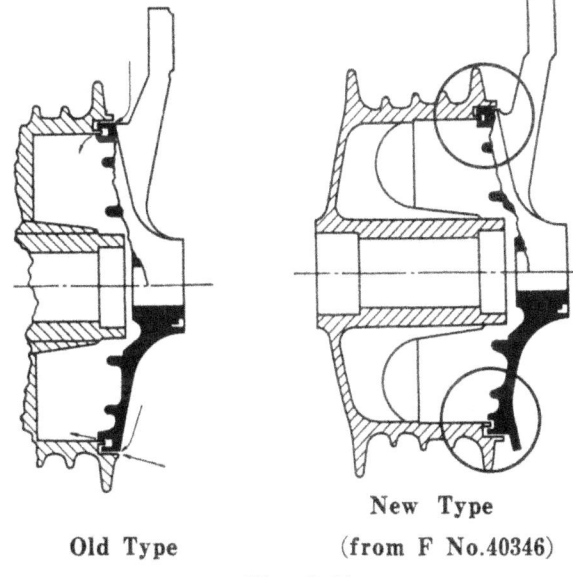

Old Type   New Type
(from F No.40346)

Fig. 2.20

of the panel have been changed from the production of Frame Serial Number. 59-40346 as shown in **fig 2.20**.

(2) Inspection & reassembling

i. Check outside diameter of panel spacer. Replace if over usable limit.
ii. Check inside diameter of panel sleeve. If over correction limit, force out and insert oversize sleeve.
iii. Check outside diameter of brake cam. If over usable limit, replace. If cam facing excessively worn replace, also.
iv. If shoe spring excessively sprung, replace.
v. Replace shoe if thickness is over usable limit.
vi. Replace oil seal if lip is distorted or damaged.
vii. Replace felt ring if not in good condition.

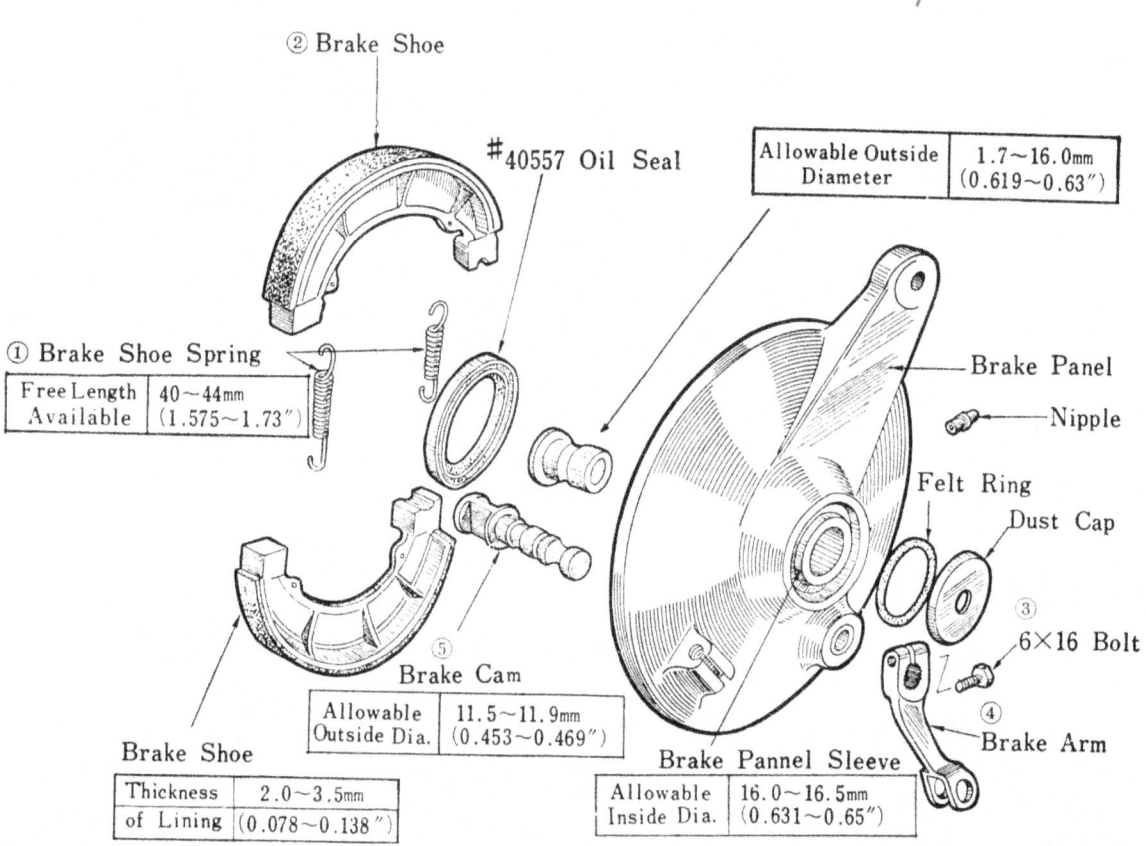

Fig. 2.21

2.7 BRAKE

To reassemble follow steps ① ~ ⑤. Sand down lining face of shoe with rough emery paper if foreign matter is found or facing is rough.

Select serration so that brake arm angle will come to correct relative position as in **fig. 2.21**, and install.

When adjusting brakes, after installing wheel and this is found to be improper, this can be repositioned by changing the serration angle, accordingly.

NOTE: Check inside facing of wheel hub drum. If found scored or uneven, reface or replace.

B. Rear Brake

Disassembling and reassembling is in the same steps as front brake ① ~ ⑤. Inspection is carried out in same manner. Only rear brakes do not have spacer. **Fig. 2.21** illustrates the mounted angle of brake arm against new brake shoe. This can be changed by the adjustment tolerance after reassembling.

Rear brake panel has same modification as front from the Frame Serial Number C 100 59 44815.

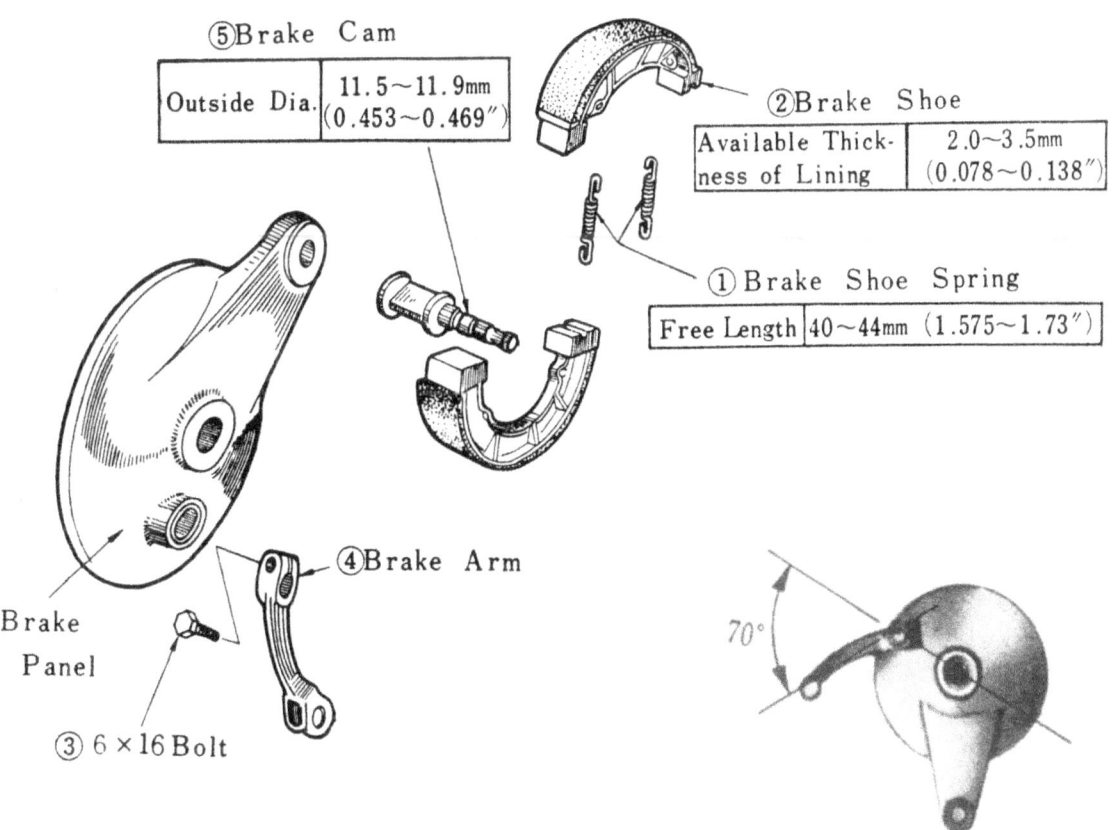

Fig. 2.22

NOTE: Servicing of wheel hub drum inside facing is same as previous.

68　　　　2. CHASSIS

2.8 Fuel Tank Saddle & Luggage Carrier

Fuel tank is bolted to top of frame body by 6mm bolts. The seat is placed on top of tank and is cushioned by rubber, underneath seat. Luggage carrier is supported by rear cushion support metal and rear fender (frame).

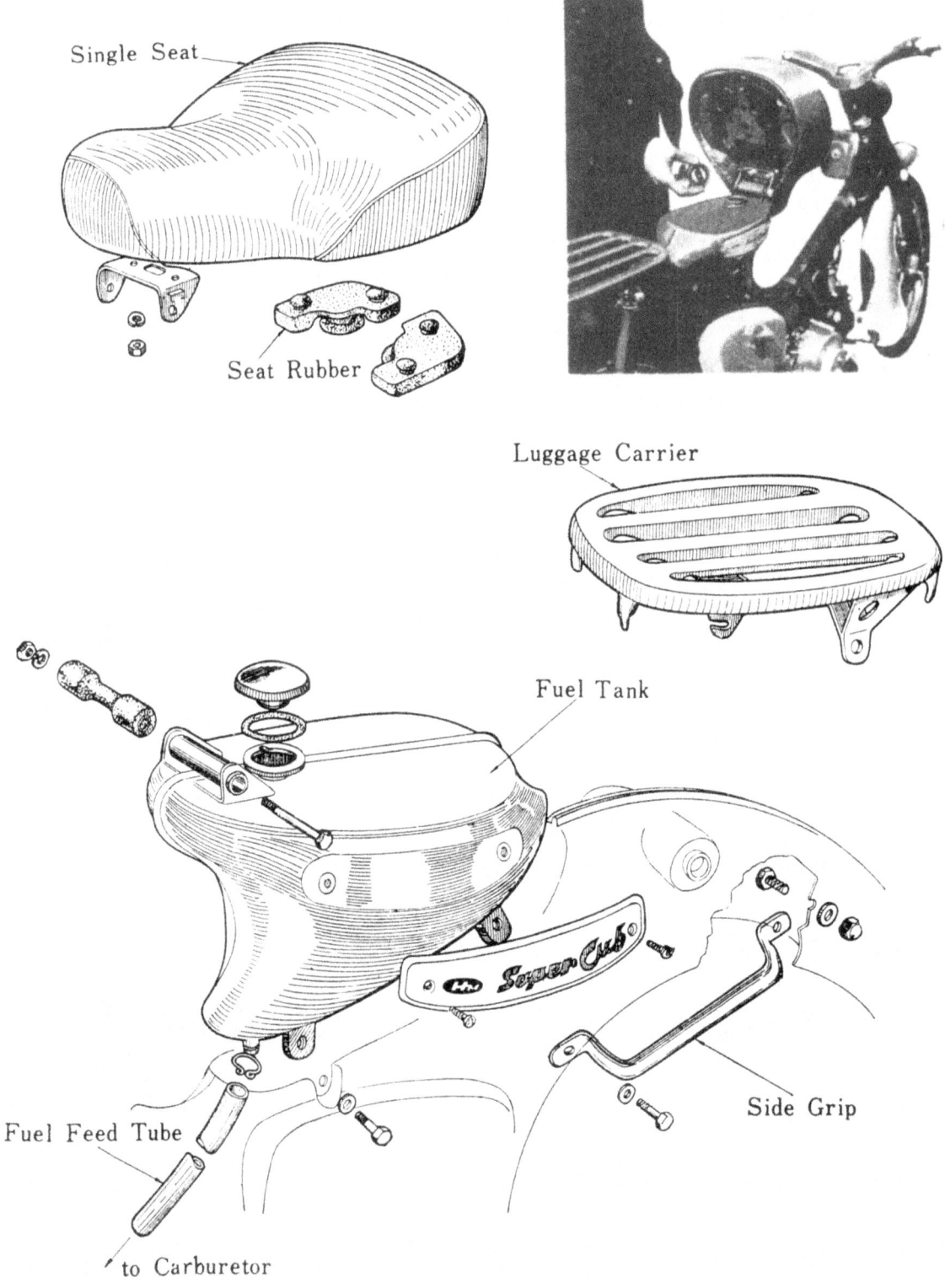

Fig. 2.23 (a)　Construction of Single Seat

2.8 FUEL TANK SADDLE & LUGGAGE CARRIER

A. Disassembly

Seat is separated by taking out seat hinge pin. Seat rubber is pressed into underpart of seat iron plate and can be taken out with a driver. Remove the four 6 mm bolts securing tank end frame and the tank will come off. Rubber tube connecting to carburetor from front end of tank is removed by taking off clips.

B. Inspection & Reassembly

① Replace damaged or worn seat cushion and seat mounting rubber
② Replace damaged or worn tank cap packing. Clean 1 mm holes of cap if clogged. (**fig. 2.23(b)**)
③ Fuel feed tube clip is to be replaced if worn.
   Following torques for tightening should be abided by.
   Tank bolts   50~60 in-lb (0.6~0.7 kg-m)
   Luggage carrier bolts   20~25 ft-lb (3.0~3.5 kg-m)

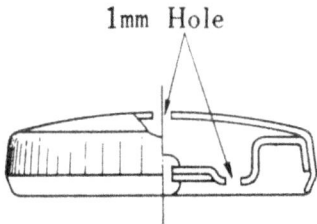

Fig. 2. 23 (b)

C. Installation of Tandem Seat

A fuel tank for tandem seat as in **fig. 2.24 (a)** is used or a bracket (**fig. 2.24 (b)**) is used with the regular tank.

Fig. 2.24 (a)

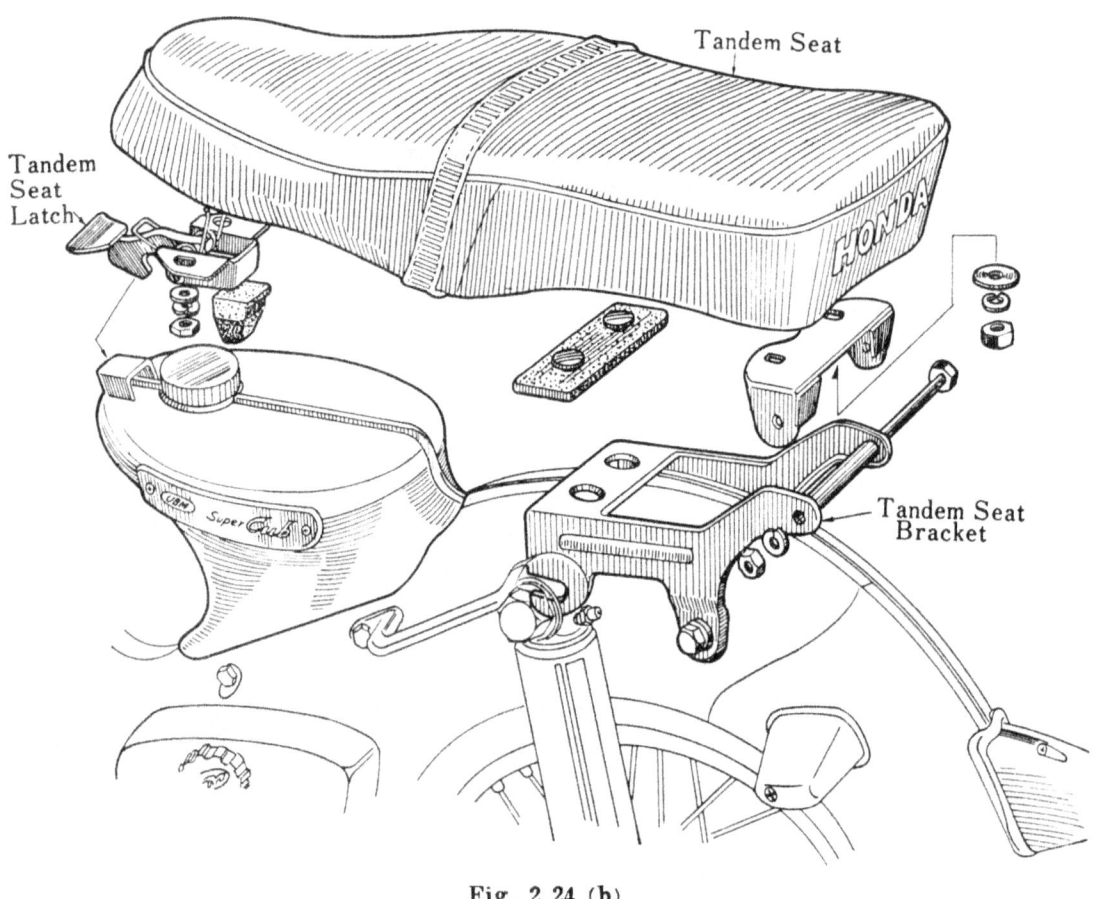

Fig. 2.24 (b)

Tandem seat bracket is installed in its place. In this case to put in fuel the front end is lifted, as the fulcrum is towards the rear.

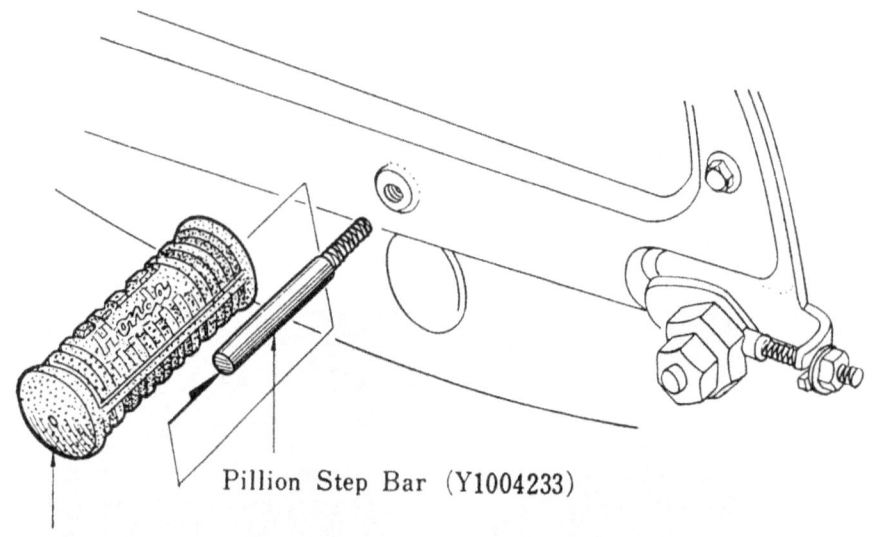

Pillion Step Bar (Y1004233)

Pillion Step Bar (Y1004231)

Fig. 2.24 (c)

MEMO

2.9 Air Cleaner

The air cleaner element is installed inside the box, inside the metal cover on the center front cover. The air sucked in is filtered here and draws to the carburetor through rubber connecting tube and pipe, which is welded to frame.

On models No. F 59-31701 and after, the construction has been modified as shown in **fig. 2.25 (b)**

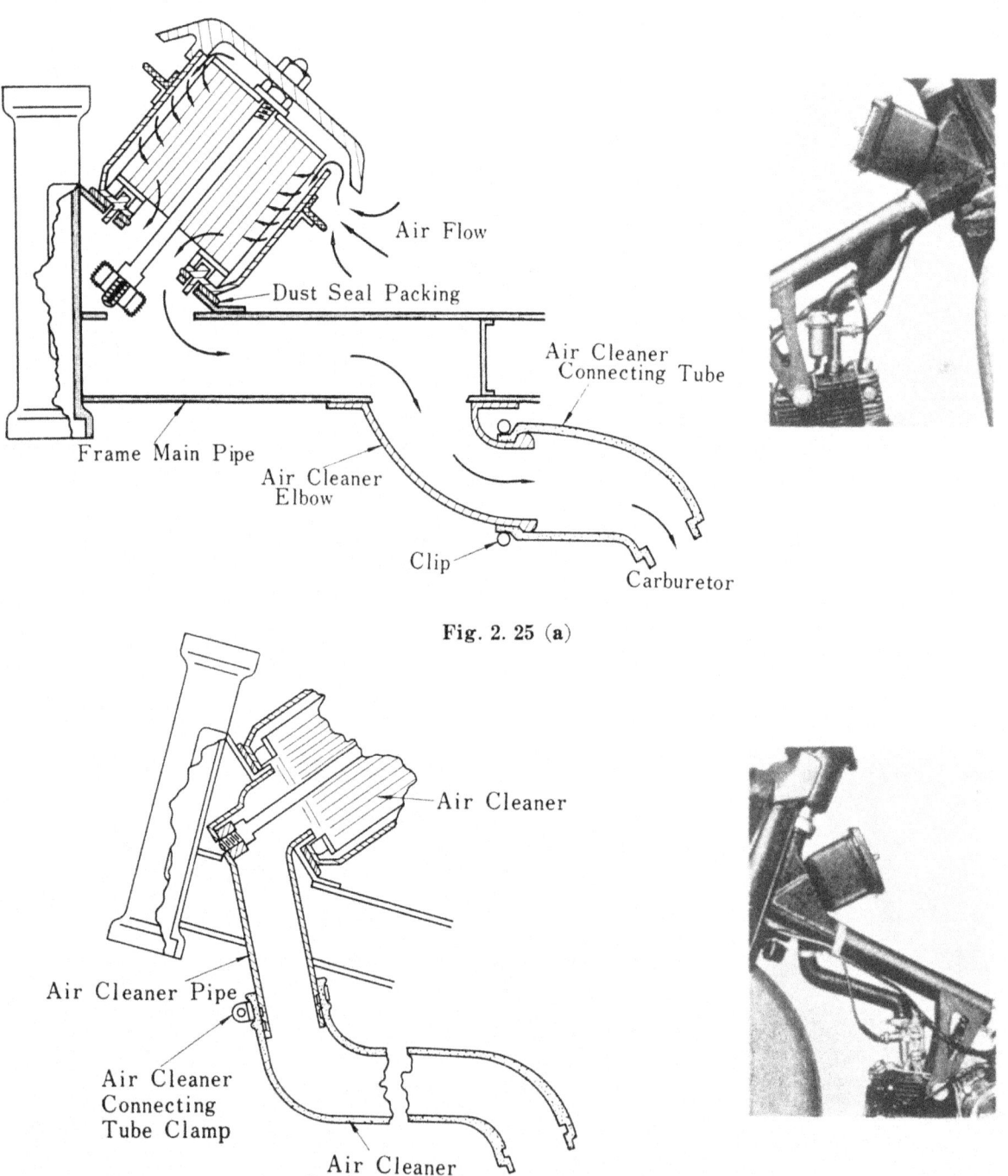

Fig. 2.25 (a)

Fig. 2.25 (b)

2.9 AIR CLEANER

A. Disassembly

This is completely disassembled by removing the parts illustrated in **fig. 2.25 (c)** from ①~⑦. Usually air cleaner is removed by taking off air cleaner cover.

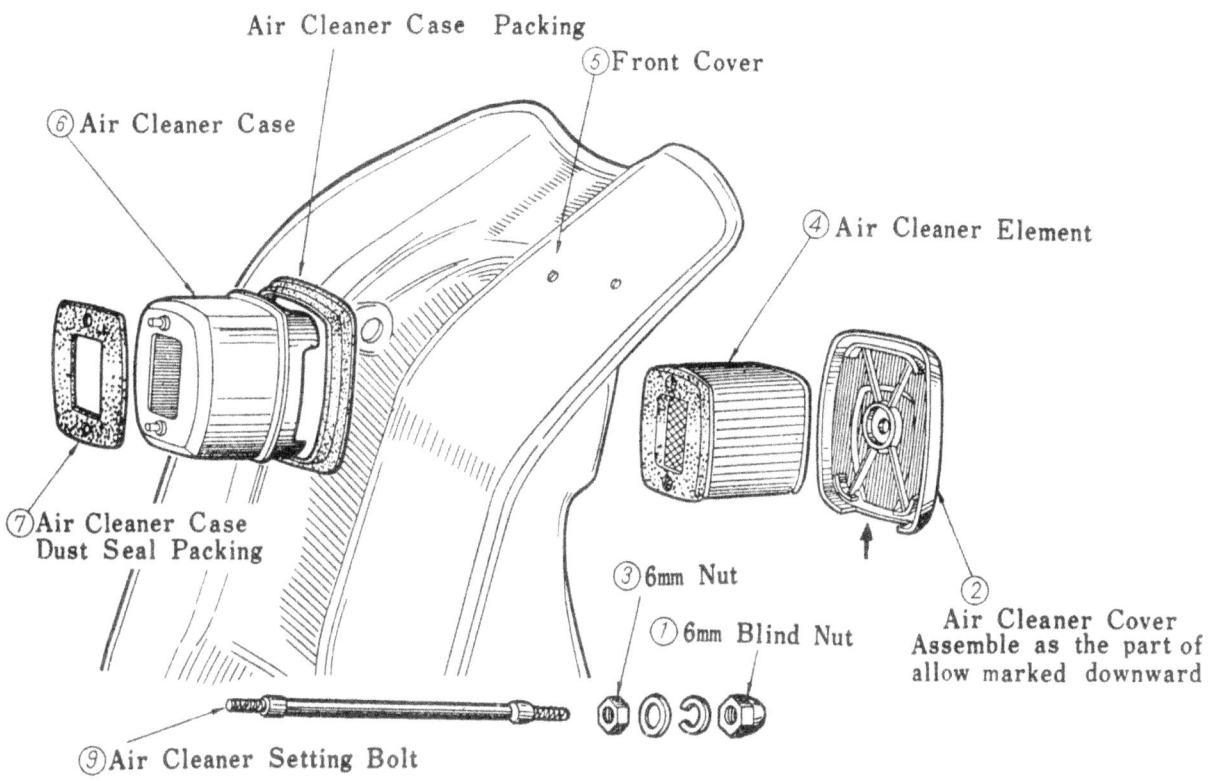

Fig. 2.25 (c) Air Cleaner System

B. Inspection & Reassembly

(1) Air cleaner element should be cleaned periodically. If damaged or oil dirty, replace this.

If this gets wet, dry thoroughly before reassembling. Replace packing at bottom of element if damaged.

(2) Replace damaged air cleaner case packing. Insert air cleaner case packing securely when reassembling and fit case hatch to hole in frame and tighten air cleaner.

Securely install clip of carburetor connecting tube.

NOTE: Be careful that air is not sucked into carburetor on the way from air cleaner element to carburetor as this would not act as air cleaner, causing dust to be drawn into engine, resulting earlier wear to engine.

2.10 Exhaust System

Exhaust gas inside engine is expelled outside through exhaust pipe and muffler. Muffler absorbs and deadens exhaust noises. Inside diagram is illustrated in **fig. 2.26(a)**

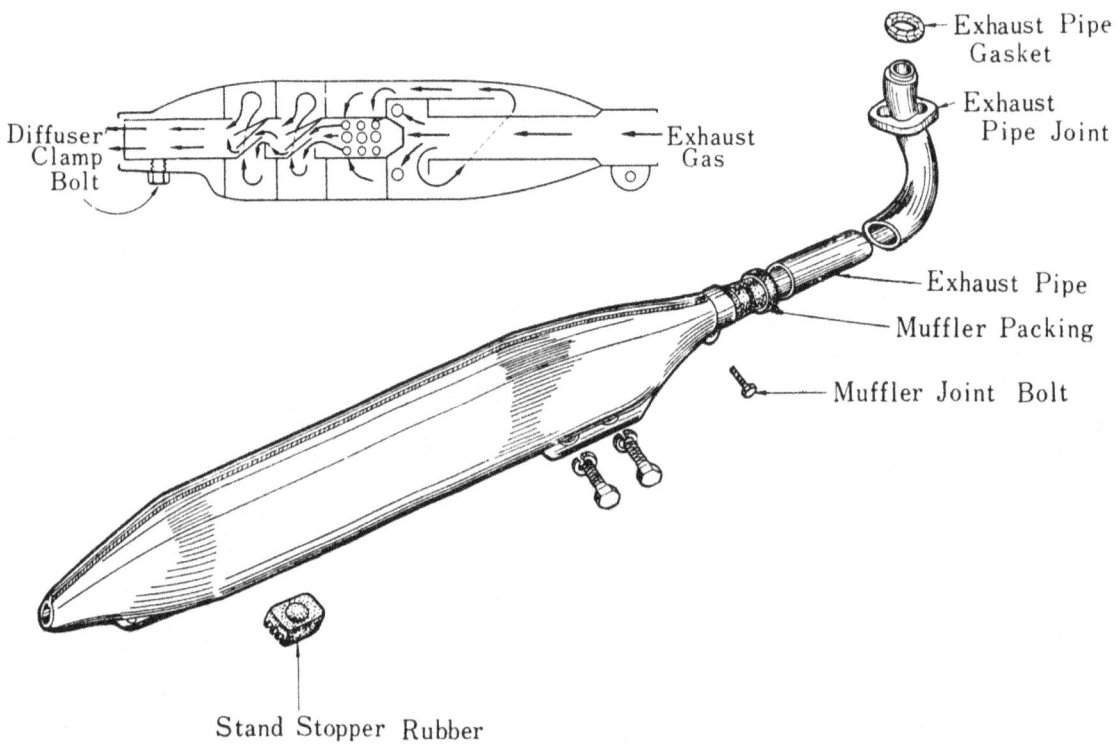

Fig. 2.26 (a)

From the Frame Serial Number C 100-59-511714 muffler diffuser pipe can be separated by removing 6 mm bolt.

When carbon has deposited on the end of the diffuser, take out and clean with wire brush.

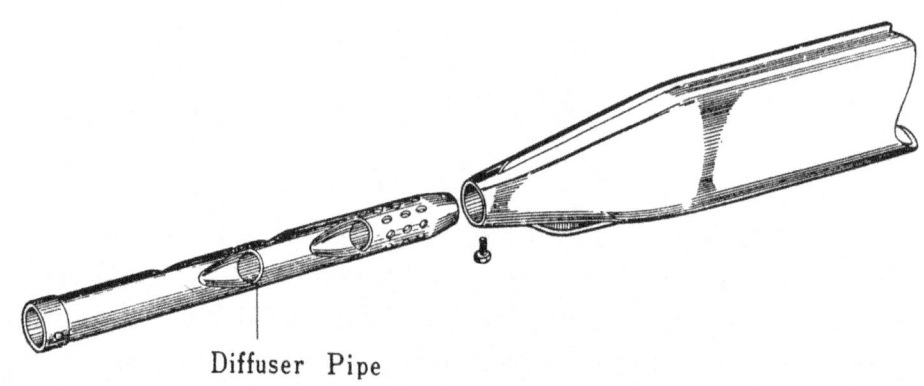

Fig. 2.26 (b)

2.10 EXHAUST SYSTEM

Inspection & Reassembly

Remove exhaust pipe joint from engine, take off bolts holding muffler (6 mm bolts -2) and this will come off as an assembly.

Replace damaged or worn muffler packing. If exhaust pipe gasket is damaged, replace this.

> NOTE: If engine smokes from muffler while driving or when racing engine, check engine right away to prevent oil up. Otherwise carbon will deposit in muffler, obstructing normal flow of exhaust gases, resulting in loss of engine power.

MEMO

2.11 Polyethylene (Hiezex) Made Parts

Polyethylene plastics are called "Heizex" as brand name and many parts illustrated in **fig. 2.27** utilize these products.

Fig. 2.27

NOTE: (1) Front fender, front cover, light cover and others should not be tightened by same torque as metal parts and are about,
        6 mm bolt-nut   30～40 in-lb (0.4 kg-m)
        8 mm bolt-nut   10～20 ft-lb (2.0～2.5 kg-m)
(2) Cracked or damaged parts cannot be fixed and must be replaced.
(3) Be careful not to mar when handling as below, as there is no way to paint or color parts, which are scratched.
   i. Wet soft cloth with water or soap water and wipe and clean surfaces.
   ii. If mud is splashed on, wash off with water first before wiping.
   iii. If oil or grease gets on, wash off cleaning solvent then wipe off.

MEMO

2.12 Step Bar, Main Stand & Brake Pedal

Disassembly & Maintenance

Remove muffler, take off end of brake rod from rear brake arm, remove pedal spring and main stand spring, remove 8 mm bolt ① and pull out rear brake pivot. Main stand and brake pedal will fall off step bar is removed by taking off nut of stud bolt on crankcase,

(1) If there is too much play in brake pivot pipe and brake pedal, adjust according to maintenance standard shown in **fig. 2.28** or replace.
(2) Replace worn or extremely rusted brake pedal spring, main stand spring and brake rod spring.
(3) Repair or replace bent main stand, wash thoroughly when reassembling and grease inside of pipes of main stand and brake pedal, well.

MEMO

2.12 STEP BAR, MAIN STAND & BRAKE PEDAL   79

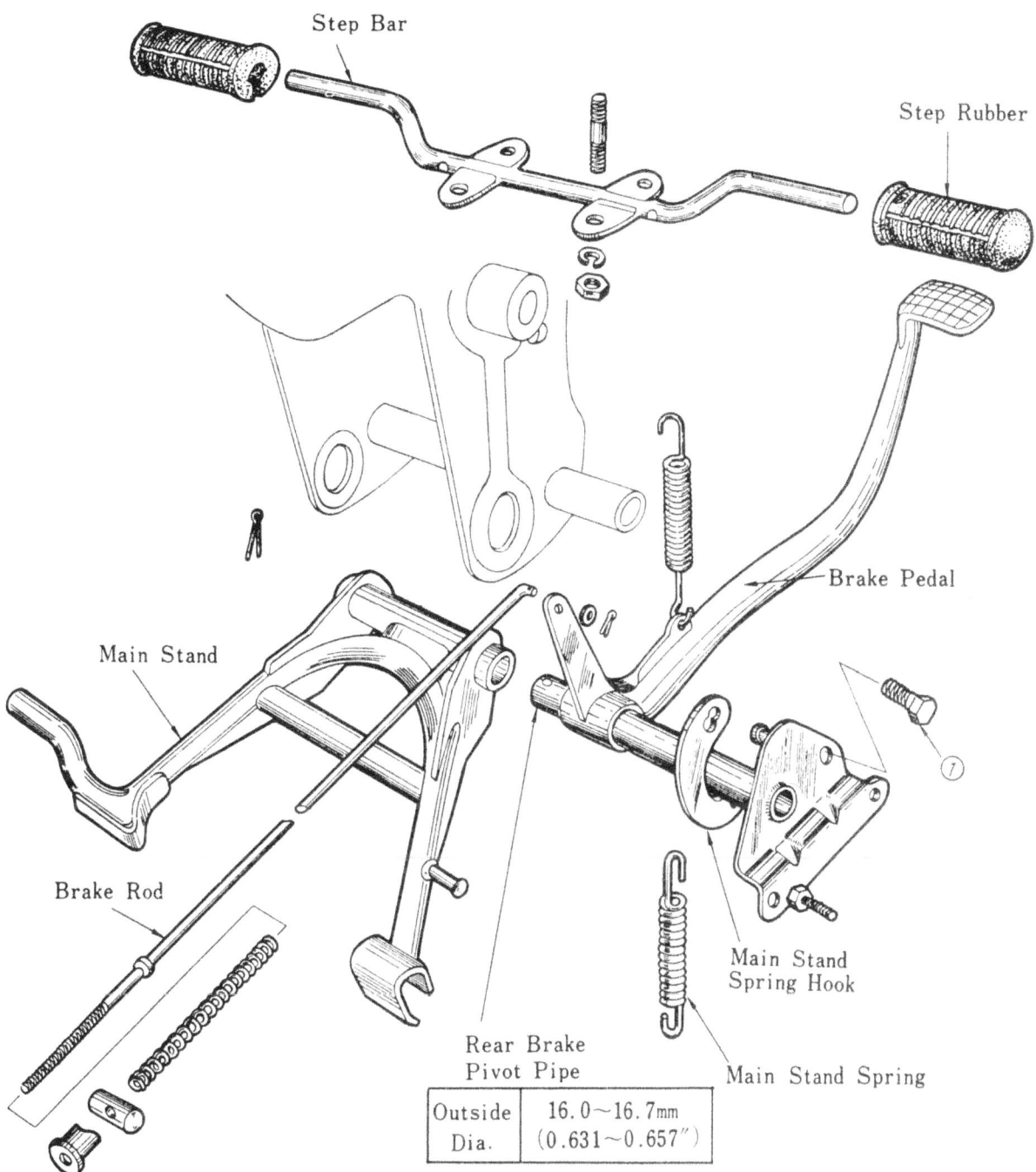

Fig. 2.28

2.13 Frame

The main parts of frame are made up by pipe-sections and pressed steel plating-sections. These two sections are welded together. In the front, steering head pipe is welded on through stiffener. Ball race is inserted into top and bottom of head pipe, consisting of twenty-one 3/16" steel balls each. Rear fork pivot pipe and bottom reinforcing pipe are welded to frame bottom plate. Air cleaner elbow and engine hanger plate are welded to middle of frame pipe section. Engine is bolted directly to frame by 8 mm bolts on rear section, but is bolted through rubber bush on front section. Head pipe plays an important part as it is the center of front wheel rotation and as angle with frame is the basis for caster angle.

Inspection & Maintenance

Frame is bared as in **fig. 2.29** by executing steps of 1.1 (Removal of Engine), 2.1-2.12 and 3.4 (Removal of Wire Harness). When disassembled inspect the following,
(1) Check for damaged welds, cracks, or distortion in pipes and pressed parts. If any are found weld and repair.
(2) If frame is twisted or out of alignment, also check angle of head pipe or distortion of head pipe. If these are found extremely defective, corrrect or replace frame.
(3) Replace damaged or worn 3/16" steel balls.
(4) If top and or bottom ball race is marred or scored, replace.
(5) Replace distorted or damaged engine rubber bush. Tightening allowance of ball race and head pipe is about $1/100 \sim 5/100$ mm, so by lightly tapping from inside with soft bar, it will come out. When installing new parts make sure ball race is not tilted and drive in evenly to its full extent. (Use wooden hammer)

MEMO

2.13 FRAME

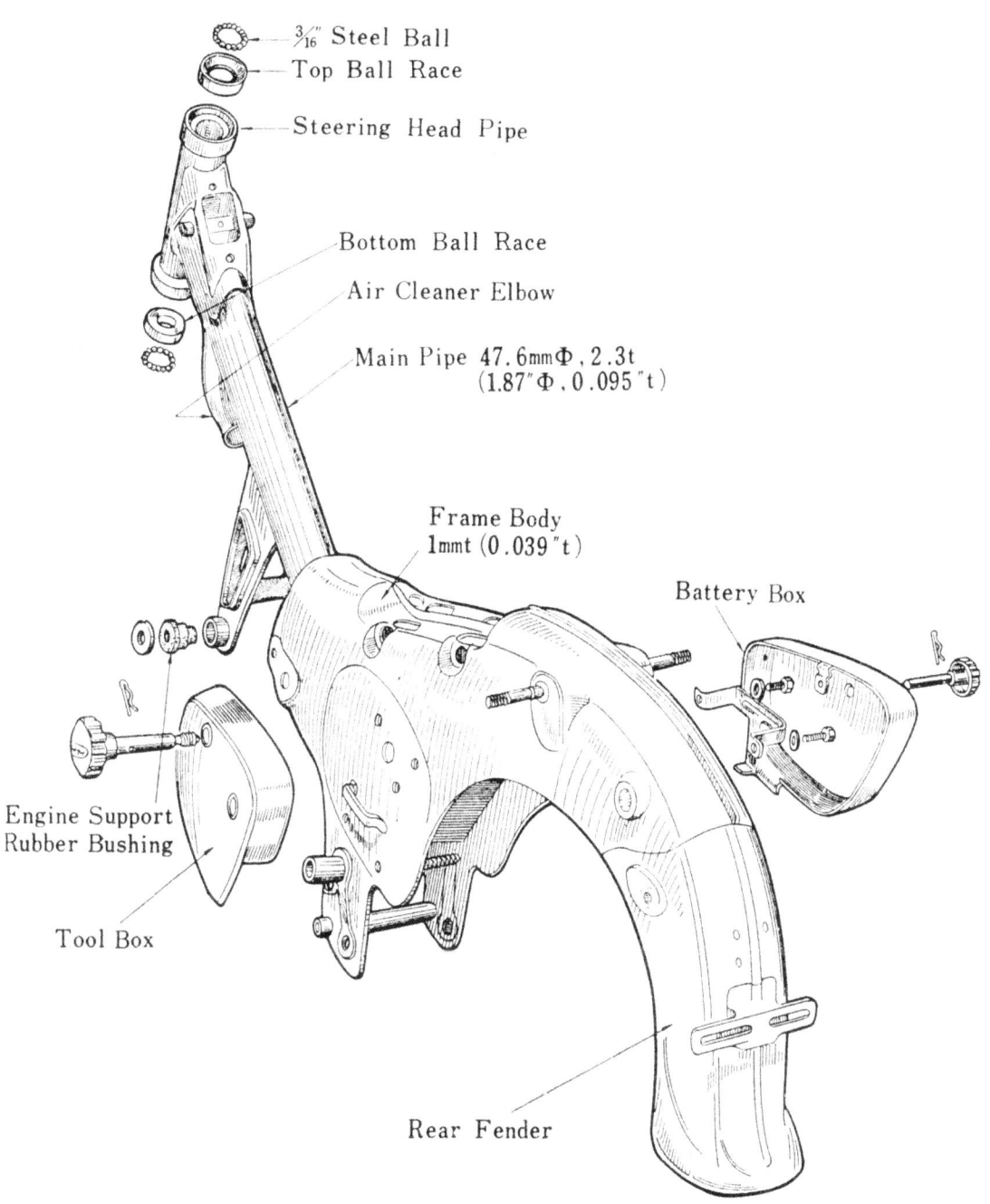

Fig. 2.29

MEMO

3. ELECTRICAL SYSTEM

3.1 Ignition System

The series of system from magneto, contact braker, condenser, spark plug and others is called the electrical system. The high tension electrical current, generated by the high tension coil of magneto, is transmitted to spark plug at specific intervals by the operation of contact braker and ignites fuel mixture.

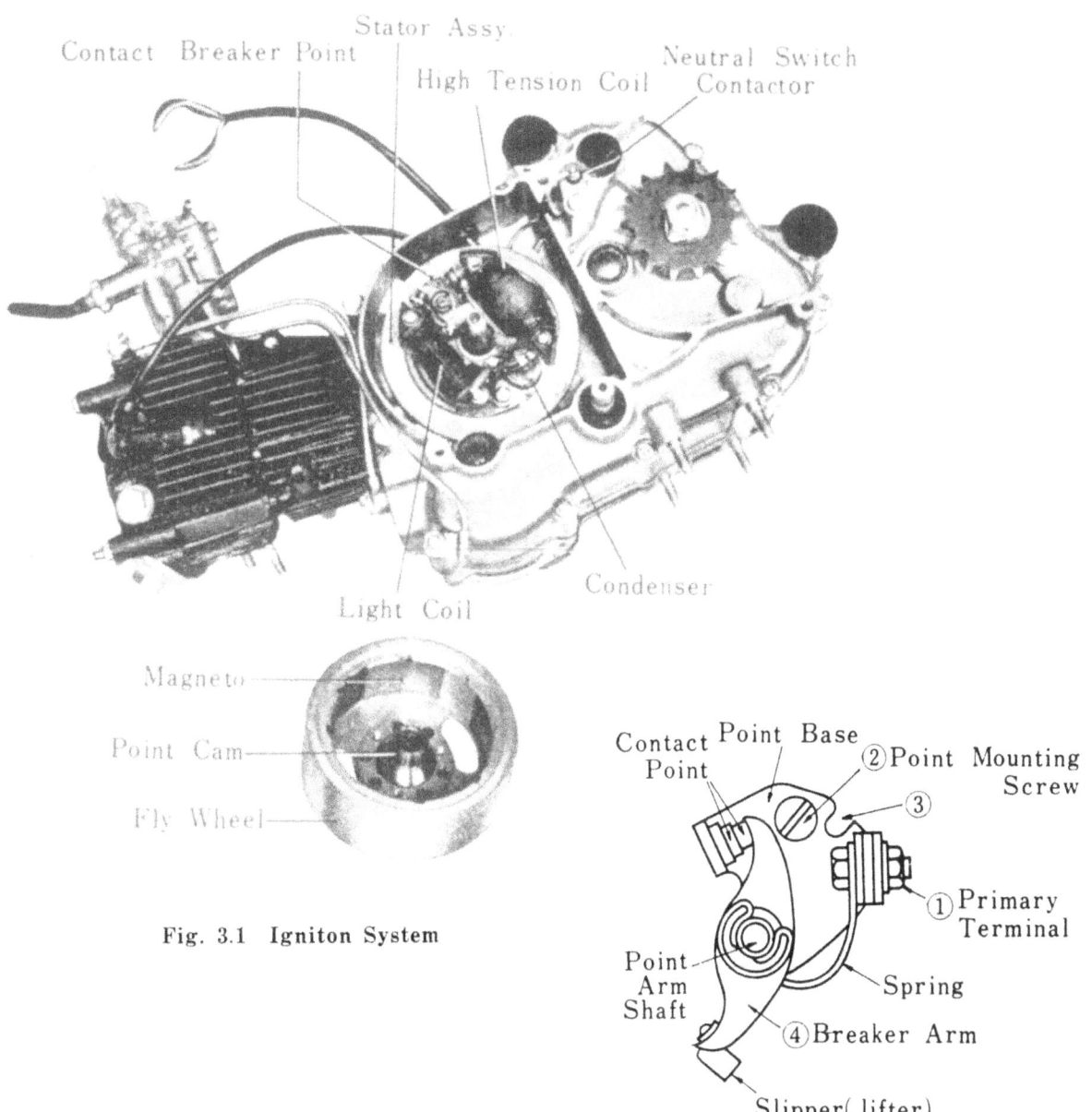

Fig. 3.1 Igniton System

Fig. 3.2 Contact Breaker Point

A. Contact Breaker

As illustrated in **fig. 3.1** the contact breaker is installed onto the stator of the magneto. Point cam is machined to boss part of flywheel and is adjusted from flywheel hole.

(1) Disassembling

Remove flywheel in manner described in engine chapter. (see p. 11)
Next remove terminal ① of contact breaker primary circuit, loosen screw ② securing breaker and take off breaker. (**fig. 3.2**)

(2) Inspection & maintenance

Contact area of point should have bright metal finish and be smooth. If discolored black or brownish or facing rough and uneven, file down both faces at the same time with a point file, if the defects are minor. If defects are major, disassemble and grind off rough or uneven face separately with oil stone. Replace as assembly if cannot be readily corrected. After furbishing, wash off points with gasoline and wipe clean, before reassembling. Be careful not to leave any oily film on facings as it will cause scoring and wear again.

(3) Reassembling & adjustments

Fit point axis to base hole and secure with screw. If oil is not penetrating oil felt at this time, penetrate with engine oil. Adjust after securing flywheel. Make sure key groove is fitted securely into woodruff key before tightening flywheel to standard torque 20 ft-lb (2.8 kg-m). After installing left cover adjust ignition timing to 35° B.T.D.C.

Adjustment is done by loosening screw ②, inserting ⊖ driver into slit ③ and turning. After adjusting, rotate flywheel about 90° and check to see that gap between points is within limit of 0.3~0.4 mm (0.012~0.016") (see p. 104).

B. Condenser

Condenser is installed onto magneto as in **fig. 3.1**. Construction and wiring is as in **fig. 3.3**. The condenser prevents arcing at the points and aids in breaking down the magnetic field in the coil, helping the operation of the contact breaker.

Capacity is 0.2~0.26 μF.

To determine condition of condenser measure insulation of condenser primary coil side terminal and shell with service tester, with point in opened position.

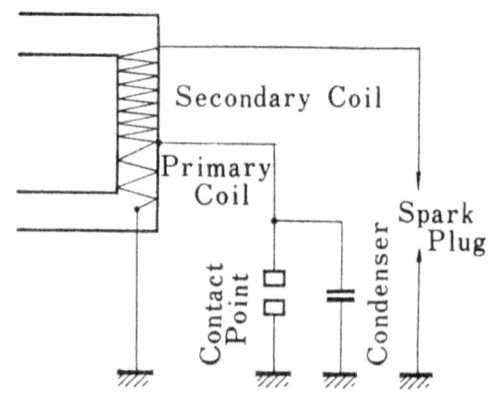

Fig. 3.3 Wiring Diagram of Ignition System

3.1 IGNITION SYSTEM

Under normal temperature, if insulation resistance measures;
- over 5 meg. ohm — good
- 1~5 meg. ohm — fairly good
- under 1 meg. ohm — no good

and determine according to the above findings. To replace, remove screw and connector and take off.

Condenser itself rarely causes trouble, only be careful of securely tighten and that point of contact is clean as these can be cause of faulty ignition.

C. Spark Plug

Standard type is N.G.K. make, C-7H type and **fig. 3.4** illustrates sectional diagram.

Use plug wrench to remove, paying caution not to damage insulator. Plug should be wholly dry and have a thin accumulation of grey or brownish coating and the insulator scorched golden brown color.

Clean if found dirty and if carbon has deposited. After cleaning, set electrode gap to 0.6~0.7 mm. Replace if spark plug is in bad condition.

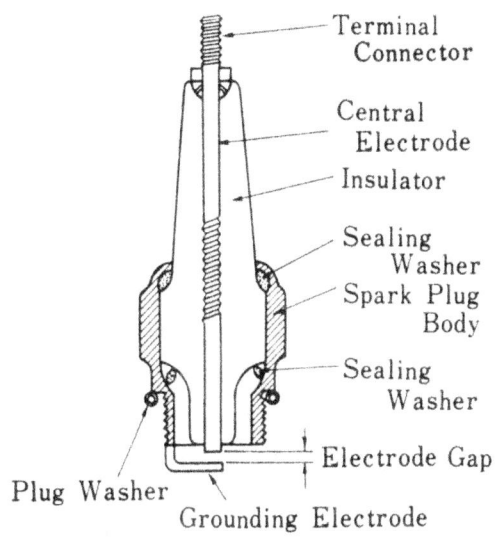

Fig. 3.4 Section View of Spark Plug

Condition of Spark Plug	Engine Condition	Probable Cause	Probable Remedy
Inside of plug dirty, sooty or wet, etc.	Hard starting, engine misfires at low speed.	Plug too cold.	Change to hot plug (C 50 H) (Consult technician).
		Carburetor mixture too rich. Excessive use of choke.	Correctly adjust carburetor.
		Driving abnormally long at low speed.	Avoid as much as possible. Change to hot type plug (C 50 H) if necessary.
		Burning oil due to worn piston rings.	If excessive, disassemble and repair engine.
		Damaged top insulator. Usage of deteriorated high tension wiring.	Replace plug.
		Contact point dirty.	Clean points.
		Firing gap too large.	Adjust gap.
Insulator is white without hardly any accumulation of foreign matter.	Poor operation at high speed and hill climbing.	Plug too hot causing preignition	Change to cold type plug. (Consult technician).
		Gas leakage due to faulty installation of plug.	Replace with new gasket. Tighten to correct torque.
		Carburetor mixture too lean.	Correct to right adjustment.
		Faulty ignition timing.	Correct to right adjustment.
Igniting part of insulator damaged.		Using too hot a plug.	Change to cold type plug.
		Overheat due to plug loosely tightened.	Tighten to correct torque.

To install, first tighten the plug "finger tight" then turn 1/4 with plug wrench. Do not forget to place plug washer. (see p. 106 for cleaning and adjusting).

Check condition of plug with plug tester after cleaning and setting. Usually bad condition of plug cannot be determined visually except for worn electrode or other visible damage. In many cases other defects are the cause of bad plugs and their probable remedies are listed in the table of p. 85.

D. Flywheel Magneto

For domestic two types, FA Type (Kokusan Denki) and HDM Type (Nippon Denso) of same performance are used, and for overseas, only HDM Type is used. This is installed on left side of engine. A permanent magnet, casted into flywheel, rotates around iron core coil. There are two coils installed on the base. One a light coil, the other an ignition coil.

(1) Testing the ignition coil.

Take off plug cap of coil secondary wiring end and connect lead line of three needles tester (On service tester). At the time of kick, measure the maximum gap that spark can constantly jump with the needles. If this gap is under 6 mm the coil is faulty or the magnet is weak and necessary action must be taken. Usually it is attributed to faulty coil. If charging performance of light coil is deteriorating probable cause could be demagnetization.

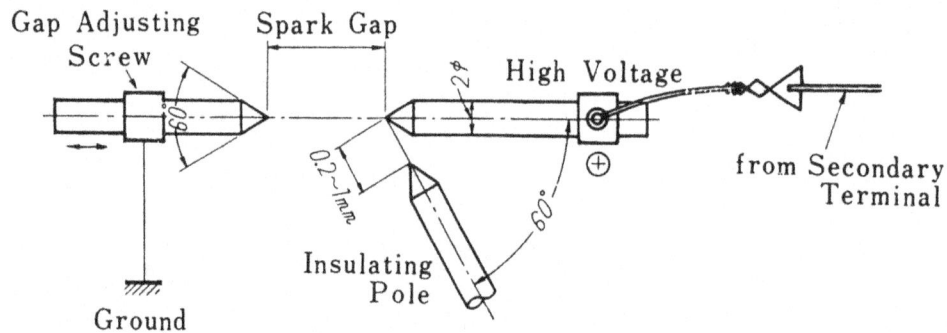

Fig. 3.5 Wiring of Three Needle Tester

(2) Disassembly, replacement & reassembly of ignition coil

Remove flywheel, take off stator assembly and pull off cord from case and unscrew ignition coil. Install ignition coil so that iron core face fits with grooved facing of stator base, in correct position. After passing cord through case, insert grommet properly and tighten on stator base. (see **fig. 3.1**)

(3) Demagnetization of flywheel magnet.

When magnet force demagnetizes have this re-magnetized at shop that specializes in this kind of work. Usually, natural loss of magnet force does not occur so it is necessary to check lead line of coil for shorts with tester.

3.2 Charging System

Charging system consists of low tension coil of magneto, selenium rectifier, battery and associated wiring.

Alternating current generated by magneto goes to head lamp, tail lamp and meter lamp and a part of this flows to charge battery. Alternating current is rectified to half wave current by selenium rectifier before going to battery.

A. Charging Coil

Low tension coil is separated into coil for lamps and for charging. For night driving this generates alternate current (6~8 V) direct to the head lamp, tail lamp and meter lamp to light these and the charging coil generates alternate current day and night to charge battery.

(1) Testing the charge coil

In order to determine condition of charge coil, connect ammeter (reading about 2 A) in series to fuse connector, start the engine and check current according to the crank revolutions.

Check with key in daytime and night-time position. Standard charging capacity for each position at different revolutions is according to following list. If charge is more or less 20~30 % than as indicated replace coil.

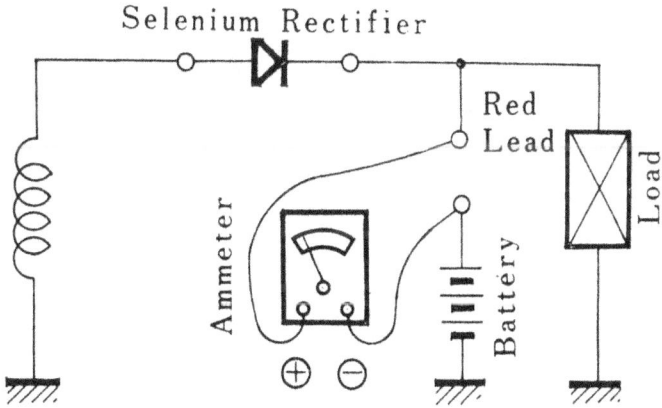

Fig. 3.6 Wiring Ammeter for Checking Coil Charge

Crank rpm		1,500	3,000	6,000	8,000
Daytime Charging Current (A)		0	0.2	0.2	1.5
Night-time	Charging Current (A)	0	0.2	0.4	0.5
	Lamp Voltage (V)	4.5	6.5	8.0	8.5

(2) Replacement

Be careful to center iron core with stator base, as with high tension coil, when installing.

B. Selenium Rectifier

Selenium rectifier is installed on right side of frame. Its structure is illustrated in **fig. 3.8.** This charges the battery by rectifing half wave the alternate current generated by the coil.

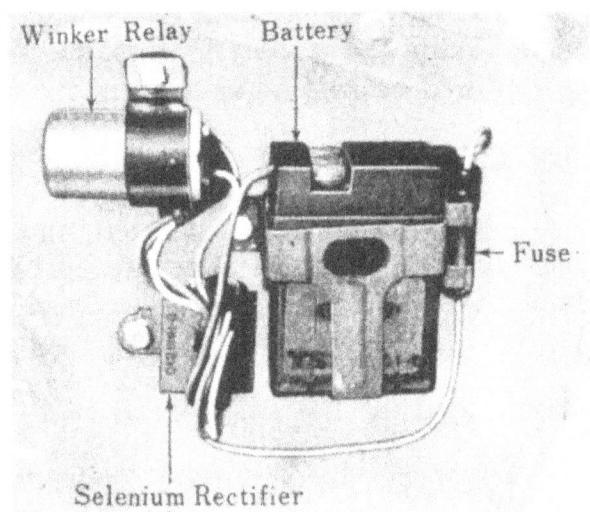

By removing the battery at daytime or running long distance at high speed without a fuse will cause reverse flow current towards selenium rectifier causing it to loose its rectifing efficiency and if this is continued for a prolonged period the rectifier will get hot and may break. Be sure to check that fuse is not blown out and is properly installed.

If battery discharges too often, check not only the coil, but also discoloring of rectifier and for short of terminals. After replacing parts, securely tighten ternimals.

Fig. 3.7

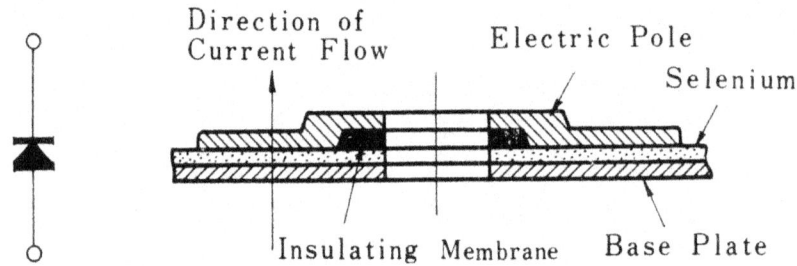

Fig. 3.8 Sectional View of Slenium Rectifier

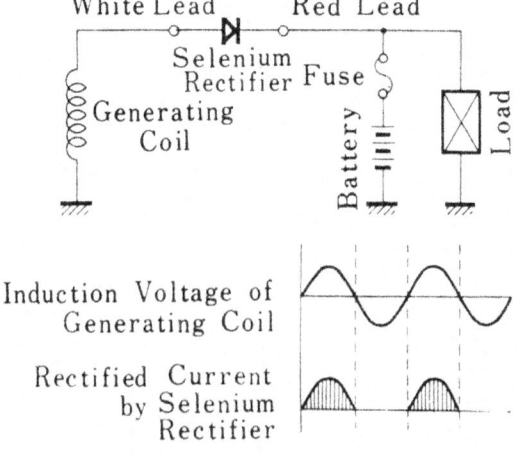

Fig. 3.9 Wiring of Selenium Rectifier

3.2 CHARGING SYSTEM

C. Battery

Horn, directional signal lamp, neutral lamp and others are run by the direct current flowing from the battery. The battery used is MBCI-6 type, which has three cells, whose plates are connected in series. Capacity is 6V-2Ah, and has discharge capacity of 10 hours at 0.2A. This is connected from selenium rectifier through fuse (red lead line), and black terminal is grounded to frame through main switch.

Battery is located on right side of frame and can be easily inspected by removing battery cover. (**fig. 3.7**)

(1) **Removal & installation of battery.**

Remove battery band, disconnect fuse connector and take battery out. Check to see fuse is in place and for short of fuse when installing battery. Always keep outside of battery washed clean and so inside can always be seen. Ground part should be checked for rust and corrosion and securely tightened.

(2) **Inspection & maintenance.**

This should be periodically checked by the user or dealer.

Just checking of electrolyte level is sufficient, but dealer should also check its specific gravity.

Specific gravity will determine batteries charging rate performance as follows.

Specific gravity	Rate of charging
1.130~1.500	0 % (full charge)
1.200~1.210	50 % (half 〃)
1.260	100 % (none 〃)

The above are for standard figures at 20°C and for approximate calculations at different temperatures use the following formula.

$$\text{Specific gravity at } 20°C = (t°C \text{ spec. grav.}) + 0.0007(t° - 20°)$$

40~50% discharge necessitates charging.

If battery discharge continues, sulphation white powder will from on plates and settle in bottom of cell.

In this case wash out cell completely and refill with battery electrolyte before charging. This is done at battery shop.

An example of a simple hydrometer is shown in **fig. 3.10**. This meter determined state of specific gravity by floating red and white balls.

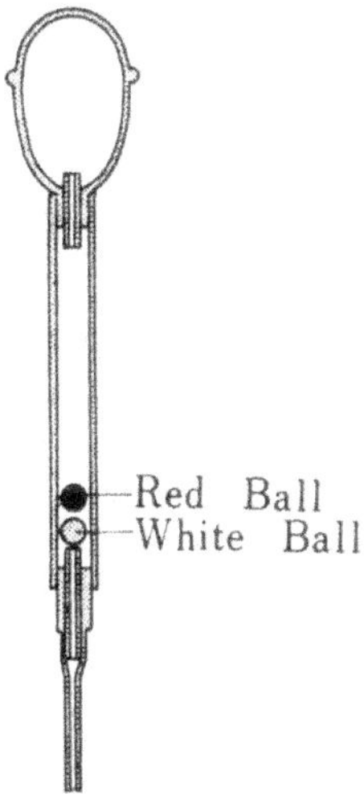

Fig. 3.10

	①	②	③
Red Ball	float	sink	sink
White Ball	float	float	sink
Rate of Charging	100%	50%	0%

There are small battery chargers (Yuasa make), which makes charging easy and sure. **Fig. 3.11** (**a**) shows one and usually these are for charging one battery, but some can charge two or more batteries at once. Connect as shown in same **fig**. (**b**) and plug into 100 V outlet and let set. When charge is completed a red light shows. It takes 10 hours with a 0.2~0.3 A current to recharge.

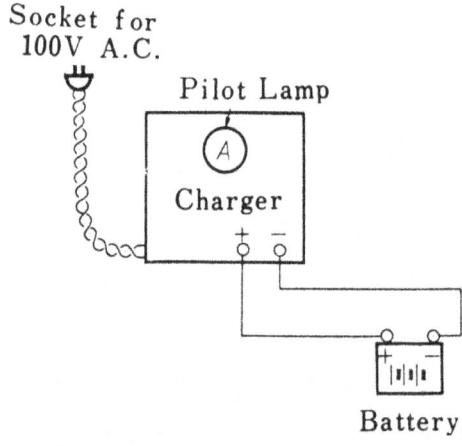

(a) Battery Charger   (b) Wiring of Battery Charger

Fig. 3.11

MEMO

3.3 Switches

A. Combination Switch

Combination switch is separated into three positions and their operations are illustrated in **fig. 3.12**

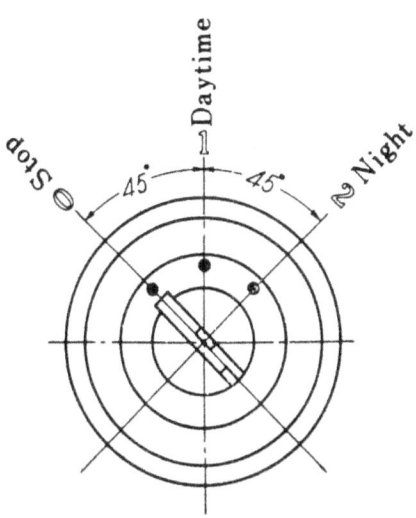

Fig. 3.12

(Position of Key)   (Operation)

0 .... Key can be removed when stopped or parked. Black wiring from contact breaker terminal is ground inside switch and engine will not start. ⊖ terminal wiring from battery is disconnected inside switch and all electrical apparatus will not function.

1 .... Daytime driving and key cannot be removed. Black wiring from contact breaker terminal is released from ground and engine will start. Battery ⊖ terminal wiring is grounded and horn, directional signal lamp and neutral lamps will operate by turning attached switch.

2 .... Night-time driving and key cannot be removed. Head lamp, meter lamp and tail lamps will light besides the functions of position 1. However as lighting is from magneto these will not light unless engine is running.

If the above three positions do not operate properly when turning switches on, first check wiring system of the defective part. If it still does not function conclude that the combination switch is defective and replace. In order to check defect of switch itself, make a conductivity test.

3. ELECTRICAL SYSTEM

In order to replace switch take off tool box cover and loosen screws securing switch. Remove connector and switch will come off easily. When wiring connectors do not mistake colors.

B. Directional Signal Lamp Switch & Head Dimmer Switch

Directional signal lamp switch is on right side of handle and head light dimmer switch is on left side of handle. These both have the same kind of construction. If control knob does not operate, or contact points are defective or if wiring system has short, these can be disassembled and repaired. Replace parts, if necessary.

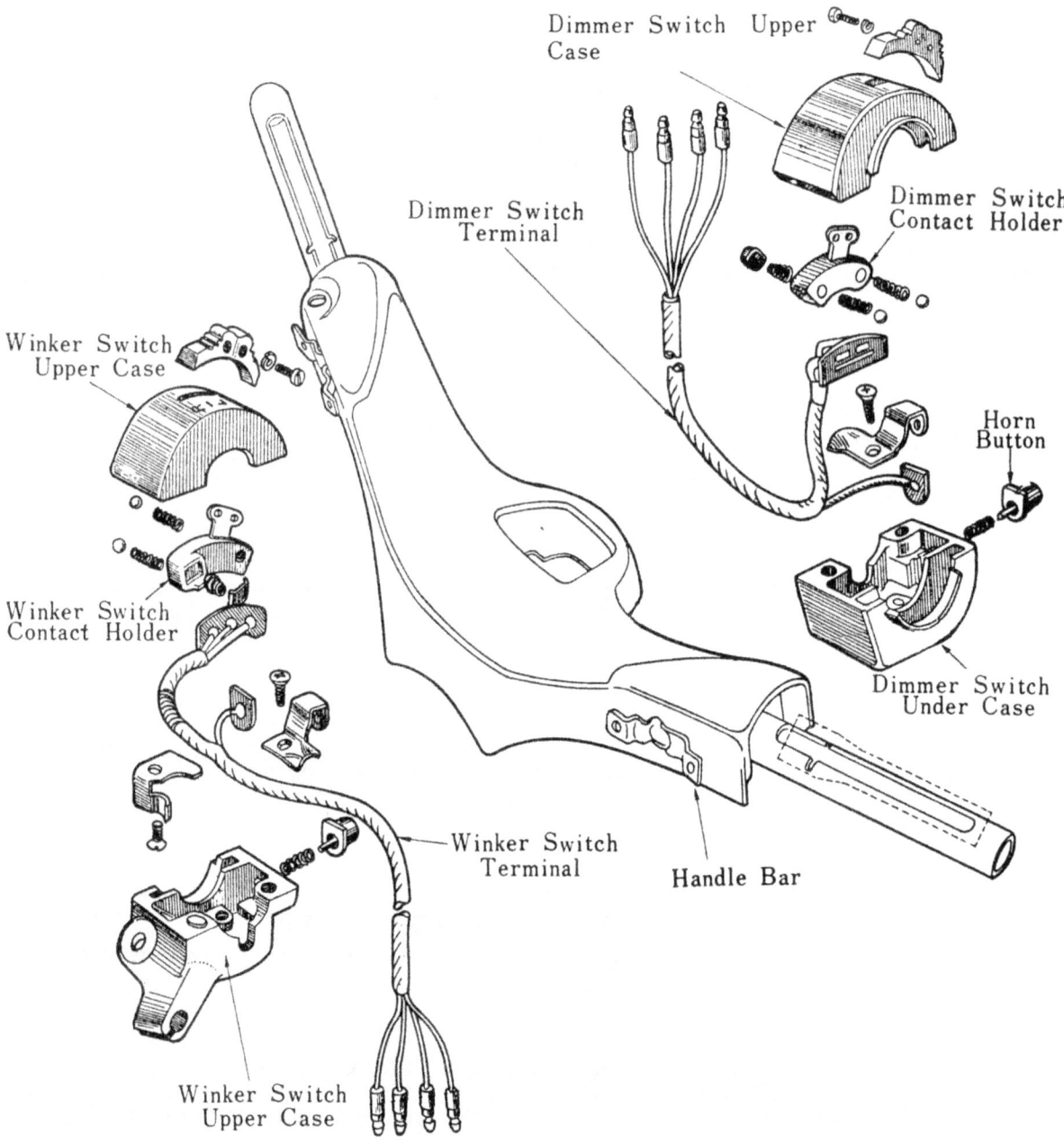

Fig. 3.13 Handle Bar Switches

3.3 SWITCHES

Disassembly & Inspection

Loosen screw holding together grip metal and disassemble into top and bottom piece. Remove metal fastener of switch terminal. If terminal or ball facing is corroded, rusted, shorted, etc., take fine emery paper and polish for better contact. If further replacement is required take off handle mounting nut, so handle can be lifted up, take off head lamp and remove concealed connector. Pull out harness on side that requires replacing. Reassembly is the opposite of this, but be careful in passing harness through and not pinch lead lines when tightening. (see **fig. 3.13**)

C. Neutral Switch

Neutral switch is located on right side of crankcase and operates together with gear shift mechanism. Refer to p. 35.

Poor functioning of neutral lamp can be sometimes attributed to the switch itself. The causes are poor contact of switch contact and switch rotor, short due to damage of resin mold part of contact, wiring cut or shorted, etc. When replacing switch also check to see if rubber ring is in good condition or not, before installing. (**fig. 3.14**)

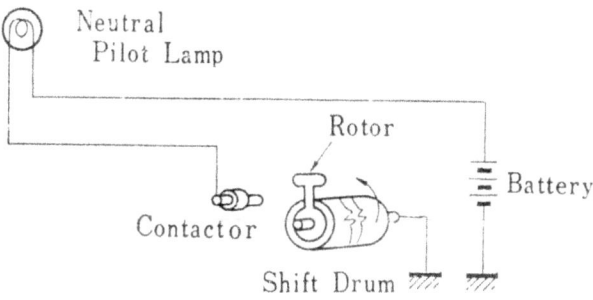

Fig. 3.14 Neutral Switch Wiring

D. Horn Button Switch

This is installed on the grip metal of left side handle. As this is a simple push button, if horn does not blow it is usually caused by poor contact of button. This can be repaired by using a fine emery paper. As the harness for this part is combined with head light dimmer switch, replacement is done together.

3.4 Various Electrical Loads, Harness & Speedometer

A. Horn

This is of direct current microphonic type and construction is as illustrated in **fig. 3.15**. Tone volume is 90~100 phone at 2 m distant and requires current of 0.6~0.8 A at this time.

When volume of sound is poor or tone is hoarse the cause is usually not the horn itself, but discharge of battery, poor contact of horn button switch, etc., so first check to see if anything is wrong with these before checking horn itself.

To disassemble remove head lamp, take off bolt (6 mm) holding head lamp case. Horn is installed behind head lamp case so remove this and connect horn to 6 V battery and check. Tone and volume is adjusted by turning in or out the adjusting screw. If this cannot be repaired, replace with new one.

Upon reassembling check all attaching places for rust and make for good ground then install securely.

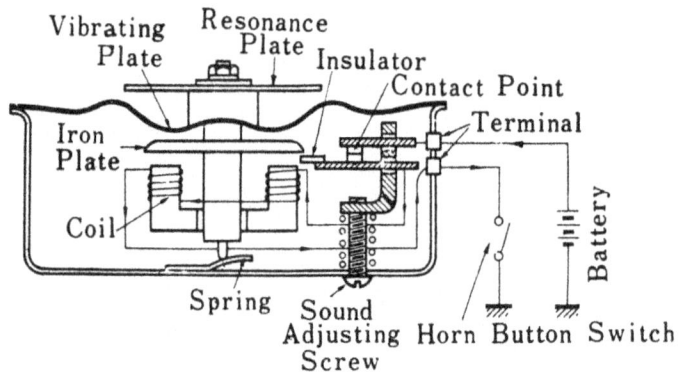

Fig. 3.15 Section View of Horn

B. Directional Signal Lamp Relay

This is installed on left side of body and is of relay type as illustrated in **fig. 3.16**. This blinks by the balance of the relay pulling power and electrical current. Standard operation is 70~110 blinks per minute.

With key in "on" position, if one lamp on same side is out the other lamp will not blink. In this case replace the lamp that is out.

When operating the switch, if one side functions correctly and the other side does not, or both sides function at the same time this trouble is not in the relay, but always in the directional signal lamp switch, wiring, lamp, etc.

With directional signal lamp switch on, if either side does not blink and stays on all the time, or the blinking is erratic, or it does not light at all the trouble is in the relay. In this case replace the relay. Also, in the event it does not light at all the trouble may be lead wiring broken from the battery to the relay or bad connection.

3.4 VARIOUS ELECTRICAL LOADS, HARNESS & SPEEDOMETER

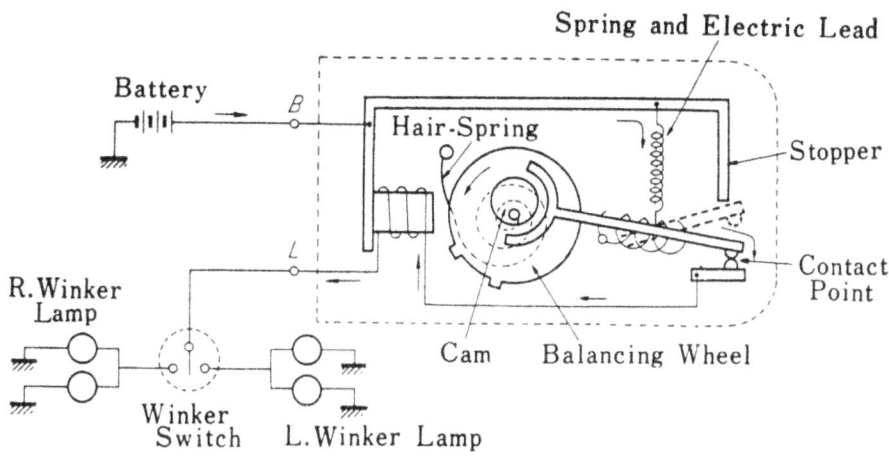

Fig. 3.16 Structure of Winker Relay

C. Speedometer

This is of magnetic eddy type and incorporates two devices—the speedometer to indicate rate of speed and odometer to record the distance traveled. Construction is illustrated in **fig. 3.17** and **3.18**.

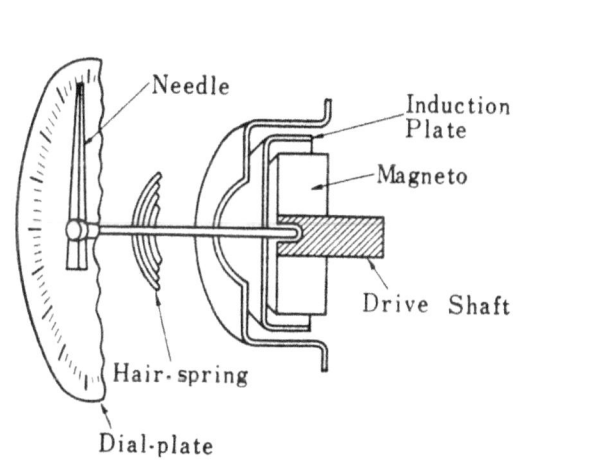

Fig. 3.17 Speedometer

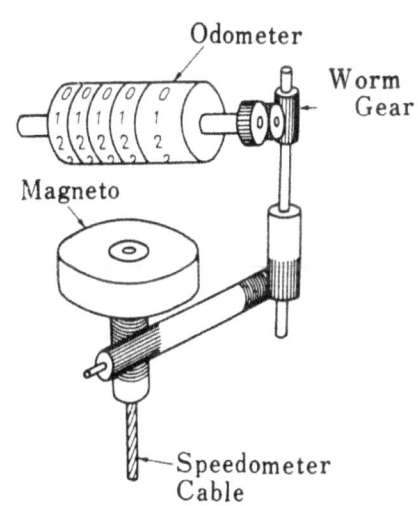

Fig. 3.18 Odometers

Speedometer reads 60 km/h when meter cable rotates at 1,400 rpm and odometer registers 1 km when meter cable rotates 1,400 rpm.

When speedometer glass breaks, inside of glass mists, indicator needle comes off or does not register correctly, replace speedometer itself. Follow steps in p.45 to disassemble handle, take off joint of speedometer cable, remove speedometer clamp and it will come off from handle.

Inner cable and speedometer axle should be correctly fitted and tightened as shown in **fig. 3.19 (a)**. **(b)** shows incorrect fit.

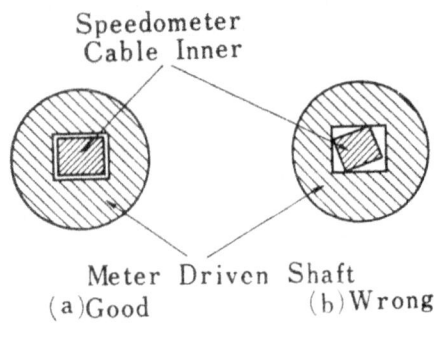

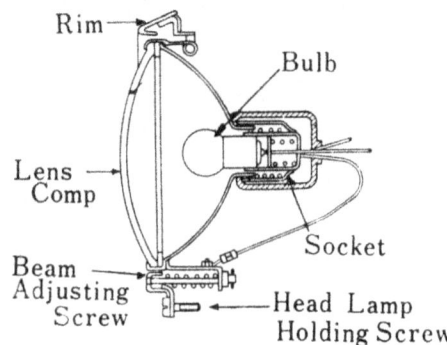

Fig. 3.19   Fig. 3.20

D. Head Lamp

Construction is illustrated in **figs. 3.20** and **3.21**.

As lens and reflector are caulked together into one piece, bulb is replaced from behind reflector. Therefore it is not necessary to touch inside the reflector, which prevents misting of the lens and reflector. This construction also prevents dust from getting inside.

Bulbs of 6~8 V, 10 W (12 W when dimmed) are specified. If specified parts are not used, not only will the set brightness not be achieved, but will burn out when revolution is increased.

To replace, remove head lamp, pull off socket cover and twist socket body and take out socket assembly. Remove bulb from socket.

When either head lamp burns out, do not run without lights, but switch over to the good lamp and ride until replacement can be made. Be careful not to run over 1~2 minutes with lamp burned out as the tail lamp and speedometer lamp will become overloaded and burn out. Head lamp beam aiming is done by screwing in beam adjusting screw with $\ominus$ driver.

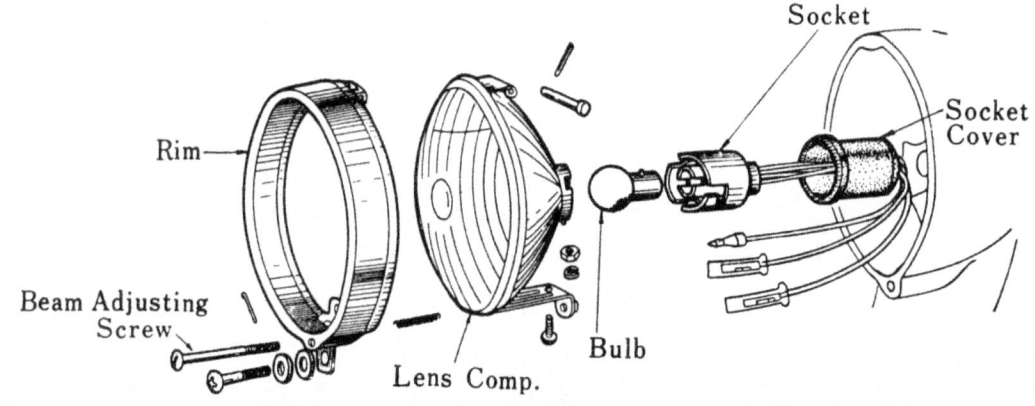

Fig. 3.21 Head Lamp

3.4 VARIOUS ELECTRICAL LOADS, HARNESS & SPEEDOMETER   97

E. Tail Lamp & Speedometer Lamp

With switch on in night position head, speedometer and tail lamps all operate together and only light when engine is running.

Tail lamp is of 6~8 V 2 W, speedometer lamp is a special type 6~8V 1W.

Only use specified tail lamp and speedometer lamp, otherwise it burn out or not light sufficiently.

For replacing, gauge lamp is done so by removing handle and tail lamp by taking off tail lens. (**fig. 3.22**)

F. Directional Signal Lamp

With engine switch on, right side front and rear directional signal lamp will function when pushing control knob forward. Pulling knob towards back will light left side.

Lamps used (4 pieces) are all 6~8 V 8 W. These are replaced by removing screws of each lens. (**fig. 3.22**)

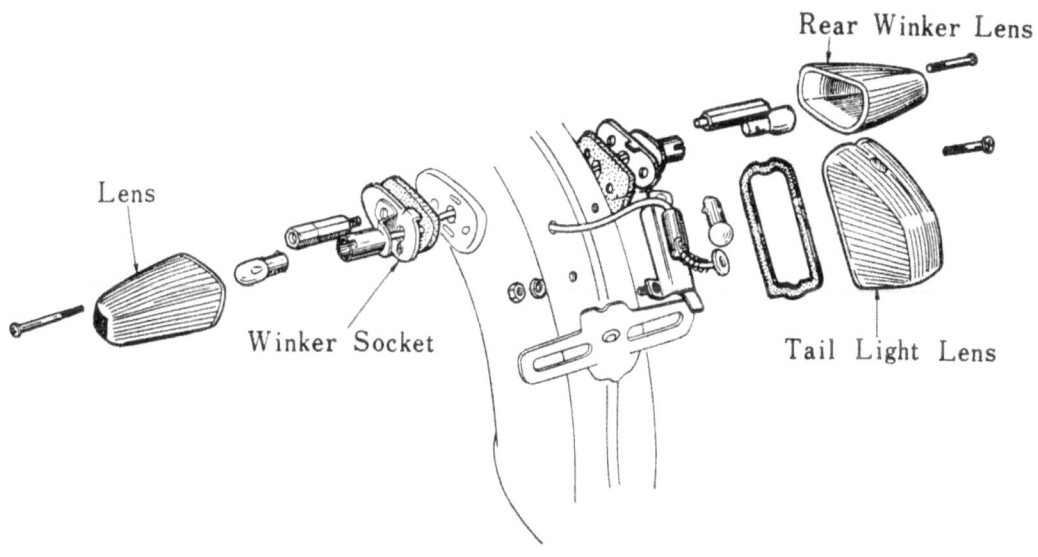

Fig. 3.22 Rear Winker Lamp

G. Fuse

As illustrated in **fig. 3.7** fuse is installed on the battery ⊕ cord. Fuse is 7 A. The cause of fuse blowing out is short in the wiring system. Repair the troubled parts and replace fuse. Never use copper wire, fuse of larger amp. than specified or any other metal object because if electrical circut shorts current of about 20 amp. will flow through circuit and burn the switches and harness and may result in a fire of wire harness.

H. Wire Harness

Electrical of wiring system are put together with the exception of the connector sections, and are protected by vinyl tubing and passed through frame. As tail lamp and left and right rear directional signal lamp wirings passed through inside of welded part of rear fender, pull out each wire one by one so as not to force, when removing harness. When installing also do not force to pass through. There are clamps at various intervals, so set and securely fasten these clamps and grommets. Be sure to match connectors with wiring colors, when connecting. (**fig. 3.23**)

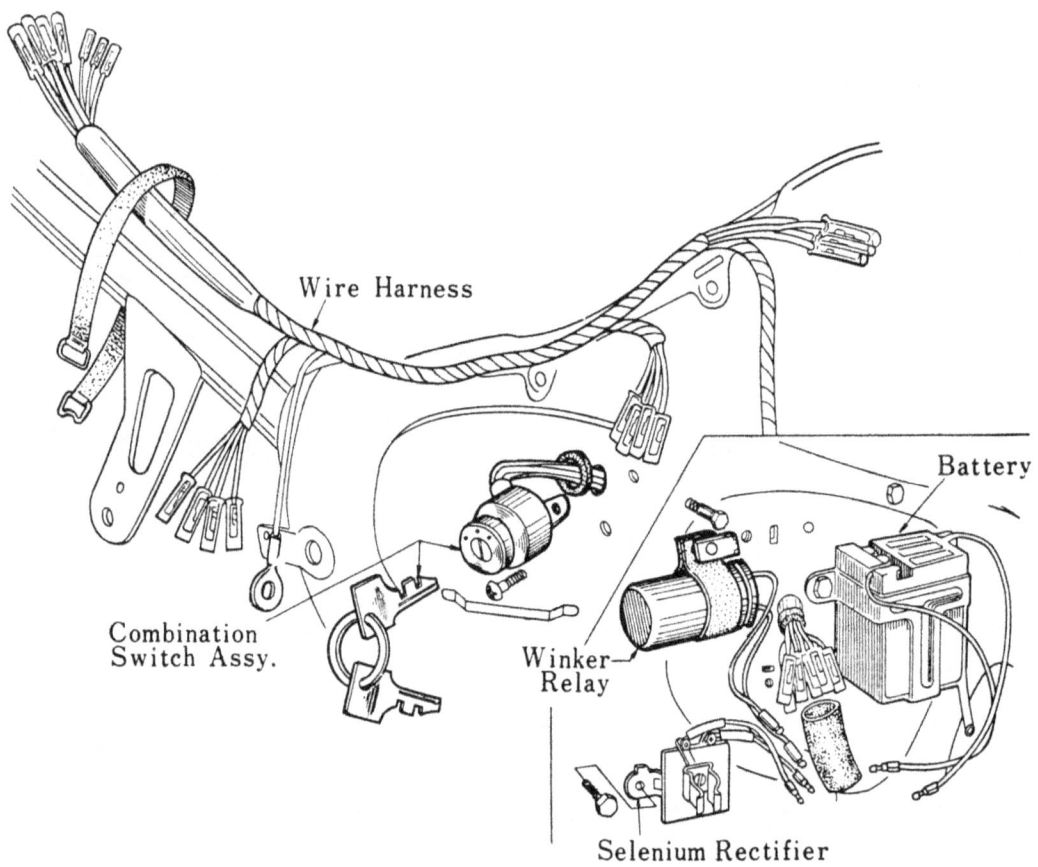

Fig. 3.23

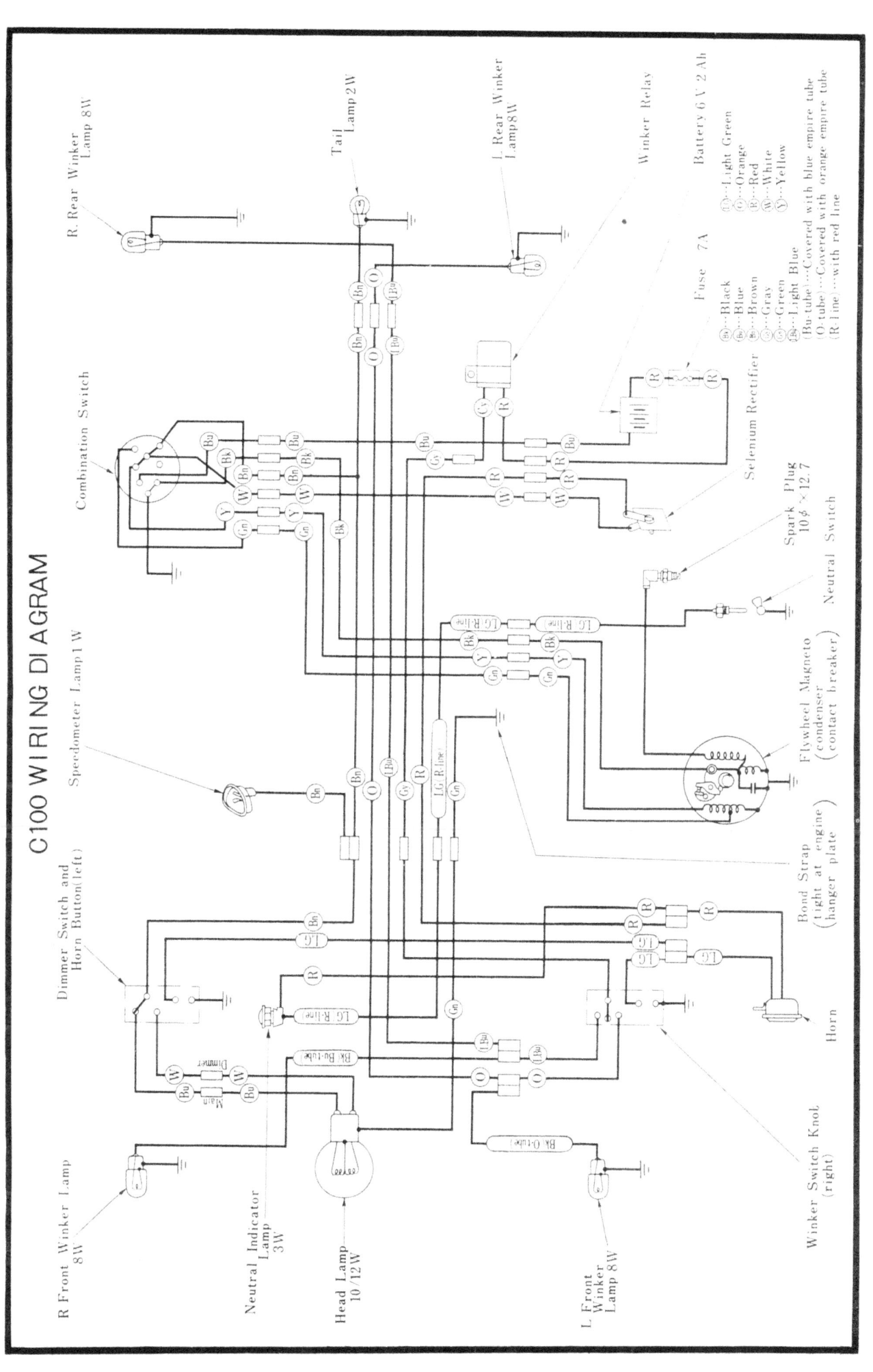

MEMO

MEMO

4. INSPECTION, MAINTENANCE & SPECIFICATION

4.1 Preventive Maintenance

In the previous chapters maintenance and adjustments have been taken up for each system or parts. "Preventive Maintenance" is to carry out diagnosis, maintenance, adjustment, etc., of these various parts and systems at periodical intervals from a different stand point. At times, maintenance is carried out partly in order to maintain the performance of the vehicle.

A. Engine Tune-Up

Engine tune-up is a means to restore the engine performance back to normal and is a rectifying operation, not just an inspection. The performance of the engine is governed by the following conditions and by rectifying these, one by one, the engine can be restored to normal operation.

    Compression System
    Ignition System
    Intake System
    Combustion System
    Fuel System

By fulfilling the requirements of these 5 basic operations, performance as an internal combustion engine will be complete. The following are the steps for checking and remedying the faults.

(1) Checking compression

If compression is low the engine will lose power and if for some reason there is compression loss the engine revolution will become uneven and will cause engine to stall at low idle.

To measure compression follow the following steps.

4. INSPECTION, MAINTENANCE & SPECIFICATIONS

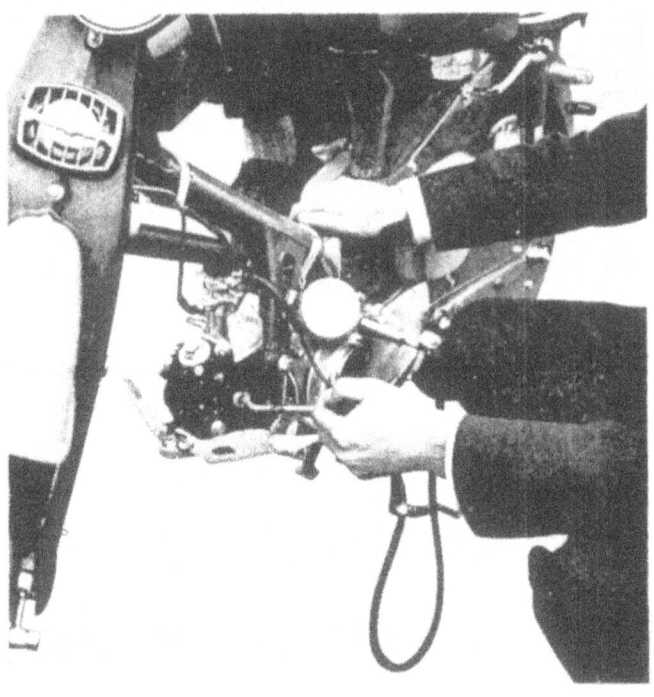

Fig. 4.1

Operation Steps	Remarks
① Remove spark plugs.	Use plug wrench
② Insert compression gauge in spark plug hole and hold tightly in place.	Make sure compression gases do not leak.
③ Open throttle grip and choke wide open, continuously kicking down kick pedal strongly.	Do not forget this or else readings will differ completely.
④ Watch gauge while kicking and take reading of needle at highest point.	Do not discontinue kicking until reading is taken as gauge will keeping rising with each kick.
⑤ Correct reading is 6.8~7.03 kg/cm^2 (95~100 lb/in^2)	Check when engine is warm.
⑥ If reading is above the correct compression, carbon has accumulated in combustion chamber.	Remove cylinder head and clean carbon. (see p. 4)
⑦ If reading is below the above limits there is compression loss in valve, piston rings, head gasket, etc.	Inspect tappets, disassemble, inspect and overhall others. (See p. 4~5)

(2) Tightening of cylinder head

When compression is low first check tappet clearance, then check to see if head is securely tightened or not.

4.1 PREVENTIVE MAINTENANCE

Operation Steps	Remarks
① Remove front cover.	
② Remove dust seal and head cover.	
③ Tighten cylinder head bolts.	Use small torque wrench.
④ Specified torque is 0.8 kg-cm (60 lb-in)	
⑤ When cylinder stud bolts are tightened as specified ④, trouble is inside. Remove head and disassemble and inspect cylinder. After disassembling head, always tighten head according to above torque. (see p.6)	Repair head. (p. 4~5) cylinder, piston (p. 7~9)

(3) Adjusting tappet clearance

Tappet clearence has a great deal to do with the operation of the valves. When compression is low the tappets still operate and are the cause for the valves not to close completely. When tappet clearance is too large the tappet noise becomes loud, causing excessive engine noise. This clearance is therefore related to the power of the engine, performance at slow idle and excessive noise and is an important function.

Adjustment is by the following steps.

Fig 4.2

4. INSPECTION, MAINTENANCE & SPECIFICATIONS

Operation Steps	Remarks
① Remove tappet cover.	
② Remove contact breaker cover.	
③ Check tappet clearance with "T" mark on flywheel and mark on case lined up.	
④ Tappet clearance is correct when 0.05 mm (0.0020″) thickness gauge (a) will clear and 0.06 mm (0.0024″) will not.	On models before ENO. 927277 thickness gauge cannot be used so place dial gauge on head of tappet adjusting screw and take reading by moving tappet.
⑤ Standard clearance is 0.05 mm (0.002″)	Check when cold.
⑥ When clearance is not correct, loosen adjusting nut and adjust with adjusting screw. After tightening adjusting nut, recheck clearance.	Use tappet adjusting box wrench and tappet lock box wrench. Be careful as clearance will change after tightening adjusting nut.

(4) Adjusting ignition timing

When the ignition timing is wrong, even if the engine has proper compression and the valves operate in order, the engine will not perform sufficiently. When the timing is too fast or too slow it will cause over-heating or back firing and have very diverse results. Also, this is always in contact operation and must be periodically checked.

The following are the adjustment steps.

Fig. 4.3

4.1 PREVENTIVE MAINTENANCE

Step of Work	Remarks
① Align mark on flywheel and punched mark on case.	Provide the point gap as 0.3~0.4mm (0.012~0.016")
② Check contact facing of points through flywheel window.	Move flywheel slightly and open points. Can be easily seen by using light.
③ If facing uneven or burnt, file with point file. If facing extensively uneven remove and correct with oil stone. Place file between points to work both facings at once.	Be sure not to install points with oil on facing.
④ Ideal ignition timing is to have point contacts open instantly when the "T" mark on flywheel passes mark on case. Use tester for adjusting as operation is difficult to follow by eye.	
⑤ Take out connector of wire harness contained inside frame on top of engine, take off black wire and connect to black wire of tester. Ground red tester wire to body and turn tester switch on (Use point or service tester).	If tester is not available use lamp to check conduct. Wiring is as **fig. 4.4**. Use 6V miniature lamp.

Fig. 4.4

| ⑥ Revolve flywheel slowly in direction of revolution and adjust so that lamp goes out instantly when mark passes case marking. | Correct timing can be obtained by adjusting as in (6). In other words ignition timing is 35° BTDC (stationary) |
| ⑦ Adjustment is done by loosening screw 'a' and turning 'b' with screw driver, **fig. 4.5**. Right turn of driver advances and left turn retards. | |

Fig. 4.5

| ⑧ When position is correct tighten 'a'. After tightening recheck to make sure. | Position may change by tightening. Be careful. |

4. INSPECTION, MAINTENANCE & SPECIFICATIONS

(5) Cleaning and adjustment of spark plugs

Spark plugs must be periodically cleaned and adjusted or else it will not spark and ignite in best condition if dirty, damaged or electrode worn. If plug electrode is sooty, wet or have carbon accumulation these must be removed or else high tension current will escape through these foreign agents. For removal of this, use sand blaster (plug cleaner) which makes cleaning of plugs very easy.

When sand blaster is not available, clean with wire brush and wipe off with dry cloth. When carbon has accumulated, pick off with sharp instrument. At this, time do not use burner and others to dry off as this will have bad effect.

After cleaning, set electrode gap. Set gap so that 0.6mm (0.024") thickness gauge will easily pass through by lifting or lightly tapping portion ⓐ.

Determine whether plug is good or bad after setting gap to standard clearance by using plug tester. In other words set at predetermined voltage and if spark is constant under various inside pressures of tester this is in good condition. Replace if found bad. (see p. 85)

Fig. 4.6

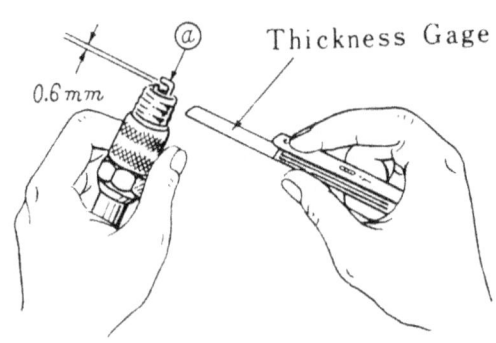

Fig. 4.7

(6) Ignition coil secondary sparking performance test

When there is trouble in the ignition coil, plug will not spark or will miss or will become weak and effect the firing.

In order to check this attach a good plug to secondary coil, kick engine over while grounding and confirm the plug sparking performance.

Also, there is a three needle spark coil tester. Connect ⊕ of tester to this ⊕ pole, ground ⊖ pole to body or engine and measure maximum gap that spark can jump, when kicking engine over. If this gap is over 6mm (0.24"), coil is in good condition. However, check to be sure that trouble is not in coil as poor condenser can also be cause of trouble. (see p. 86)

(7) Condenser test

Spark plug will not operate correctly when insulator inside condenser is poor and performance of condenser is defective and this is sometimes

4.1 PREVENTIVE MAINTENANCE

mistaken for bad ignition coil. Condition of condenser can be determined by measuring the insulator resistence of primary coil side and outside covering of condenser with service tester. (see p. 84).

(8) Fuel supplying system

When fuel system is stopped up engine will miss when accelerating or stop at high speed as fuel supply to carburetor is insufficient.

In this case check by the following steps.

Step for Work	Remarks
① If tank has sufficient fuel, check flowing condition by disconnecting fuel feed tube from carburetor elbow.	
② If flow is insufficient remove tank and clean out tank and inside of tube.	
③ Also reconnect fuel feed tube with carburetor and remove fuel cock. Check flow of gasoline when shutter is opened.	Check fuel cock by removing screw attaching to carburetor.
④ If cock is plugged up disassemble and clean.	

(9) Cleaning & adjustment of carburetor

Remove and clean carburetor every 8 months or 8,000 km. Other adjustments are to be performed as required. Steps for work and adjustment are as follows (detailed in chapter 1.14.)

i. Set throttle stop screw ⓑ to engine rpm 800~1,000 rpm.

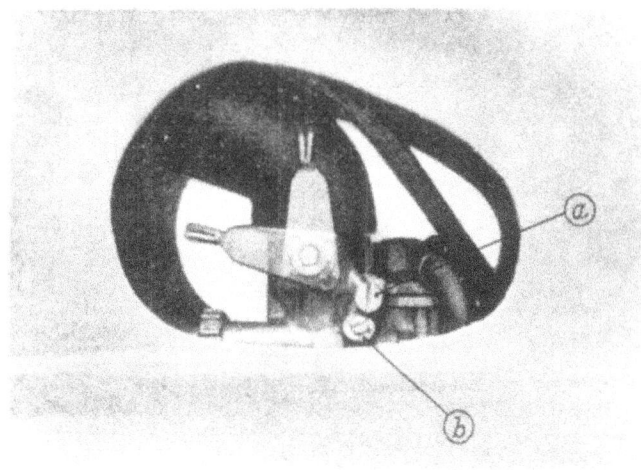

Fig. 4.8

4. INSPECTION, MAINTENANCE & SPECIFICATIONS

Steps For Work	Remarks
① Remove 6 mm nut holding carburetor.	
② Remove throttle wire, air cleaner connecting tube, fuel feed tube & etc.	
③ Disassemble carburetor.	See p. 36
④ Wash disassembled parts with cleaning solvent.	
⑤ Blow out each nozzle with compressed air, wash and clean, then adjust after reassembling and installing. Adjusting is usually done by idle adjustment.	

ii. Adjust air-fuel mixture by air screw ⓐ. Proper position is when air screw is turned fully in then turned back about 1–1¼ turns and when exhaust noise will not change even if body is tilted inside of 10° both ways. If engine stops when tilted to left the mixture is too rich and if engine stops when tilted to right mixture is too lean.

iii. Jet needle calibration alteration or adjustment of main jet, etc. is required if vehicle will not accelerate along with slow opening of grip when running vehicle or if maximum speeds exceeding 60 km/hr (38 mile/hr) cannot be obtained with grip fully opened. (see p. 38).

(10) Cleaning of air cleaner

When air cleaner is clogged up with dust, intake air meets strong resistance and cannot be readily sucked in. Therefore, vehicle will lose power and when accelerating this cannot keep up with it. Periodically perform cleaning of air cleaner so the above events do not occur.

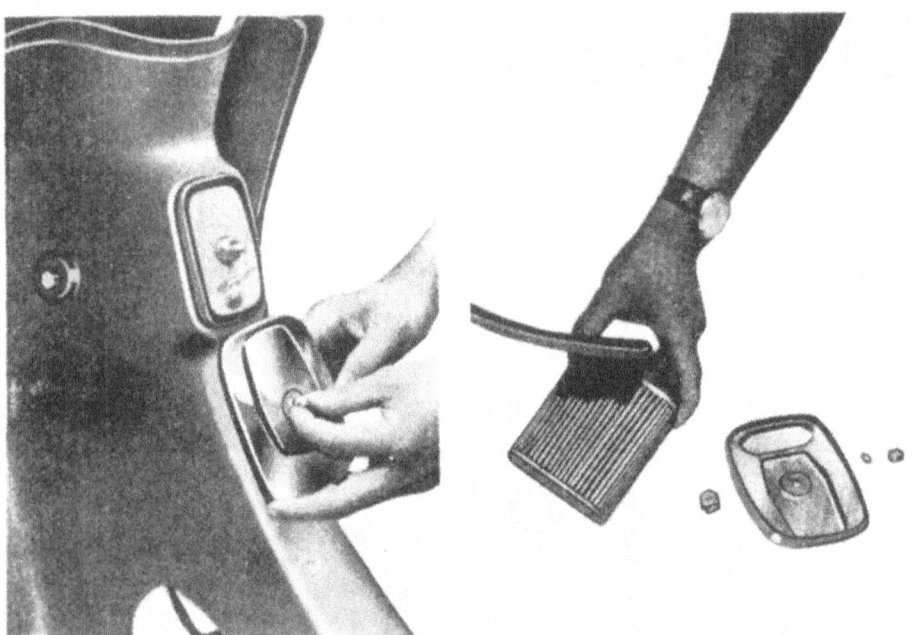

Fig. 4.9

Steps for Work	Remarks
① Remove air cleaner cover.	
② Take out air cleaner and knock off dust by lightly tapping cleaner. Then blow out with compressed air from the inside or clean with brush.	As cleaner is made of paper, if this is wet or torn, change with new one.

4.1 PREVENTIVE MAINTENANCE

(11) Adjusting clutch

If clutch adjustment is faulty, no matter how excellent the engine is performing, it cannot exert its power fully and vehicle cannot be driven in its complete state.

When clutch will not release completely, when starting, vehicle will start moving with change engaged. In the opposite case if clutch slips vehicle speed will not coincide even when engine revolution is risen.

Steps for adjusting is as follows.

Fig. 4.10

Steps of Work	Remarks
① Loosen ⓐ bolt.	Use 9mm spanner wrench.
② By screwing in screw ⓑ clutch will be harder to release and by turning out clutch will release easier.	
③ To check clutch, a) Engine should start easily without kick slipping, when kicking. b) Vehicle should not start moving (or engine should not stall) when shifting into second gear with engine running. Vehicle should not jump out even when depressing down on change arm further than 10° and opening grip. c) Engine stalls with shift in second gear and releasing pedal, depressing on brakes and opening throttle to increase revolution.	Disassembling & maintenance (see p. 33). a) Clutch does not slip. b) Clutch releases. 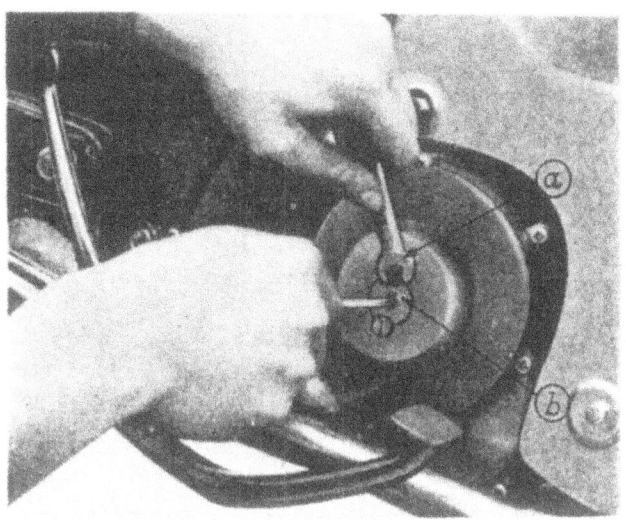 Fig. 4.11 c) Clutch does not slip.

B. Adjustment of Drive Chain

Drive chain should always be tightened properly or it will create chain knock while running and hit against chain case if too slack. If chain tension is too strong this will create resistance and sufficient power will not be transmitted to rear wheels. Steps for adjusting are as follows.

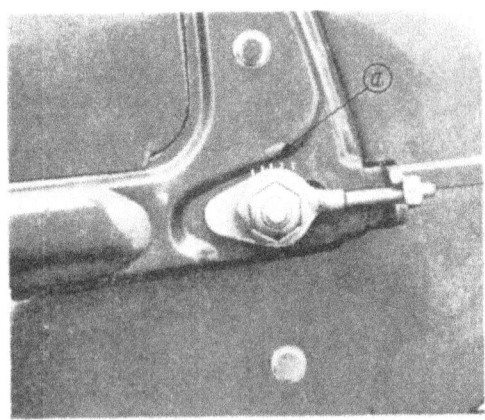 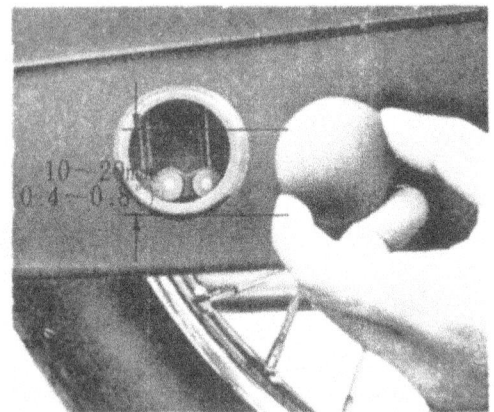

Fig. 4.12

Steps of Work	Remarks
① Remove peep hole cap of chain case	
② Loosen large and small nut securing rear wheel axle. Adjust rear wheel axle chain adjuster so that chain deflection is at its maximum 10~20mm, through chain case peep hole.	Set marking ⓐ of adjuster and fork at same position on both sides.
③ Chain will tighten by tightening chain adjuster nut.	

C. Adjusting Brakes

As brakes are the staff of life these of course must be checked periodically and driver should also habitually check these before driving vehicle every day.

(1) Adjustment of front brakes

Adjust play of handle lever for front brake.

Steps for Adjusting	Remarks
① Free play will decrease by tightening nut (a) and increase by loosening.	It is best to push arm in all the way.
② Free play is the width the end of lever travels from position (a) when releasing lever and position (b) when brake begins to take hold. This is normally 30~40mm. (1.2~1.6″)	When adjusting allowance of nut is gone, change angle of arm and readjust for the time being. (see p. 66).

4.1 PREVENTIVE MAINTENANCE 117

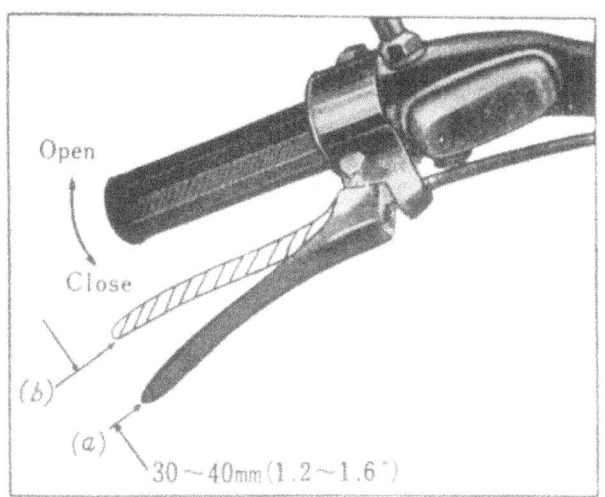

Fig. 4.13

(2) **Adjustment of rear brake free play.**

Adjust free play of pedal for brake.

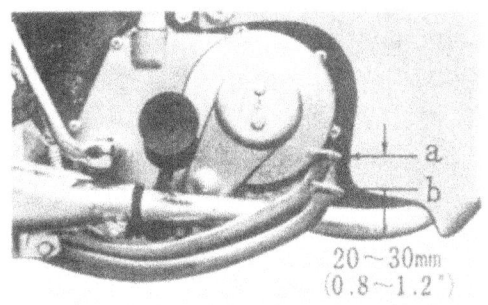

Fig. 4.14

Steps for Adjusting	Remarks
① As same as front brake, free play will decrease by tightening nut (a) and increase by loosening.	
② Required free play is 20~30 mm (0.8~1.2″) from when pedal is in natural position till it starts to hold.	When adjusting allowance is gone, change angle of arm or replace brake shoe. (see p. 67)

D. Care of Battery

Electrolyte of battery should be replenished at set intervals as it loses water after long usage.

When liquid level is lower than plates it shows that the battery capacity will decrease and discharge rapidly. Therefore liquid should always be filled to correct quantity. When liquid drops down to minimum level, distilled water

4. INSPECTION, MAINTENANCE & SPECIFICATIONS

should be added to the maximum level line. All three cells should be filled to same level when seen from side. Water is added from top of battery by removing red cap.

NOTE:
(1) Do not use sulphuric acid.
(2) Be sure not to impair breather pipe.
(3) If liquid diminishes extremely fast, check battery charging capacity. (see p. 89)

Fig. 4.15

E. Lubrication

Lubricating oils are necessary on parts where two faces contact and move such as rotating or sliding parts in order to decrease the friction and disperse heat from the over-heated parts to prevent excessive wear and scoring. When lubricating oil is not sufficient this not only shortens the machines life, but will result in impeding the overall mechanical performance. This also of course pertains to the SUPER CUB and the major parts must be replaced or replenished with guaranteed high-quality oil at periodical intervals.

(1) Lubricating service where periodical replacement or replenishment is not required.

Some parts only require replacement or replenishment of lubricating oils when parts are disassembled for repair or when complete overhaul is performed, and not periodically.

In the other words,

Steering Stem Ball Race Cone	
Front and Rear Brake Cam	Grease
Throttle Grip	
Brake Pedal Shaft	

Fig. 4.16

4.1 PREVENTIVE MAINTENANCE

Steps for Changing Oil	Remarks
① Set vehicle on stand, start engine and warm up oil.	When oil is warm it is easy to change.
② Remove drain bolt on bottom of crankcase. Drain oil.	
③ Insert drain bolt. Pour oil in through oil filler.	
④ After pouring in 0.6*l* check to see if oil comes up to oil level (a) with oil guage on cap. Fig. 4.17	Check in position when cap is not tightened.

⑤ "Oil brand and number. HONDA's Honda Ultra Oil" and the recommended brands for overseas are,
   Caltex   RPM
   Pennsylvania PENDRAKE
   Mobil oil   A
   Summer over 15°C (59°F) # 30
   Winter under 15°C (59°F) # 20W
   (Under 0°C (32°F)   # 10W)
	"Honda Ultra" oil is a HD high-quality diesel oil, specially made for HONDA engines.

NOTE: ① Do not exceed standard oil level when putting oil in. Excessive oil will result in oil pumping and insufficient horse power.
    ② Always change oil at set intervals as oil gets dirty easily.
    ③ Do not use unknown brands of oil.
    ④ Do not use oils that contain water or dust.

(2) Changing of crankcase oil

This should be changed according to Periodical Inspection Chart.

(3) Replenishing of grease

Periodically grease nipples and others.
a) Greasing Nipples
Grease all places with nipples. Use grease pump. Grease until excessive grease overflows from portion requiring lubrication.
Use "fiber" grease.

NOTE: Replace faulty nipples, which do not accept grease.

4. INSPECTION, MAINTENANCE & SPECIFICATIONS

b) Front and Rear Axle Bearings

Replace front and rear wheel bearing grease every 5,000km (or every 5 months)

Steps for Work	Remarks
① Remove front and rear wheels.	
② Remove bearings by hand.	If tight, lightly tap from inside.
③ Take off old grease and wash bearing with cleaning solvent then dry thoroughly.	
④ Pack bearings with grease, putting some in hub and insert bearings.	Be sure to pack grease so balls are well greased.
⑤ Use "fiber grease".	

NOTE: Be careful not to get any dirt or dust in bearings when removing wheels to repair flats, etc.

(4) Drive chain lubrication

Normally lubrication is done by dropping oil in through peep hole when monthly inspection is performed and to prolong chain life follow the proceeding steps about every 5,000 km (Every 5 months).

Lubricating Procedure	Remarks
① Remove chain case cover.	
② Remove drive chain.	
③ Wash drive chain with cleaning solvent thoroughly and dry.	Thorough cleaning is required as chain is always dirty.
④ Melt grease by warming in container and put chain inside container so that grease can penetrate inside roller of chain.	
⑤ Take out chain from container and wipe off excess grease and install.	
⑥ Preferably use "chain grease" or else "gear oil".	

F. Inspection for Tightening of Various Parts

(1) Retightening of bolts and nuts of important parts.

In order to prevent loosening of bolts and nuts caused by vibration and wear, etc., from long use it is necessary to tighten the major parts (see following chart). Use torque wrench and tighten to specified capacity.

4.1 PREVENTIVE MAINTENANCE 115

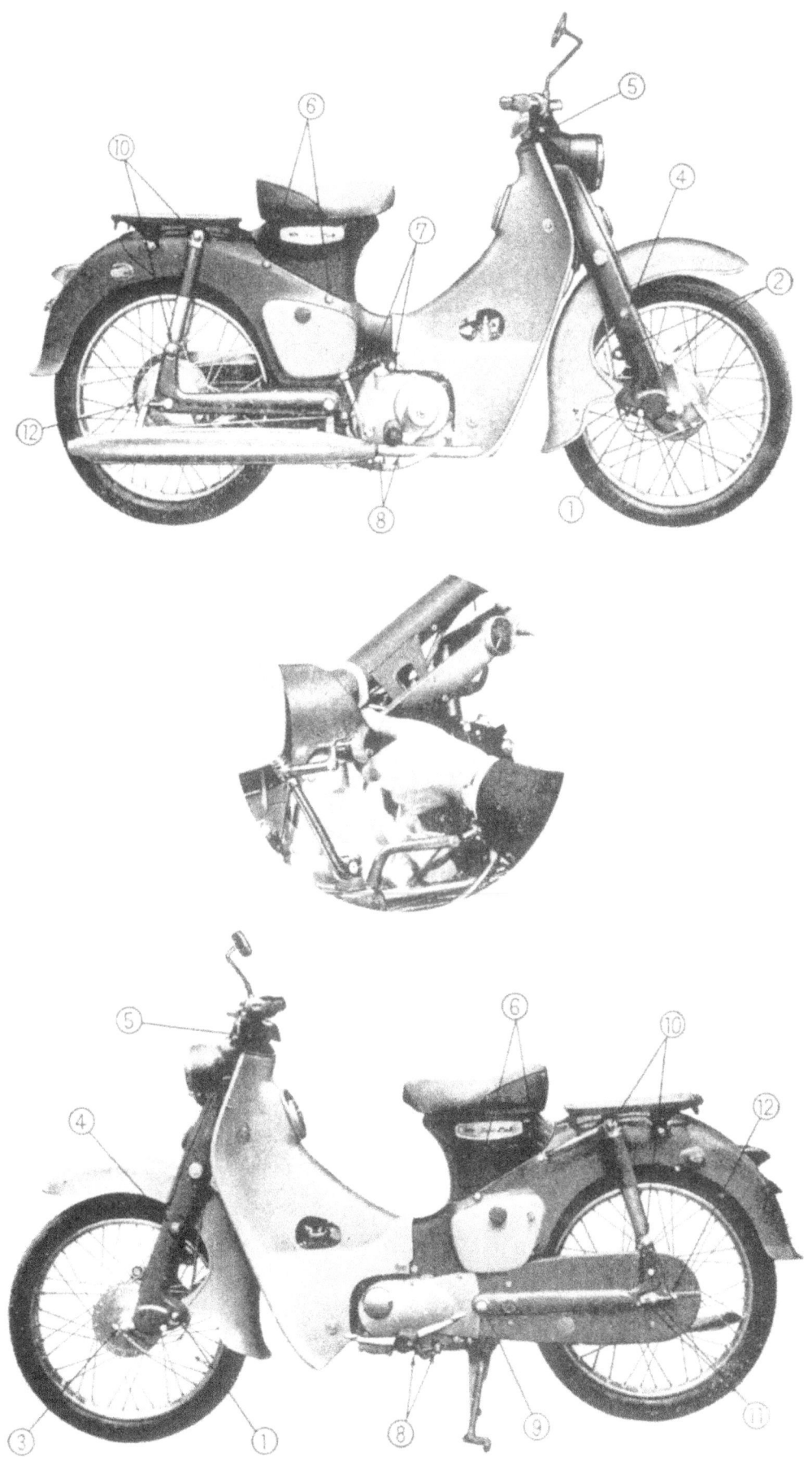

Fig. 4.18

4. INSPECTION, MAINTENANCE & SPECIFICATIONS

Tightening torque is as following chart.

Parts Name	Tightening Torque			
① Front arm pivot bolt.	3.0	kg-m	20	ft-lb
② Front brake torque link.	3.0	〃	20	〃
③ Front wheel axle nut (1).	3.5~4.5	〃	25~35	〃
④ Front cushion upper bolt (2).	3.0	〃	20	〃
⑤ Steering handle mounting bolts (2).	3.0	〃	20	〃
⑥ Fuel tank mounting bolts (4).	0.7	〃	60	in-lb
⑦ Engine spoting bolts (2).	3.0	〃	20	ft-lb
⑧ Step bar mounting nuts (4).	2.7	〃	18	〃
⑨ Rear fork pivot bolt nut.	6.0	〃	40	〃
⑩ Rear cushion mounting nuts (4).	4.5	〃	30	〃
⑪ Rear wheel axle nut.	3.5~4.5	〃	25~35	〃
Rear cnshion sleeve nut.	6.0~6.3	〃	40~50	〃
⑫ Drive chain adjuster nut (2).	0.7	〃	60	in-lb

(Prefixed number is matched to the number of **fig. 4.18**)

(2) Tightening of wheel spokes.

It is necessary to tighten loose spokes periodically or else when vehicle is run with some spokes loose this will effect the rim and the strength of the other spokes. Prescribed period is every 5,000 km (5 months). Check each spoke by turning the nipple, with the wheels off the ground, and tighten any loose spokes to the same amount as others. Use nipple wrench. Check both front and rear wheels.

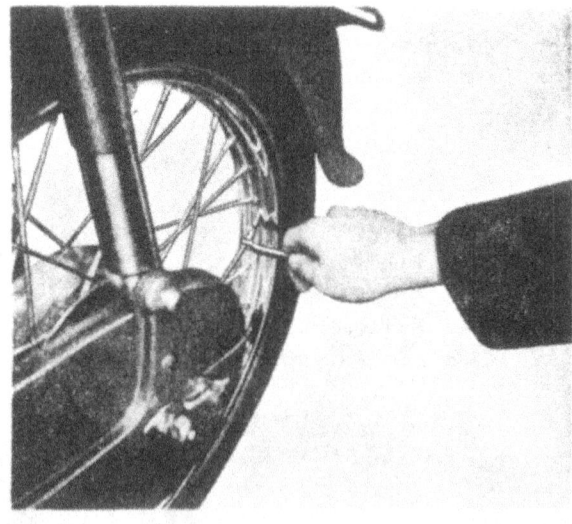

Fig. 4.19

4.2 Periodic Inspections & Maintenance

For the protection of the vehicle, perform inspections and maintenance periodically, to prevent troubles from occurring entirely and at the same time do not neglect to take care of vehicle to always keep it in best condition. There is the daily inspection to be performed by the driver every day and the periodic inspections to be performed by the driver or dealer at set intervals.

A. Daily Inspection

The following items should be habitually done by the driver before use every day.

These items should be included and repeated in the periodic inspection and maintained. (See **fig. 4.20**)

① Check front and rear tire pressure.
   Front tire   22 psi   Rear tire   28 psi
② Check brake appliance and condition of free play.
   Condition of brakes when depressed on or gripped.
   Free Play   End of front brake lever   30~40 mm (1.2~1.6")
               Top of brake pedal (see p. 111) 20~30 mm (0.8~1.2")
③ Check operation of clutch.
   Releasing action.
   Slipping action. (see p. 109)
④ Check oil level of crankcase.
   Check condition of oil. (see p. 113)
⑤ Check fuel level of gasoline tank.
⑥ Check horn.
⑦ Check headlamp, directional signal lamp, tail lamp, neutral lamp, etc.

B. Periodic Inspections

The following is chart of contents and time for periodic inspections and maintenances.

MEMO

118   4. INSPECTION, MAINTENANCE & SPECIFICATIONS

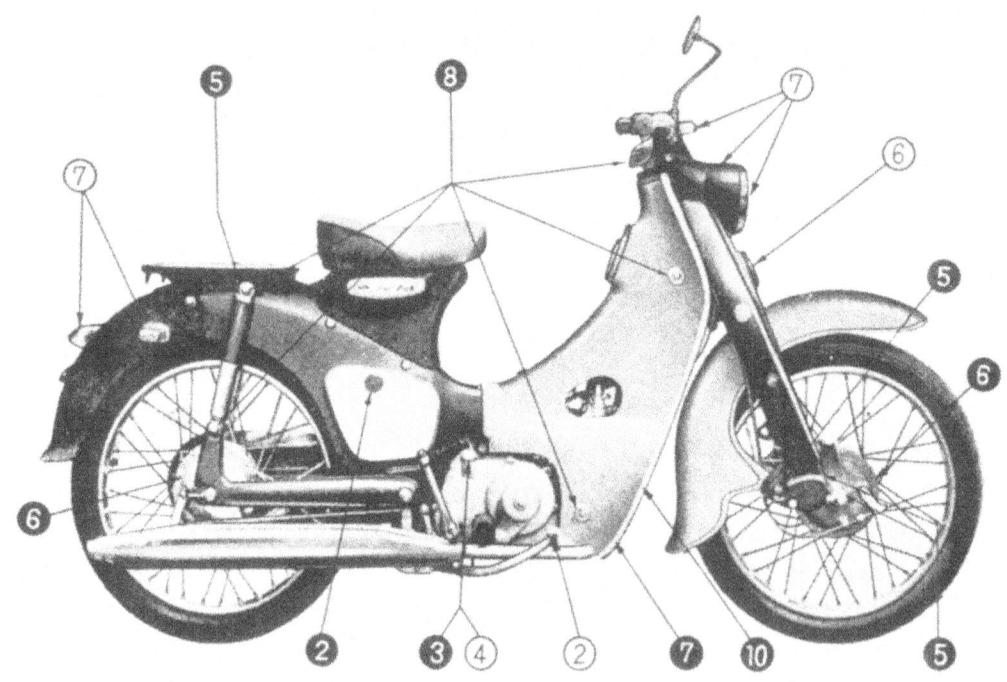

(⑪ refer to fig. 4.18)

Fig. 4.20

4.2 PERIODIC INSPECTIONS & MAINTENANCE — 119

No.	Item	200 km	1 Mon.	2	3	4	5	6	7	8	9	10	11	12
❶	Adjust and service drive chain.	●	○	●	○	○	●	○	○	●	○	○	●	○
❷	Check battery.	●	○	●	○	○	●	○	○	●	○	○	●	○
❸	Change engine oil.	●	○	●	○	○	●	○	○	●	○	○	●	○
❹	Clean air cleaner.			●			●			●			●	
❺	Grease nipples.			●			●			●			●	
❻	Grease wheel bearing.						●						●	
❼	Adjust tappet clearance.	●		●			●			●			●	
❽	Adjust ignition timing.	●		●			●			●			●	
❾	Clean carburetor.									●				
❿	Clean and adjust spark plug.			●			●			●			●	
⓫	Check tightness for bolts and nuts.			●			●			●			●	

NOTE: ● Should be done at service shop.
○ Should be done by owner or service shop.

MEMO

4. INSPECTION, MAINTENANCE & SPECIFICATIONS

4.3 Diagnosis of Troubles

It is important to detect the origin of the trouble when it occurs with the vehicle. The following chart lists the ways and means for best and correct detection of the trouble. As the steps for diagnosis and the probable cause is listed according to the trouble, once the cause is discovered, proper steps for maintenance can be taken.

NOTE: ○ Shows the vehicle with trouble.
△ Shows the vehicle accomplished remedy.

A. Engine Does Not Start or Difficult to Start.

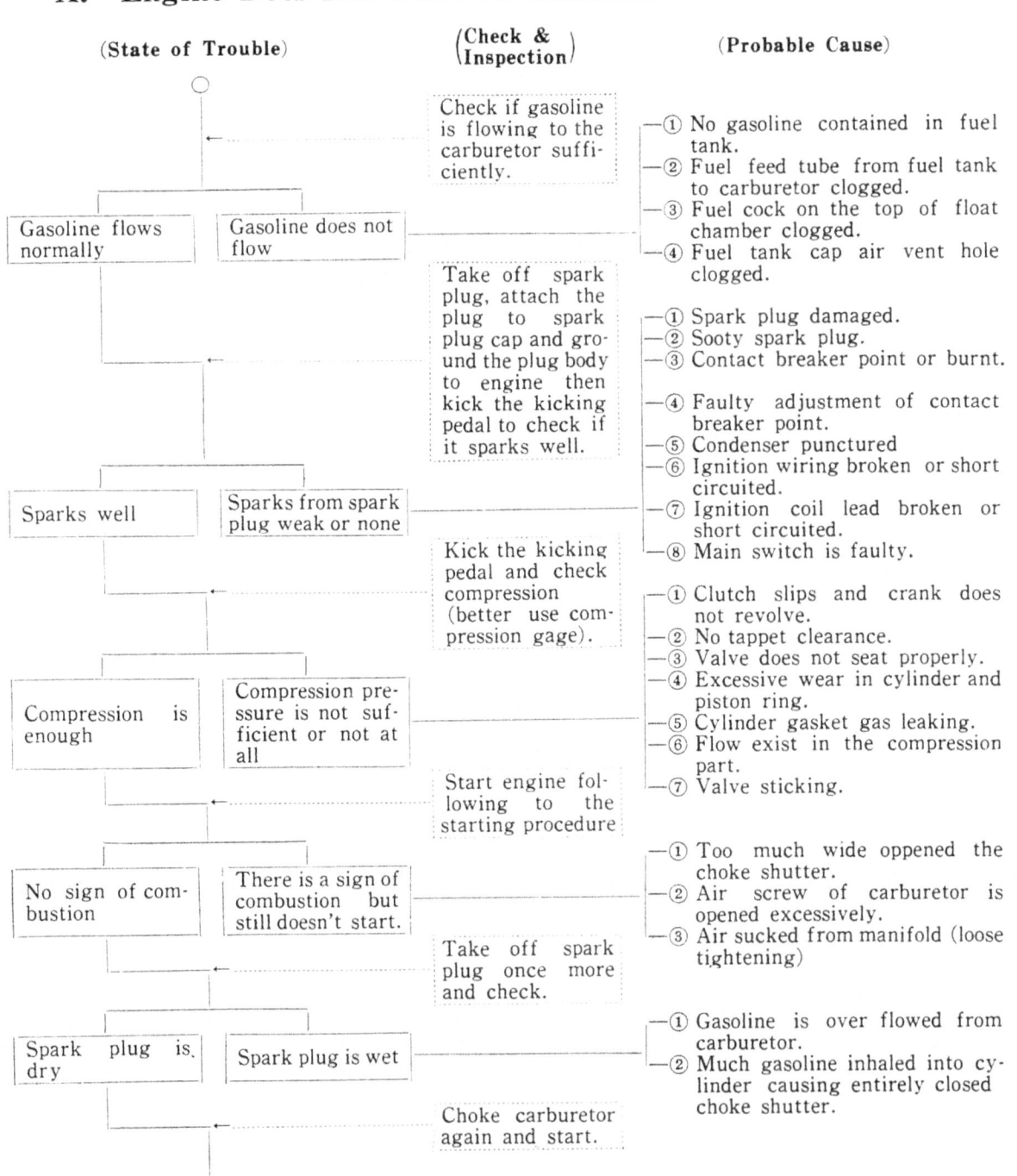

(State of Trouble) — (Check & Inspection) — (Probable Cause)

Check if gasoline is flowing to the carburetor sufficiently.
- ① No gasoline contained in fuel tank.
- ② Fuel feed tube from fuel tank to carburetor clogged.
- ③ Fuel cock on the top of float chamber clogged.
- ④ Fuel tank cap air vent hole clogged.

Gasoline flows normally / Gasoline does not flow

Take off spark plug, attach the plug to spark plug cap and ground the plug body to engine then kick the kicking pedal to check if it sparks well.
- ① Spark plug damaged.
- ② Sooty spark plug.
- ③ Contact breaker point or burnt.
- ④ Faulty adjustment of contact breaker point.
- ⑤ Condenser punctured
- ⑥ Ignition wiring broken or short circuited.
- ⑦ Ignition coil lead broken or short circuited.
- ⑧ Main switch is faulty.

Sparks well / Sparks from spark plug weak or none

Kick the kicking pedal and check compression (better use compression gage).
- ① Clutch slips and crank does not revolve.
- ② No tappet clearance.
- ③ Valve does not seat properly.
- ④ Excessive wear in cylinder and piston ring.
- ⑤ Cylinder gasket gas leaking.
- ⑥ Flow exist in the compression part.
- ⑦ Valve sticking.

Compression is enough / Compression pressure is not sufficient or not at all

Start engine following to the starting procedure

No sign of combustion / There is a sign of combustion but still doesn't start.
- ① Too much wide oppened the choke shutter.
- ② Air screw of carburetor is opened excessively.
- ③ Air sucked from manifold (loose tightening)

Take off spark plug once more and check.

Spark plug is dry / Spark plug is wet
- ① Gasoline is over flowed from carburetor.
- ② Much gasoline inhaled into cylinder causing entirely closed choke shutter.

Choke carburetor again and start.

4.3 DIAGNOSIS OF TROUBLES

B. Machine Does Not Develop Full Power or Not Make Enough Speed

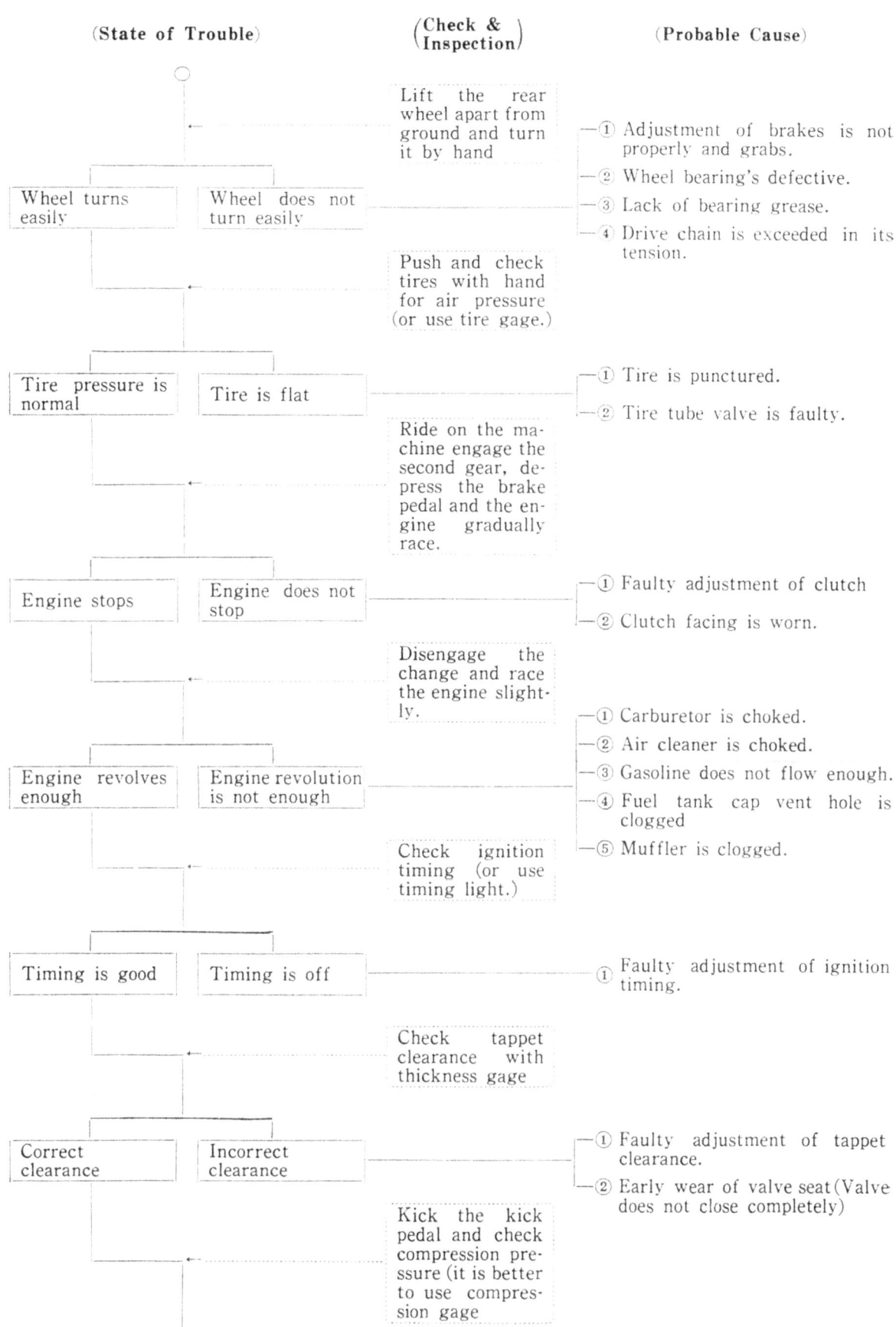

4. INSPECTION, MAINTENANCE & SPECIFICATIONS

Check	Result (OK)	Result (Problem)	Causes
	Compression is enough	None or less compression	① Valve does not seat properly. ② Excess wear in cylinder and ring. ③ Gas leaks from cylinder or cylinder gasket. ④ Valve timing is not correct.
Check fuel lines and carburetor for fuel flow	Fuel flows good	Fuel lines are clogged	① Clogged fuel lines and carburetor.
Check spark plug	Plug is clean and colored normal	Plug is dirty or changed color	① Cleaning of plug in not enough. ② Heat range of plug is not suited.
Check containing oil level and quality	Oil contains properly	Oil containing is not proper	① Too much or too less oil. ② Diluted excessively.
Check circulation of oil to head, removing oil pipe clamp bolt at cylinder head	Oil flows good	Oil does not flow good	① Oil pipe is clogged ② Oil grooves of cam shaft is clogged.
Check for the cooling of engine	Engine cools properly	Engine over heats	① Carbon deposits in the combustion chamber. ② Low grade of gasoline is used. ③ Clutch is slipping. ④ Gas and air mixtue is too weak.
Accelerate and continue high speed testing	Engine does not ping	Engine develops pings or knocks	① Wear of piston ring and cylinder. ② Fuel/air mixture is lean.

△

4.3 DIAGNOSIS OF TROUBLES 123

C. Engine Missfires at Idling or Low Speed Running

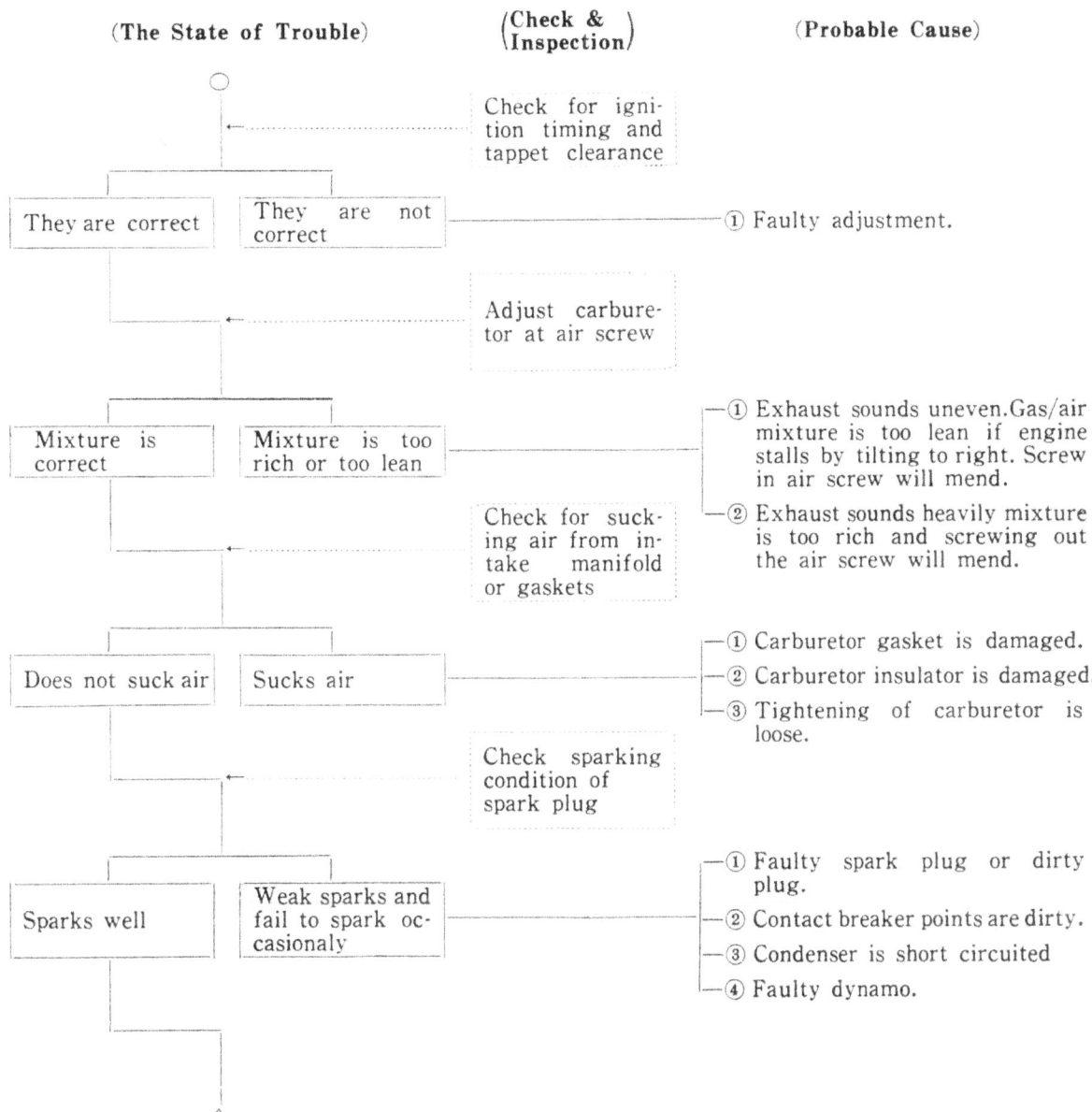

4. INSPECTION, MAINTENANCE & SPECIFICATIONS

D. Engine Missfires at High Speed.

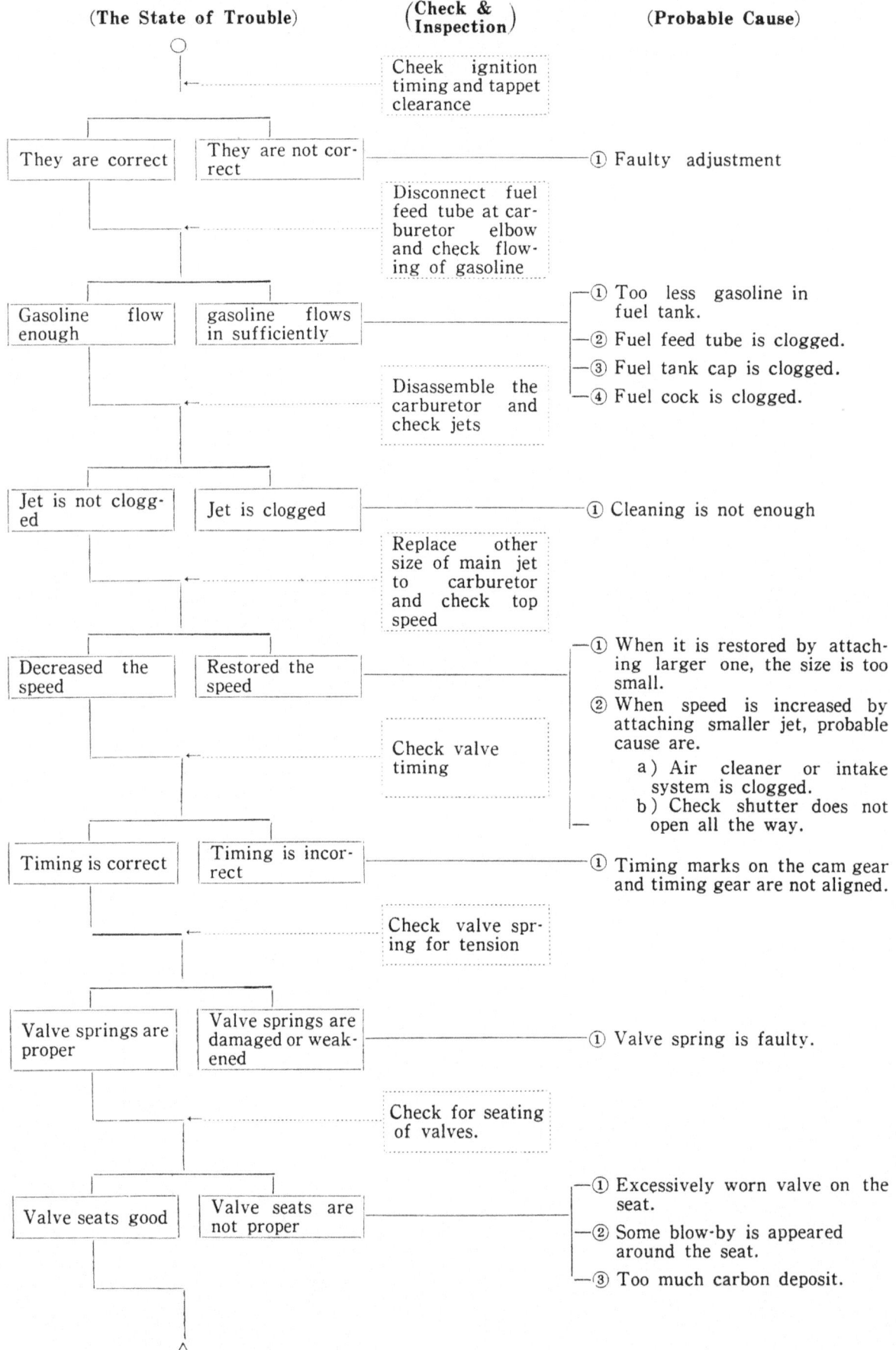

4.3 DIAGNOSIS OF TROUBLES 125

E. Engine Consumes Excess Oil in Combustion Chamber
(Muffler exhaust white or black smoke)

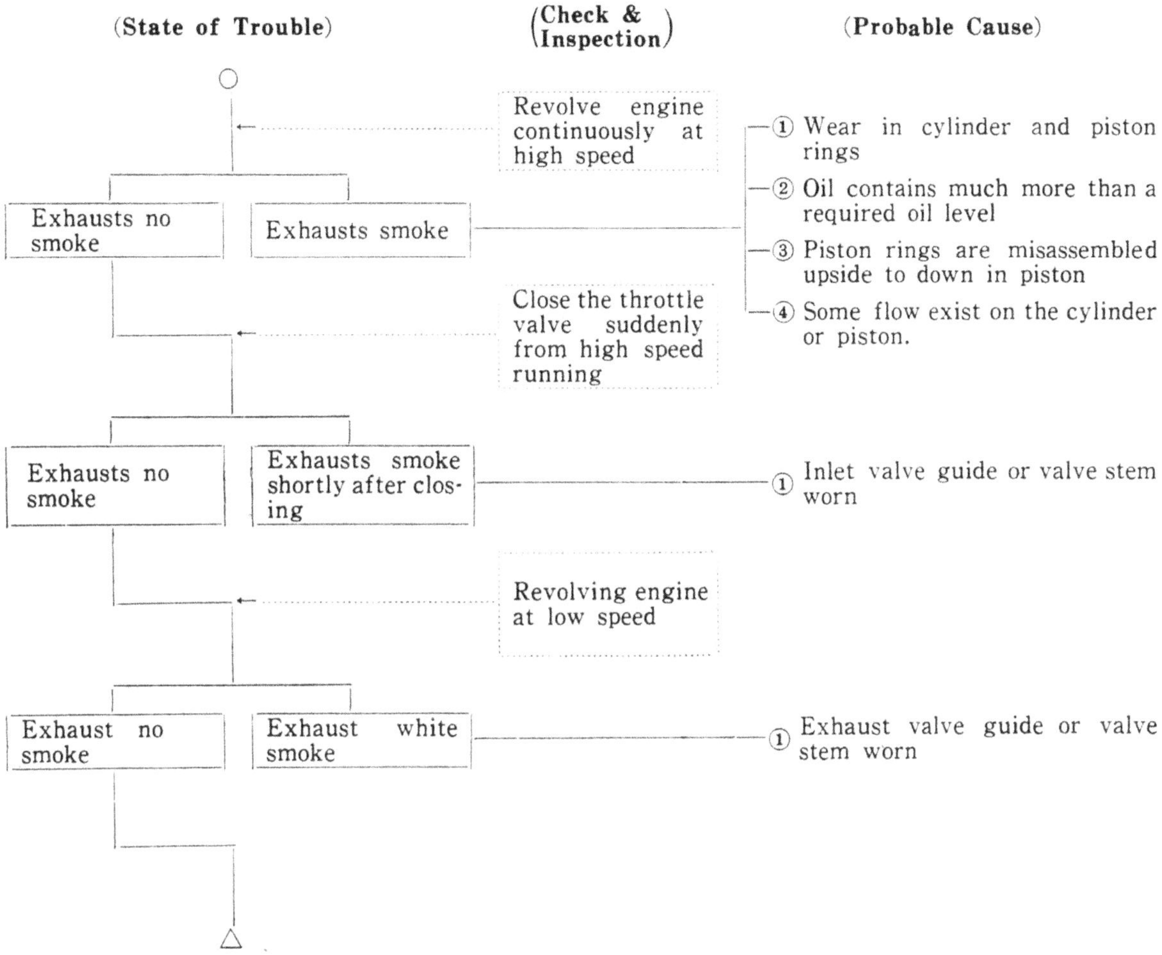

(State of Trouble)　　(Check & Inspection)　　(Probable Cause)

- Revolve engine continuously at high speed
  - ① Wear in cylinder and piston rings
  - ② Oil contains much more than a required oil level
  - ③ Piston rings are misassembled upside to down in piston
  - ④ Some flow exist on the cylinder or piston.

Exhausts no smoke / Exhausts smoke

- Close the throttle valve suddenly from high speed running

Exhausts no smoke / Exhausts smoke shortly after closing
  - ① Inlet valve guide or valve stem worn

- Revolving engine at low speed

Exhaust no smoke / Exhaust white smoke
  - ① Exhaust valve guide or valve stem worn

F. Clutch Doesn't Function Properly

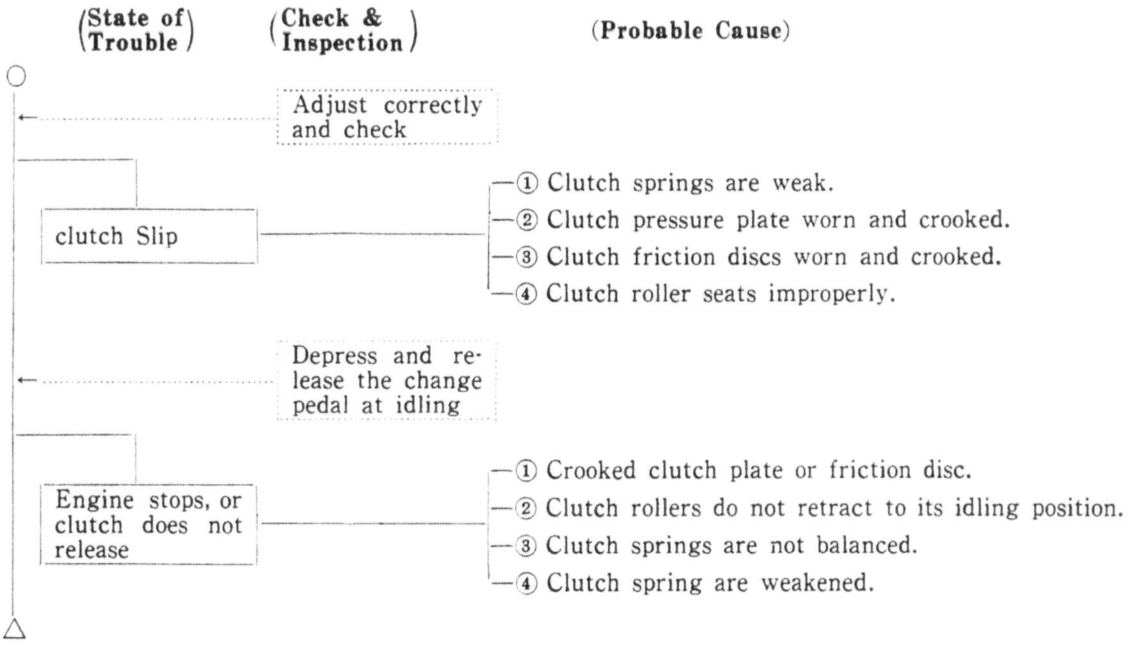

(State of Trouble)　(Check & Inspection)　(Probable Cause)

- Adjust correctly and check

clutch Slip
  - ① Clutch springs are weak.
  - ② Clutch pressure plate worn and crooked.
  - ③ Clutch friction discs worn and crooked.
  - ④ Clutch roller seats improperly.

- Depress and release the change pedal at idling

Engine stops, or clutch does not release
  - ① Crooked clutch plate or friction disc.
  - ② Clutch rollers do not retract to its idling position.
  - ③ Clutch springs are not balanced.
  - ④ Clutch spring are weakened.

G. Change Does Not Function Properly

(State of Trouble)   (Probable Cause)

[Clutch functions properly]

Changing device fails to work
- ① Notch on the shift drum is broken
- ② Notch of the shift arm is broken
- ③ Shift forks are sticked on the shift drum
- ④ Shift fork is broken

Change pedal does not release
- ① Shift return spring is broken
- ② Clutch thrust ball don't roll smoothly
- ③ Shift shaft bent

Changing gear jumps out of itself
- ① Worn pins of shifter gear
- ② Worn or crooked shift fork
- ③ Broken or weakened stopper spring of shift drum

H. Engine Emmits Noise

(The State of Trouble)   (Probable Cause)

Tappet noise
- ① Too much clearance of tappets
- ② Bent push rod
- ③ Worn tappet

Piston knock
- ① Worn piston and cylinder
- ② Carbon deposit in combustion chamber
- ③ Worn piston pin or correcting rod end

Cam and timing gear noise
- ① Worn cam shaft journal
- ② Worn cam and timing gear

Chutch noise
- ① Exceed gap between teeth of clutch outer and clutch plate
- ② Weakened clutch damper spring

Primary drive & driven gear noise
- ① Worn-out rubber dampers in driven gear
- ② Worn gears

4.3 DIAGNOSIS OF TROUBLES

I. Unstable Steering

(State of Trouble) — (Probable Cause)

[Correct tire pressure on both front and rear]

- Hard steering
  - ① Excessive tightness of steering head thread
  - ② Broken steering head ball
  - ③ Bent steering stem

- Front or rear wheel wobbles
  - ① Worn wheel bearing
  - ② Loosen or broken spokes
  - ③ Deformed rim
  - ④ Worn out rear fork pivot rubber bushing
  - ⑤ Twisted frame
  - ⑥ Misadjustment of drive chain adjuster (crooked rear wheel)

- Steering pulling to one side
  - ① Unbalanced front or rear shock absorbers
  - ② Offset front and rear wheel
  - ③ Crooked front or rear fork

J. Front and Rear Spring and Shock-absorber Function Inaccurately

(State of Trouble) — (Probable Cause)

[Correct tire air pressure on front and rear]

- Weak cushions
  - ① Weakened springs
  - ② Excessive load

- Stiff cushion
  - ① Front shock absorber damper valve not function
  - ② Greased excessively in rear damper

- Cushion noise
  - ① Squeak from contacting spring case and spring
  - ② Broken stopper rubber
  - ③ Lack of oil in front damper
  - ④ Weakened spring in rear damper

4. INSPECTION, MAINTENANCE & SPECIFICATIONS

K. Brake Functions Inaccurate

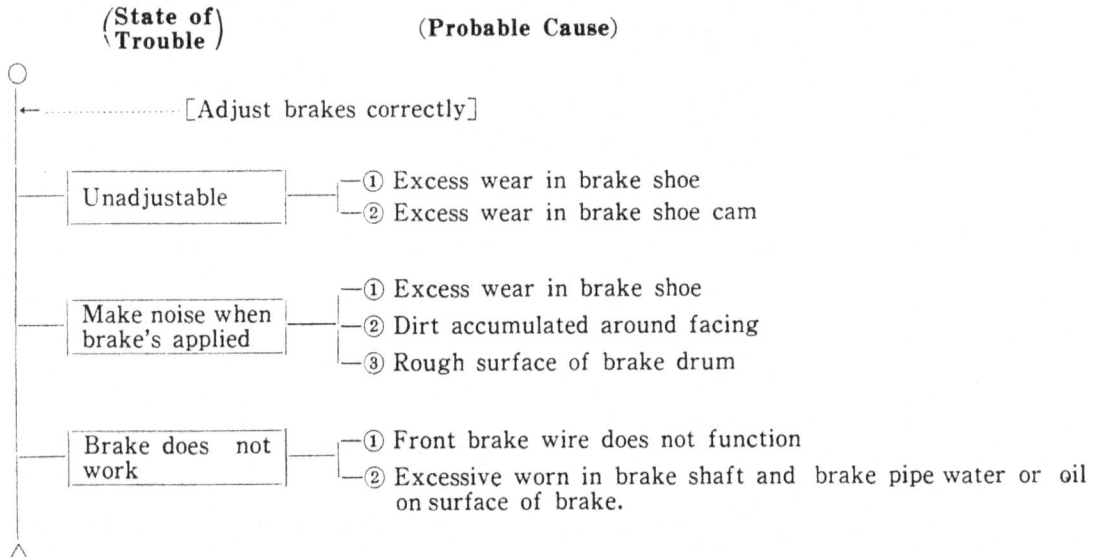

```
(State of Trouble)              (Probable Cause)

○
├─ ·············· [Adjust brakes correctly]
│
├─ [Unadjustable] ──┬─ ① Excess wear in brake shoe
│                   └─ ② Excess wear in brake shoe cam
│
├─ [Make noise when ──┬─ ① Excess wear in brake shoe
│   brake's applied]  ├─ ② Dirt accumulated around facing
│                     └─ ③ Rough surface of brake drum
│
├─ [Brake does not ──┬─ ① Front brake wire does not function
│   work]            └─ ② Excessive worn in brake shaft and brake pipe water or oil
│                          on surface of brake.
△
```

L. Excess Wear in Drive Chain

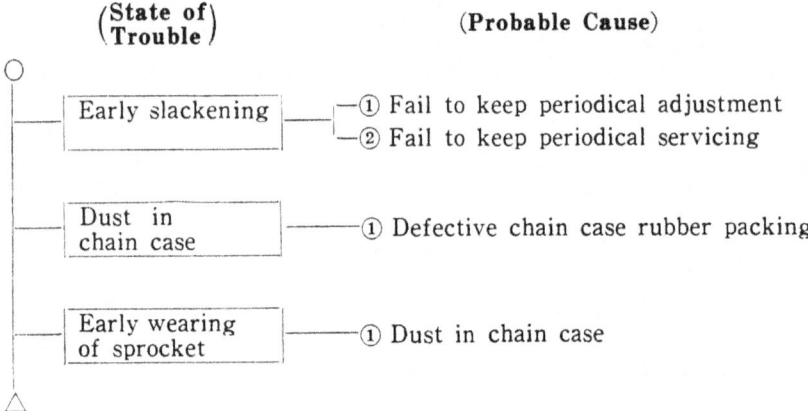

```
(State of Trouble)              (Probable Cause)

○
├─ [Early slackening] ──┬─ ① Fail to keep periodical adjustment
│                       └─ ② Fail to keep periodical servicing
│
├─ [Dust in chain case] ─── ① Defective chain case rubber packing
│
├─ [Early wearing of sprocket] ─── ① Dust in chain case
△
```

4.4 Maintenance Data & Specifications

A. Maintenance Data

In order to operate the vehicle in best condition and also extend its life it is necessary to perform without fail the preceeding periodic inspections and prevent trouble from occurring from the beginning. Use the following standards to determine whether overhaul is required or not.

	Standard Value	Unavailable Limit	Procedure on Measuring
Compression Pressure	100 lb/in² (7.0 kg/cm²)	65 lb/in² (4.5 kg/cm²)	Use compression gage, check with kick and while engine is warm.
Fuel Consumption	85~90 km/l (240~255 mile/gal) gal : British gal	50 km/l (140 mile/gal)	Use fuel consumption gage, test on level road (paved) running with constant speed 30 km/hr (19 mile/hr) in the top gear.
Max. Top Speed	75 km/hr (43 mile/hr)	50 km/hr (35 mile/hr)	Test on a level road, when it is no wind, with full throttle, top gear and the posture is leaning forward the upper half of body.
Stopping Ability (distance)	max. 5 m (16.5 ft)	over 10 m (33 ft)	Test on a dry level road (paved), with solo and initial speed is 25 km/hr (16 mile/hr), front and rear brake applied at same time.

When interior noise and oil consumption, in other words oil pumping, is excessive determine cause according to diagnosis of trouble means and service.

B. Specifications of Performances

The following chart lists assembly performance specifications and parts size standards, which should be used for reference when performing service.

MEMO

4. INSPECTION, MAINTENANCE & SPECIFICATIONS

Dimension	Overall length	1,780mm (70.5")	Engine	Crankcase oil capacity	0.6 l (1.05 Pts)
	Overall width	575 (22.6")	Power transmission	Transmission gear	3 forward constant mesh
	Overall height	945 (37.2)		Gear ratio (gear box)	Low 3.08 / 2nd 1.45 / Top 0.96
	Wheel base	1,180 (47.0)		Primary sprocket ratio	4.66 (driven with gear)
	Min. ground clearance	140 (5.5)		Secondary sprocket ratio	2.86 (driven with chain)
Weight	Total weight	55kg (dry)	Power Plant	Steering angle	45°
	Weight distribution			Caster	63°
	Front	25kg (55 lb)		Trail	70mm (2.76")
	Rear	30kg (66 lb)		Tire size (front)	2.25-17 (air press 22lb/in^2)
Performance of Vehicle	Min. turning radius	1,700mm (67.0")		" (rear)	2.25-17 (28lb/in^2)
	Max. top speed	70km/hr (43mile/hr)		Spoke (front)	#12~#13 (36pcs)
	Hill climbing ability	1/4		" (rear)	#11~#12 (36pcs)
	Stopping ability	within 5m (16.5ft) at 25km/hr (16m/hr)		Brake drum size	120φ (4.73")
			Electric System	Power of head light bulb	10W ; 1.43 A
				"	12W ; 1.87 A
	Fuel consumption	90km/l (255mile/gal) at 30km/hr (19m/hr)		Neutral lamp bulb	3W
				Speedometer lamp	1W ; 0.15 A
Engine	Disposition of valves	O. H. V.		Tail light lamp	2W
	Bore × Stroke	40×39mm (1.58×1.54")		Front & rear winker lamp	8W ; 1.23 A
	Capacity	49cc		Celenium rectifier	
	Compression ratio	8.5 : 1		Output voltage	6~10V
	Max. horsepower	4.5HP/9,500rpm		Input current	2 A
	Max. torque	0.33kg-m/8,000rpm		Horn	
	Engine weight	15kg (33 lb)		Sound volume	95~100ph
	Carburetor	DDBHOV (bore 13mm)		Fuse capacity	6V/7A
	Battery	MBC 1-6 (6V 2Amp. h)		Battery	
				Electrolite capacity	0.1 l
	Spark plug	NGK 6HW (10mmφ)		Current capacity	2 A.h
	Ignition timing	35° BTDC		Specific gravity of electrolite	1.26 (20°C)
	Valve timing				
	Inlet open	56° BTDC			
	" close	86° ABDC	Carburetor	Main jet	#75 / #85
	Exhaust open	79° BBDC		Air jet	#1.5
	" close	47° ATDC		Air screw opening	1~1 1/4
		(at 1mm (0.039") lift of cam)			

C. Specification of Parts

(1) Maintenance of common parts.

Even parts not listed in the next chart should always be checked and inspected for the following points and acted upon with proper judgement.

The following is also a standard chart for dealers to determine whether parts are beyond limit of repair.

① Rubber made parts.... Especially oil seal rubber bushing and cushion parts should be replaced when found too old, distorted, damaged and elasticity gone, etc.

② Bearing parts.... Ball, roller, needle bearing, etc., should be replaced when found worn, damaged, movement not smooth, etc.

③ Packing, gasket parts.... All should be replaced. Especially when liquid packing is used, clean thoroughly repack and use.

④ Replace snap rings, end rings, set rings, etc., that have lost their tension. End ring as a rule should be replaced.

⑤ Replace deformed or damaged bolts, screws, nuts, washers, etc.

⑥ Only use geniune HONDA parts when newly installing (Purchased through authorized HONDA dealers).

(2) Definition of words used in chart.

Standard Value.... This indicates the manufacturer's standard size or the standard size after newly assembling or adjusting, and shows the size-limit of completed part or the permissable limit of adjustment.

Repairing limit..... Unusable wear limit of parts requiring correction or replacement, function-wise.

Remarks..... Additional instructions on measuring or servicing.

Items..... Items to be inspected, service-wise.

(3) Units in chart.

Unmarked numbers are mm unit and inch unit in parenthesis, and others according to the unit indicated.

4. INSPECTION, MAINTENANCE & SPECIFICATIONS

	Item	Standard	Repairing Limit	Remarks
1. Cylinder & Cylinder Head Block	Cylinder bore	40.0~40.01 mm (1.575~1.576)	max. 40.1 mm (1.580)	
	Max. Cylinder out of round	0.01 (0.0004)	max. 0.05 (0.002)	
	" taper	0.01 (0.0004)	max. 0.05 (0.002)	
	Height of cylinder	63.2~63.4 (2.49~2.497)	min. 63.1 (2.485)	
	Over size of cylinder	0.25, 0.5, 0.75 (0.009, 0.019, 0.029)		
2. Crankshaft include (piston connecting rod)	Piston top diameter	39.63~39.68 (1.561~1.563)		
	Piston skirt diameter	39.98~49.0 (1.575~1.930)		Thrust
	Width of piston ring groove Top and second	1.51~1.53 (0.059~0.06)	max. 1.6 (0.063)	
	Oil	3.51~3.53 (0.138~0.139)	max. 3.6 (0.141)	
	Min. clearance of piston to cylinder	0.01~0.03 (0.0003~0.001)	max. 0.14 (0.005)	
	Thickness of piston rings Top and second	1.47~1.49 (0.057~0.058)	min. 1.40 (0.055)	
	Oil	3.47~3.49 (0.136~0.137)	min. 3.40 (0.133)	
	Piston ring end gap	0.1~0.3 (0.003~0.01)	max. 1.0 (0.039)	
	Piston & ring oversize	0.25, 0.50, 0.75 (0.009, 0.019, 0.029)		
	Diameter of connecting rod small end	13.02~13.05 (0.512~0.514)	max. 13.1 (0.516)	
	Clearance of piston pin to connecting rod	0.03~0.05 (0.0011~0.0019)	max. 0.08 (0.003)	
	Diameter of connecting rod large end	26.09~26.1 (1.027~1.028)	max. 26.2 (1.032)	
	Radial play of connecting rod	0.006~0.03 (0.0002~0.001)	max. 0.01 (0.0003)	
	Axis play of connecting rod	0.1~0.35 (0.003~0.013)	max. 1.0 (0.039)	
	Diameter of R.L. crankshaft	16.99~17.0 (0.6694~0.6698)	max. 16.9 (0.665)	
	Crankshaft run-out	0.03 (0.001)	max. 0.3 (0.011)	
3. Cam and Valve	Diameter of valve stem Ex.	5.44~5.45 (0.2143~0.2147)	min. 5.40 (0.212)	
	In.	5.46~5.47 (0.2151~0.2155)	min. 5.42 (0.213)	
	Valve seat angle	45°		In. & ex.
	Clearance of valve stem to guide Ex.	0.06~0.08 (0.002~0.003)	max. 0.1 (0.003)	
	In.	0.04~0.06 (0.0015~0.002)	max. 0.1 (0.003)	

4.4 MAINTENANCE DATA & SPECIFICATIONS 133

	Iten	Standard	Repairing limit	Rdmarks
3. Cam and Valve	Valve spring compression			
	Outer	6.3~6.9kg (13.891~15.214 lb)	min. 5.4 (0.212 lb)	at 23.5mm (0.925") test length.
	Inner	2.6~2.9kg (5.733~6.394 lb)	min. 2.2 (0.086 lb)	at 22.5mm (0.886")
	Diameter or cam shaft jounal			
	Large end	30.95~30.98 (1.2194~1.2206)	min. 30.9 (1.217)	
	Small end	18.96~18.98 (0.7470~07.478)	min. 18.9 (0.744)	
	Height of cam	24.5 (0.965)	min. 23.0 (0.906)	
4. Clutch	Clutch center guide			
	Outside diameter	19.94~19.96 (0.7856~0.786)	min. 19.55 (0.770)	
	Inner 〃	17.0~17.01 (0.6968~0.670)	min. 17.15 (0.675)	
	Friction disc thickness	2.5~2.8 (0.098~0.110)	min. 2.3 (0.090)	
	Clutch spring free length	23.23 (0.915)	min. 22.07 (0.869)	
5. Transmission & Others	Diameter of main shaft	13.91~13.98 (0.548~0.550)	min. 13.5 (0.531)	
	Diameter of counter shaft	16.98~16.99 (0.6690~0.6694)	min. 16.0 (0.630)	
	Shift drum			
	Large end	41.95~41.97 (1.652~1.653)	min. 41.9 (1.650)	
	Small end	11.97~11.98 (0.4716~0.4720)	min. 11.9 (0.468)	
6. Frame	Stroke of front cushion	36.0 (1.418)		Containing 9.5cc of #60 spindle oil
	Free length of front cushion spring	122.5 (4.826)	min. 117 (4.609)	
	Stroke of rear cushion	63.8 (2.513)		Shock absorb with damper spring
	Free length of rear cushion spring	205.1 (8.080)	min. 193 (7.604)	
	Thickness of brake lining (front & rear)	3.5 (0.137)	min. 2.0 (0.078)	
	Diameter of brake drum (front & rear)	119.8~120.2 (4.720~4.735)	max. 123 (4.836)	
	Run-out of wheel rim (front & rear)	0~1.0 (0~0.039)	max. 3.0 (0.118)	

A SAMPLE LIST OF OTHER BOOKS AVAILABLE FROM

www.VelocePress.com

PLEASE CHECK OUR WEBSITE FOR THE MOST UP-TO-DATE INFORMATION

MOTORCYCLE WORKSHOP MANUALS, MAINTENANCE & TECHNICAL TITLES

ARIEL WORKSHOP MANUAL 1933-1951
BMW FACTORY WORKSHOP MANUAL R26 R27 (1956-1967)
BMW FACTORY WSM R50 R50S R60 R69S R50US R60US R69US (1955-1969)
BSA SERVICE & REPAIR ALL PRE-WAR MODELS TO 1939, SV & OHV 150cc TO 1,000cc
DUCATI FACTORY WORKSHOP MANUAL SINGLE CYLINDER NARROW CASE OHC ENGINES 160cc, 250cc, 350cc - MONZA JUNIOR, MONZA, 250GT, MARK 3, MACH 1, MOTOCROSS & SEBRING
HONDA FACTORY WORKSHOP MANUAL 250cc TO 305cc C/CS/CB 72 & 77 SERIES 1960-1969
HONDA FACTORY WORKSHOP MANUAL 125cc TO 150cc C/CS/CB/CA 92 & 95 SERIES 1959-1966
HONDA FACTORY WORKSHOP MANUAL 50cc C110 (1962-1969)
HONDA SERVICE & REPAIR 50cc TO 305cc C100, C102, MONKEY BIKE, CE 105H TRIALS BIKE, C110, C114, C92, CB92, BENLEY, C72, CB72, C77 & CB77
NORTON FACTORY WORKSHOP MANUAL 1957-1970
NORTON WORKSHOP MANUAL 1932-1939
ROYAL ENFIELD 736cc INTERCEPTOR & ENFIELD INDIAN CHIEF
SUZUKI T10 FACTORY WORKSHOP MANUAL 250cc 1963-1967
SUZUKI T20 & T200 FACTORY WORKSHOP MANUAL 200cc X-5 INVADER & STING RAY SCRAMBLER, 250cc X-6 HUSTLER 1965-1969
TRIUMPH FACTORY WORKSHOP MANUAL NO. 11 (1945-1955)
TRIUMPH WORKSHOP MANUAL 1935-1939
TRIUMPH WORKSHOP MANUAL 1937-1951
VESPA SERVICE & REPAIR ALL MODELS 125cc & 150cc 1951-1961
VINCENT SERVICE & REPAIR 1935-1955

CLASSIC AUTO TITLES & REFERENCE BOOKS

ABARTH BUYERS GUIDE
CARRERA PANAMERICANA 1950 ~ THE STORY OF THE 1950 MEXICAN ROAD RACE
DIALED IN ~ THE JAN OPPERMAN STORY
FERRARI 308 SERIES BUYER'S AND OWNER'S GUIDE
FERRARI BERLINETTA LUSSO
FERRARI BROCHURES & SALES LITERATURE 1946-1967
FERRARI SERIAL NUMBERS PART I ~ STREET CARS TO SERIAL # 21399 (1948-1977)
FERRARI SERIAL NUMBERS PART II ~ RACE CARS TO SERIAL # 1050 (1948-1973)
FERRARI SPYDER CALIFORNIA
IF HEMINGWAY HAD WRITTEN A RACING NOVEL ~ THE BEST OF MOTOR RACING FICTION 1950-2000
LE MANS 24 ~ WHAT THE MOVIE COULD HAVE BEEN
MASERATI BROCHURES AND SALES LITERATURE ~ POSTWAR THROUGH INLINE 6 CYLINDER CARS

All VelocePress titles are available through your local independent bookseller, Amazon.com, or they may be purchased directly through our website at www.VelocePress.com. Wholesale customers may also purchase directly from us or from the Ingram Book Group.

A SAMPLE LIST OF OTHER BOOKS AVAILABLE FROM

www.VelocePress.com

PLEASE CHECK OUR WEBSITE FOR THE MOST UP-TO-DATE INFORMATION

AUTOBOOKS SERIES OF WORKSHOP MANUALS

ALFA ROMEO GIULIA 1750, 2000 1962-1978 WORKSHOP MANUAL
AUSTIN HEALEY SPRITE, MG MIDGET 1958-1980 WORKSHOP MANUAL
BMW 1600 1966-1973 WORKSHOP MANUAL
FIAT 1100, 1100D, 1100R & 1200 1957-1969 WORKSHOP MANUAL
FIAT 124 1966-1974 WORKSHOP MANUAL
FIAT 124 SPORT 1966-1975 WORKSHOP MANUAL
FIAT 125 & 125 SPECIAL 1967-1973 WORKSHOP MANUAL
FIAT 126, 126L, 126DV, 126/650 & 126/650DV 1972-1982 WORKSHOP MANUAL
FIAT 127 SALOON, SPECIAL & SPORT, 900, 1050 1971-1981 WORKSHOP MANUAL
FIAT 128 1969-1982 WORKSHOP MANUAL
FIAT 1300, 1500 1961-1967 WORKSHOP MANUAL
FIAT 131 MIRAFIORI 1975-1982 WORKSHOP MANUAL
FIAT 132 1972-1982 WORKSHOP MANUAL
FIAT 500 1957-1973 WORKSHOP MANUAL
FIAT 600, 600D & MULTIPLA 1955-1969 WORKSHOP MANUAL
FIAT 850 1964-1972 WORKSHOP MANUAL
JAGUAR E-TYPE 1961-1972 WORKSHOP MANUAL
JAGUAR MK 1, 2 1955-1969 WORKSHOP MANUAL
JAGUAR S TYPE, 420 1963-1968 WORKSHOP MANUAL
JAGUAR XK 120, 140, 150 MK 7, 8, 9 1948-1961 WORKSHOP MANUAL
LAND ROVER 1, 2 1948-1961 WORKSHOP MANUAL
MERCEDES-BENZ 190 1959-1968 WORKSHOP MANUAL
MERCDEDS-BENZ 220/8 1968-1972 WORKSHOP MANUAL
MERCEDES-BENZ 230 1963-1968 WORKSHOP MANUAL
MERCEDES-BENZ 250 1968-1972 WORKSHOP MANUAL
MG MIDGET TA-TF 1936-1955 WORKSHOP MANUAL
MINI 1959-1980 WORKSHOP MANUAL
MORRIS MINOR 1952-1971 WORKSHOP MANUAL
PEUGEOT 404 1960-1975 WORKSHOP MANUAL
PORSCHE 911 1964-1969 WORKSHOP MANUAL
PORSCHE 911 1970-1977 WORKSHOP MANUAL
RENAULT 8, 10, 1100 1962-1971 WORKSHOP MANUAL
RENAULT 16 1965-1979 WORKSHOP MANUAL
ROVER 3500, 3500S 1968-1976 WORKSHOP MANUAL
SUNBEAM RAPIER, ALPINE 1955-1965 WORKSHOP MANUAL
TRIUMPH SPITFIRE, GT6, VITESSE 1962-1968 WORKSHOP MANUAL
TRIUMPH TR2, TR3, TR3A 1952-1962 WORKSHOP MANUAL
TRIUMPH TR4, TR4A 1961-1967 WORKSHOP MANUAL
VOLKSWAGEN BEETLE 1968-1977 WORKSHOP MANUAL

All VelocePress titles are available through your local independent bookseller, Amazon.com, or they may be purchased directly through our website at www.VelocePress.com. Wholesale customers may also purchase directly from us or from the Ingram Book Group.

A SAMPLE LIST OF OTHER BOOKS AVAILABLE FROM

www.VelocePress.com

PLEASE CHECK OUR WEBSITE FOR THE MOST UP-TO-DATE INFORMATION

OTHER WORKSHOP MANUALS, MAINTENANCE & TECHNICAL TITLES

AUSTIN HEALEY SIX CYLINDER CARS 1956-1968
BMW ISETTA FACTORY REPAIR MANUAL
FERRARI 250/GT SERVICE AND MAINTENANCE
FERRARI GUIDE TO PERFORMANCE
FERRARI OPERATING, MAINTENANCE & SERVICE HANDBOOKS 1948-1963
FERRARI OWNER'S HANDBOOK
FERRARI TUNING TIPS & MAINTENANCE TECHNIQUES
MASERATI OWNER'S HANDBOOK
OBERT'S FIAT GUIDE
PERFORMANCE TUNING THE SUNBEAM TIGER
PORSCHE 356 SERVICE AND MAINTENANCE MANUAL 1948-1965
PORSCHE 912 WORKSHOP MANUAL
SOUPING THE VOLKSWAGEN IMPROVING THE PERFORMANCE OF YOUR VW
TRIUMPH TR2, TR3 & TR4 WORKSHOP MANUAL
VOLVO ALL MODELS 1944-1968 WORKSHOP MANUAL

BROOKLANDS ROAD TEST PORTFOLIOS

FIAT DINO 1968-1973
MV AGUSTA F4 750 & 1000 1997-2007
JAGUAR MK1 & MK2 1955-1969
LOTUS CORTINA 1963-1970
FIAT 500 1936-1972
FERRARI ROAD CARS 1946-1956

All VelocePress titles are available through your local independent bookseller, Amazon.com, or they may be purchased directly through our website at www.VelocePress.com. Wholesale customers may also purchase directly from us or from the Ingram Book Group.

www.ingramcontent.com/pod-product-compliance
Lightning Source LLC
Chambersburg PA
CBHW080436230426

43662CB00015B/2295